Language as an Ecological Phenomenon

Bloomsbury Advances in Ecolinguistics

Series Editors:
Arran Stibbe and Mariana Roccia

Advisory Board:
Nadine Andrews (Lancaster University, UK)
Maria Bortoluzzi (University of Udine, Italy)
Martin Döring (University of Hamburg, Germany)
Sue Edney (University of Bristol, UK)
Alwin Fill (University of Graz, Austria)
Diego Forte (University of Buenos Aires, Argentina)
Amir Ghorbanpour (Tarbiat Modares University, Iran)
Nataliia Goshylyk (Vasyl Stefanyk Precarpathian National University, Ukraine)
Huang Guowen (South China Agricultural University, China)
George Jacobs (Independent Scholar)
Kyoohoon Kim (Daegu University, South Korea)
Katerina Kosta (Oxford Brookes University, UK)
Mira Lieberman-Boyd (University of Sheffield, UK)
Keith Moser (Mississippi State University, USA)
Douglas Ponton (University of Catania, Italy)
Robert Poole (University of Alabama, USA)
Alison Sealey (University of Lancaster, UK)
Nina Venkataraman (National University of Singapore, Singapore)
Daniela Francesca Virdis (University of Cagliari, Italy)
Sune Vork Steffensen (University of Southern Denmark, Denmark)

Bloomsbury Advances in Ecolinguistics emerges at a time when businesses, universities, national governments and many other organisations are declaring an ecological emergency. With climate change and biodiversity loss diminishing the ability of the Earth to support life, business leaders, politicians and academics are asking how their work can contribute to efforts to preserve the ecosystems that life depends on.

This book series explores the role that linguistics can play in addressing the great challenges faced by humanity and countless other species. Although significant advances have been made in addressing social issues such as racism, sexism and social justice, linguistics has typically focused on oppression in human communities and overlooked other species and the wider ecosystems that support life. This is despite the disproportionate impact of ecological destruction on oppressed groups. In contrast, this book series treats language as an intrinsic part of both human societies and wider ecosystems. It explores the role that different areas of linguistic enquiry, such as discourse analysis, corpus linguistics, language diversity and cognitive linguistics can play at a time of ecological emergency.

The titles explore themes such as the stories that underpin unequal and unsustainable industrial societies; language contact and how linguistic imperialism threatens the ecological wisdom embedded in endangered languages; the use of linguistic analysis in ecocriticism, ecopsychology and other ecological humanities and social sciences; and emerging theoretical frameworks such as Harmonious Discourse Analysis. The titles also look to cultures around the world for inspirational forms of language that can lead to new stories to live by. In this way, the series contributes to linguistic theory by placing language fully in its social and ecological context, and to practical action by describing the role that linguistics can play in addressing ecological issues.

Titles published in the series:
Corpus-Assisted Ecolinguistics, Robert Poole
Language and Ecology in Southern and Eastern Arabia, edited by Janet C.E. Watson, Jon C. Lovett and Roberta Morano
Storytelling and Ecology, Anthony Nanson
TESOL and Sustainability, edited by Jason Goulah and John Katunich

Language as an Ecological Phenomenon

Languaging and Bioecologies in Human-Environment Relationships

Edited by
Sune Vork Steffensen, Martin Döring,
and Stephen J. Cowley

BLOOMSBURY ACADEMIC
LONDON • NEW YORK • OXFORD • NEW DELHI • SYDNEY

BLOOMSBURY ACADEMIC
Bloomsbury Publishing Plc, 50 Bedford Square, London, WC1B 3DP, UK
Bloomsbury Publishing Inc, 1359 Broadway, New York, NY 10018, USA
Bloomsbury Publishing Ireland, 29 Earlsfort Terrace, Dublin 2, D02 AY28, Ireland

BLOOMSBURY, BLOOMSBURY ACADEMIC and the Diana logo are
trademarks of Bloomsbury Publishing Plc

First published in Great Britain 2024
Paperback edition published 2026

Copyright © Sune Vork Steffensen, Martin Döring, Stephen J. Cowley,
and Contributors, 2024, 2026

Sune Vork Steffensen, Martin Döring, Stephen J. Cowley and Contributors
have asserted their right under the Copyright, Designs and Patents Act, 1988,
to be identified as Authors of this work.

For legal purposes the Acknowledgements on p. 247 constitute an
extension of this copyright page.

Series design: Ben Anslow

All rights reserved. No part of this publication may be: i) reproduced or transmitted in
any form, electronic or mechanical, including photocopying, recording or by means of
any information storage or retrieval system without prior permission in writing from the
publishers; or ii) used or reproduced in any way for the training, development or operation
of artificial intelligence (AI) technologies, including generative AI technologies. The rights
holders expressly reserve this publication from the text and data mining exception as per
Article 4(3) of the Digital Single Market Directive (EU) 2019/790.

Bloomsbury Publishing Plc does not have any control over, or responsibility for, any
third-party websites referred to or in this book. All internet addresses given in this
book were correct at the time of going to press. The author and publisher regret
any inconvenience caused if addresses have changed or sites have ceased
to exist, but can accept no responsibility for any such changes.

A catalogue record for this book is available from the British Library.

Library of Congress Cataloging-in-Publication Data
Names: Steffensen, Sune Vork, editor. | Döring, Martin, 1966- editor. |
Cowley, Stephen J. (Stephen John), 1955- editor.
Title: Language as an ecological phenomenon : languaging and bioecologies in human-environment
relationships / edited by Sune Vork Steffensen, Martin Döring and Stephen Cowley.
Description: London ; New York : Bloomsbury Academic, [2024] | Series: Bloomsbury advances in
ecolinguistics | "First published in Great Britain 2018." | Includes bibliographical references and index. |
Summary: "Examining a significant conceptual change within ecolinguistics, this book presents a
process view in which language is substituted by languaging, emphasising the bioecologies that
we cohabit with numerous other species. Drawing on examples from across the World, it
addresses topics such as climate catastrophes, corporate narratives, questions of ecological
leadership, the bioecological implications of the COVID pandemic, and relational landscapes. It also
makes use of data from across multiple bioecological settings, including the dairy
and agricultural industries" – Provided by publisher.
Identifiers: LCCN 2023048577 (print) | LCCN 2023048578 (ebook) | ISBN 9781350304482 (hardback) |
ISBN 9781350304529 (paperback) | ISBN 9781350304505 (epub) | ISBN 9781350304499 (ebook)
Subjects: LCSH: Ecolinguistics.
Classification: LCC P39.5 .L35 2024 (print) | LCC P39.5 (ebook) |
DDC 306.44–dc23/eng/20240208
LC record available at https://lccn.loc.gov/2023048577
LC ebook record available at https://lccn.loc.gov/2023048578

ISBN:	HB:	978-1-3503-0448-2
	PB:	978-1-3503-0452-9
	ePDF:	978-1-3503-0449-9
	eBook:	978-1-3503-0450-5

Series: Bloomsbury Advances in Ecolinguistics

Typeset by Integra Software Services Pvt. Ltd.

For product safety related questions contact productsafety@bloomsbury.com.

To find out more about our authors and books visit www.bloomsbury.com
and sign up for our newsletters.

Contents

List of Figures — viii
List of Tables — ix
List of Contributors — x

1. Ecolinguistics: Living and Languaging United *Sune Vork Steffensen, Martin Döring and Stephen J. Cowley* — 1

Part One Energizing Ecolinguistics

2. How (Dairy) Cows and Human Intertwine Languaging Practices *Leonie Cornips* — 29
3. Ecolinguistics and the Cognitive Ecology of Global Warming *Sune Vork Steffensen and Edward Baggs* — 55
4. Regeneration: From Language Use to Languaging *Stephen J. Cowley* — 83
5. The Epistemological Conundrum of Language: Humans as Ecologically Special and Ecologically Destructive *Alexander Kravchenko* — 107
6. Varieties of Expression and Enlanguaged Cognition in the Context of a Radicalized Ecolinguistics *Rasmus Gahrn-Andersen* — 127

Part Two From Discourse to Worldly Action

7. Ecolinguistics for Ethical Leadership *Arran Stibbe* — 147
8. Landscape Sentience *Elizabeth Oriel, Deepta Sateesh and Amal Dissanayaka* — 169
9. Considering Cows in Australian Dairy Discourse *Alison Rotha Moore* — 191
10. Learning About, Learning From, Learning With: Towards a Critical Practice and Theory of Situated Language Sciences *Chris Sinha and Vera da Silva Sinha* — 221

Index — 254

Figures

1.1	Language as a complex ecological phenomenon	8
1.2	Impact of language on life-sustaining relations	10
1.3	Two poles in contemporary ecolinguistics	10
1.4	Dialectics of enlanguaged practices and life-sustaining relations	12
2.1	'Human' space with the canopy behind the blue barrel	40
2.2	Noor and her youngest calf Saar	40
2.3	Noor receives a 'cattle-cookie' as the human responds to co-articulation	41
2.4	Snapshots of the five co-articulations by Noor	42
2.5	Spectrogram of the five consecutive vocalizations by Noor	42
2.6	Snapshot of the five consecutive sounds in time	45
2.7	Spectrogram of the five consecutive vocalizations by the Fleckvieh cow	46
2.8	Intensity as a function of relative time for five consecutive calls directed to the farmer	47
3.1	Global Surface Temperature, 1880–2013	61
3.2	Global atmospheric CO_2 concentration	62
3.3	Climate spiral	63
6.1	Varieties of expression	129
8.1	Vayal, Human–Elephant 'conflict' area, village and forest edge	173
8.2	Vayal, ground of multiple practices and inhabitants, Muthanga area	176
8.3	Elephant browsing, Uda Walawe National Park, Sri Lanka	182
9.1	Cohesive Harmony of Legendairy Text	204
9.2	Dairy has been through some tough times	208
9.3	Once a hero of our health and wealth	209
9.4	It's our people	209
9.5	Jobs for generations	210
10.1	Tamahet Kamaiura demonstrates the use of the knotted string for counting days	244
10.2	Untitled painting by Rahul Shyam	245

Tables

2.1	Two fieldwork sites in this chapter	38
9.1	Transcription of Legendairy campaign principal video, 2013–20	202
10.1	Life stage names in three Amazonian languages	238
10.2	Event-based time intervals of day and night in Kamaiurá	242

Contributors

Edward Baggs is Assistant Professor at the Department of Culture and Language at the University of Southern Denmark, and Fellow at the Danish Institute for Advanced Study. His work focuses on the ecology of perception and processes of human enculturation. With Guilherme Sanches de Oliveira he is the co-author of the book *Psychology's WEIRD Problems* (2023).

Leonie Cornips is affiliated with the research group NL-Lab, Humanities Cluster of the Royal Netherlands Academy of Arts and Sciences, and is Professor of Languageculture in Limburg at Maastricht University. Since 1994 she examined sociosyntax methods in dialectology, and bidialectal child acquisition. More recently her research focused on local identity constructions through language practices including linguistic place-making and belonging. At present she examines intraspecies and interspecies interactions of dairy cows in various settings. She is conducting ethnographic fieldwork among different barns in the Netherlands.

Stephen J. Cowley is Emeritus Professor of Organizational Cognition at the University of Southern Denmark. His work offers an ecological view of distributed agency based on using radical embodied cognitive science to connect up human prosody, mother–infant interaction, classroom activity, workplace social organizing and, centrally, languaging. In the ecolinguistics of languaging, he links theoretical biology with practice theory by placing human life cycles in historically evolving bioecologies. He has authored over a hundred academic papers and edited/co-edited: *Distributed Language*, *Cognition beyond the Brain*, *Biosemiotic Perspectives on Language and Linguistics* and *Organizational Cognition: The Theory of Social Organizing*.

Amal Dissanayaka is doing his master's degree (MRES) at the University of West of England, UK. He is an action researcher, freelance practitioner and former research officer at the Hector Kobbekaduwa Agrarian Research and Training Institute (HARTI), based in Colombo. Amal actively works in the field of human–animal interaction and conducts research on human wildlife conflict

(HWC), which has become a prominent socio-economic issue in his country. He recently published a paper titled 'The Changing Role from Defenders to Challengers in the Context of Wildlife Protection Measures Implemented in the Moneragala District, Sri Lanka'.

Martin Döring holds a PhD in Romance linguistics and works at the University of Hamburg in the Institute of Geography. He is a long-standing member of the ecolinguistic research community and has published on eco-critical discourses and the ecology of minority languages. He is a co-editor of the online journal *metaphorik.de* and the book series *MatteRealities* with Transcript. His current research is devoted to constructing a participative and co-constructive climate change adaptation in the areas of coastal protection and fisheries on the North German coast.

Rasmus Gahrn-Andersen is Associate Professor in the Department of Culture and Language at the University of Southern Denmark. He is currently researching human socio-practical activity from an interdisciplinary perspective. He focuses primarily on phenomena such as concept and non-concept involving perception, basic and distributed cognition, social organizing, human–technology entanglements as well as how linguistic competencies and skills enable human practical behaviour.

Alexander V. Kravchenko is Professor of Theoretical and Applied Linguistics at Baikal State University, Russia. Recently, he has developed a new curriculum for the BA program in TEFL offered by Baikal State University, and is trying, with the help of his colleagues, to apply ecological ideas about language and cognition in training would-be teachers capable of seeing language in new light and developing more effective skills in teaching a foreign language. He is the author of *Sign, Meaning, Knowledge* (2003), *Biology of Cognition and Linguistic Analysis* (2008), and the editor of *Cognitive Dynamics in Linguistic Interactions* (2012). His latest book (published in Russian) is *Rediscovering Language: A New Agenda for Linguistics* (2021).

Alison Rotha Moore has a long-standing interest in how linguistic enquiry can build pathways for positive social change. Currently Associate Professor at the University of Wollongong in Australia, Alison has held research and teaching positions at Macquarie University and the University of Sydney, and nationally competitive awards from the Australian Research Council and other agencies.

Ongoing interests include health discourses, the representation and treatment of animals, and Hasanian approaches to register and semantic variation, especially in spoken interaction. Across these areas, key unifying concerns are the construal of agency and identity, and the role of embodiment. An edited collection (with Daniel Lees Fryer) on *Social Semiotics and the Animal Other* is due out in 2024.

Elizabeth Oriel is a postdoctoral researcher in the School of Communication and Culture at Aarhus University, Denmark. Her current work explores language in the news media, the climate crisis and phenology, and is generating new language for journalists to speak of climate-driven changes to lifecycles. Previous research and numerous publications examine human–wildlife conflict, nature–culture relations, learning from place, and interstitial patterns that build coexistence. She is writing a book about how plants shape humans in their subjectivities and collectives. Elizabeth is a researcher, artist, fiction writer and plant medicine practitioner.

Deepta Sateesh is Head of the Research Centre DWEEPA (Design with Environment through Education, Planning and Advocacy) at the Srishti Manipal Institute of Art, Design and Technology, Manipal Academy of Higher Education, Manipal, India. Deepta is a design researcher, educator, architect and planner, working in contentious landscapes. Her design activism, towards synchronous nature-culture futures, is focused on creating new pathways in design, eco-pedagogies and policy. Deepta's research, primarily situated in monsoonal terrains, is framed by new ontologies gathered through situated practices, movement arts, and politics of the colonial eye. She is a trained dancer, equestrian, novice cellist, wanderer and photographer.

Vera da Silva Sinha is an anthropologist, linguist and social scientist who seeks to understand how the human mind is shaped by culture and language. She gained her PhD in Linguistics from the University of East Anglia, UK and she has recently held positions at the Universities of Oxford, Bergen and Brasilia. She has worked for many years with Indigenous communities of Brazilian Amazonia, and is passionate about understanding their languages, worldviews and what we can learn from them. Her doctoral research was an in-depth study of cultural and linguistic conceptualizations of event-based time in three Indigenous minority language communities in Brazil, and her current research focuses on the cognitive, communicative and linguistic relationship between time and number in these communities.

Chris Sinha is Honorary Professor at the University of East Anglia, UK and has taught at universities in Brazil, Britain, China, the Netherlands, Denmark, India and Sweden. He has authored three monographs and more than 150 articles in the fields of anthropology, linguistics, education, evolutionary biology, connection science, as well as developmental and cultural psychology. He is co-Editor of the *Oxford Handbook of Human Symbolic Evolution*. He is Past President of both the UK and the International Cognitive Linguistics Associations. His central research interest is in the relations between language, cognition and culture, and his research aims to integrate cognitive with sociocultural approaches to language, communication and human development.

Sune Vork Steffensen is Professor of Language, Interaction, and Cognition at the University of Southern Denmark (SDU), and Senior Fellow at the Danish Institute for Advanced Study. Focusing on how language and cognition intersect in complex social and dialogical systems in ways that transform social and ecological systems, his research draws on ecological, dialogical, and distributed approaches to language, interaction and cognition. He has contributed to the theoretical development of ecolinguistics. He has edited five issues on ecological and distributed approaches to language and ecology, and he authored more than fifty articles/chapters in journals and books. He is currently the Editor-in-Chief of the journal *Language Sciences*.

Arran Stibbe is Professor of Ecological Linguistics at the University of Gloucestershire, UK. He has an academic background in both linguistics and human ecology and combines the two in his research and teaching. He is the founder of the International Ecolinguistics Association, and is author of *Ecolinguistics: Language, Ecology and the Stories We Live By* (Routledge) and *Econarrative: Ethics, Ecology and the Search for New Narratives to Live By* (Bloomsbury Academic).

1

Ecolinguistics: Living and Languaging United

Sune Vork Steffensen, Martin Döring and Stephen J. Cowley

Introduction

For half a century, ecolinguistics has aspired to study how language affects the ecosystems that sustain all life on Earth. Not only does language have psychological and sociological implications, but it contributes to human impacts on life-sustaining relations. This volume extends this tradition by pursuing how language interlaces with ecological factors. In treating linguistic phenomena as part of living, it engages with a blind spot that contemporary ecolinguistics inherited from the theoretical foundations of twentieth-century linguistics. Rather than treat 'language' as an object that speakers use to communicate content or meaning within a social 'circuit de la parole' (Saussure 1972), this volume argues that activities involving language are ecological and that, consequently, much is masked by the verbal focus of linguistic theories. This conceptual move intentionally reaches out to ecolinguistic scholars[1] who address issues like climate change, the worldwide loss of biodiversity, harmful agro-industrial practices, or the degradation of the land leading to desertification.

In spite of a burgeoning of such interests, the field has seen little if any theoretical development. While the recent *Routledge Handbook of Ecolinguistics* (Fill & Penz 2018) exhibits a rich range of applications of linguistic methodology to environmental issues, few contributors address foundational issues. Little or nothing is said about ecology, linguistic theory, practices, or how languages extend living (Steffensen 2011). Rather, contemporary ecolinguistics draws on or hybridizes methods of cognitive linguistics, functional linguistics, corpus linguistics, etc.

Given the pressing urgency of the current ecological crisis, some might see such an analytical focus as an obvious priority. One might stress the need to *say* that the planet is feverishly warm, and that animals, plants and other living creatures are being wiped out. And one might feel the need to *explain* that this is because human beings overrun the Earth with their livestock, degrade the soil, pollute the sea and feed human excess with resources from below the surface. As Greta Thunberg said in what became a catchphrase for the fifth International Conference on Ecolinguistics held at Liverpool University in April 2021: 'I want you to act as if the house is on fire, because it is.' Since the house is burning, the only logical thing is to get out, using all means at your disposal. One should not sit down and theorize about the nature of combustion. Likewise, some may say that there is no time to engage in theoretical discussions. In reframing languages as ecological phenomena, we offer strong reasons to disagree.

With this volume we want to pick up the baton from the innovators in ecolinguistics in the 1990s and focus on theoretically important ecolinguistic issues that are oriented towards practical application. In this introduction, we situate this endeavour in the joint history of ecolinguistics and applied linguistics (Section 1). Having pointed to linguistic assumptions that hold back the field, we present language as ecological: it is coordinative activity embedded in practices that have epistemic and ontological effects on ecosystems (Section 2). After a short interim in Section 3 that shows how traditional linguistic theorising limits ecolinguistics, Section 4 addresses what follows from tracing languaging to human practices that co-evolve with vital process. We emphasize that languaging is an epistemic and practical tool that can be used to mitigate and reverse noxious environmental effects by raising bioecological awareness, changing people's attitudes and engendering positive action that can influence social organization. Finally, in Section 5, we sketch how the contributions to this book bear on bioecological change in life-sustaining relations that draw on how people engage with properties of the material world as part of enlanguaged practices.

Ecolinguistic continuity in discontinuity

For those with an interest in the history of the field, it is an important fact that in the 1990s, ecolinguistics emerged out of, and contributed to, applied linguistics. In 1990, Halliday (1992) gave his famous 'New ways of meaning' address at the Thessaloniki *International Association of Applied Linguistics* (AILA) conference. In this keynote Halliday highlighted the devastating aspects of a then-looming climate crisis. The subsequent AILA conferences, in 1993, 1996 and 1999, all included ecolinguistic workshops and symposia. As the field matured, its institutional anchoring grew in a rhizomatic way. Arran Stibbe, the world's first professor of ecological linguistics, established an *International Association of Ecolinguistics* (IEA) and, since 2016, there has been an annual (now biennial) *International Conference on Ecolinguistics* (administered by Guowen Huang and Sune Vork Steffensen).[2] There are two academic journals devoted to ecolinguistics: the online journal *Language & Ecology* (edited by Amir Ghorbanpour and published by the IEA) and the Brazil-based *Ecolinguística: Revista brasileira de ecologia e linguagem*, edited by Hildo Honório do Couto. Among more established academic journals both *Language Sciences* (edited by Sune Vork Steffensen) and *Journal of World Languages* (edited by Wei He) publish extensively on ecolinguistics. In 2018 Alwin Fill and Hermine Penz edited the *Routledge Handbook of Ecolinguistics* (Fill & Penz 2018). Given this development, ecolinguistics has a well-established institutional status.

Even if less closely tied to applied linguistics today, ecolinguistics derived from a tradition where the concepts of *language use* and *discourse* were applied to, inter alia, issues of education, class and sex/gender. This tradition arose in the 1950s when the label *applied* 'was commonly meant to reflect the insights of structural and functional linguists that could be applied directly to second language teaching and also in some cases to first language (L1) literacy and language arts issues as well' (Grabe 2010: 34). Today, however, the field of general or theoretical linguists has largely diverged from the concerns of applied linguists. Given an interest in practice, applied linguistics has its own epistemological horizons, theoretical positions, methodological approaches and research programmes. Indeed, in comparison to linguistics, many regard applied linguistics and its theory as more innovative. For instance, in the 1990s, Larsen-Freeman conceptually foregrounded dynamical systems (Larsen-Freeman & Cameron 2008), and, shortly after that, Kramsch offered an ecological approach (Kramsch 2002). More recently, the Douglas Fir group placed socialization at the core of language use (The Douglas Fir Group 2016), and in studying thinking and identity, new weight fell on phenomena of translanguaging (García & Li Wei 2014).

Picking up on seminal work by Einar Haugen (1972), who introduced the focus on 'the ecology of language', ecolinguistics extends the applied focus on social issues to a range of ecosystemic challenges. Yet Haugen's (1972) original vision of showing how languages 'interact' with the environments on which we depend remains unfulfilled. We trace this failing back to how, like many others, Haugen adopted theoretical assumptions that were as inappropriate then as the methods which shaped applied linguistics were in the 1950s and 1960s.

In parallel to the realization that the toolbox of theoretical linguistics was not adequate for applied linguistics, we hold that today's linguistic toolbox fails to address both central theoretical issues in ecolinguistics (cf. the discussion in Section 3) and the normative application to life-sustaining relations (cf. Sections 4 and 5). To those who reject theory, we thus respond: Yes, the house is on fire, but without adequate tools, ecolinguists will merely douse the flames with latex flippers and lawn rakes. Thus, while social debates can be informed by the analysis of language use and discourse, we also need to consider how socially produced 'reality' arises from (and changes) human and non-human agents. Indeed, the discursive focus slides all too quickly over the question of how (the future of) living beings are entangled with languages, practices and the world's changing ecosystems. Hence, we look beyond conceptual, theoretical, methodological and analytical tenets of linguistics to ask how human ways of living co-evolve with practices, languages and the ecology.

In treating language as part of living, practices and ecosystems, we bring discontinuity to continuity. As ecolinguists, we explicitly address how languages and practices impact on the life-sustaining future of both humans and non-humans. We extend the field's scope by bringing discontinuity to the theoretical tools that can be used to enable practical outcomes. Yet, there is also 'deep continuity' with the theoretical innovations that a few decades ago allowed ecolinguistics to inform pragmatics (e.g. Fill 1993) and bring new insight to applied linguistics (Van Lier 2004). Equally, we build on how challenging post-Chomskyan theory, as outlined by Peter Mühlhäusler and colleagues (e.g. Harré, Brockmeier & Mühlhäusler 1999; Mühlhäusler 2003), offered an important new perspective on diversity in languages (Mühlhäusler 1996). In other words, this volume attempts to re-establish the innovative ecolinguistic thinking that flourished in centres such as Bielefeld (Peter Finke and Wilhelm Trampe), Graz (Alwin Fill and Hermine Penz), Odense (Jørgen Christian Bang and Jørgen Døør; see Steffensen 2007) and Adelaide (Mühlhäusler).

Ecolinguistics: One or many?

As documented by the *Routledge Handbook of Ecolinguistics* (Fill & Penz 2018), the field addresses a multifaceted array of concerns and topics. Though not always theoretically driven or empirically explicit, this diversity is generally united by a normative orientation of seeking to work for life-sustaining relations. In characterizing a multitude of concerns and styles, Steffensen and Fill (2014: 16) present ecolinguistics as an archipelago of 'insulated scientific programs that offer different views on both the language ecology and the theories and methods that are most appropriate for study'. As noted as early as 1998, the field is riddled with discontinuity, and steps towards a theoretical and methodological consolidation have so far been largely unsuccessful or remain implicit. In the influential 'Ecolinguistics: State of the Art', Alwin Fill (1998) identifies 'two approaches to ecolinguistics'. On the one hand, 'ecology' is 'understood metaphorically and transferred to "language(s) in an environment"'. On the other, '"ecology" is understood in its biological sense' (Fill 1998). Today, whereas some are content to use ecolinguistics as an 'umbrella term' (e.g. Fill 2018: 3), others use the 'eco' prefix (e.g. Stibbe 2015: 183) to urge innovation based on parallels with ecopsychology, ecotheology, ecofeminism, etc. On this view, as in expanding psychology, theology or gender studies, emphasis is to fall on ecological and environmental domains that are influenced by linguistic framings and features.

Steffensen and Fill's 2014 state-of-the-art also identifies discontinuities while offering a productive means of overcoming them. They find four strands in the history of ecolinguistics that 'differ in how they interpret what the environment of (a) language is' (Steffensen & Fill 2014: 7). The four strands posit symbolic, natural, sociocultural, and cognitive ecologies as the environment of language. Unfortunately, some have used the distinction metaphorically and thus envisage an ecological super-domain. For Steffensen and Fill, by contrast, the whole point of identifying the four discontinuous ecologies is to work for their elimination. Accordingly, they call for 'a naturalised model of language' that integrates the ecological approaches. In such a model, they suggest, the four realms will become '*descriptive* dimensions of a single *explanatory* framework' (Steffensen & Fill 2014: 19).

Language as an Ecological Phenomenon works to unify ecolinguistics by seeing the ecolinguistic archipelago as a single, continuous geological formation immersed in the sea. While the volume's contributors differ in their views of 'explanation', all regard theoretical innovation as crucial to the field's normative orientation. If ecolinguistics and ecolinguists are to work for life enhancing relations, this innovation must, as suggested in Haugen's (1972) original vision, include seeing languages as part of a wider ecology. However, rather than to stick to a model of languages in 'interaction' with the ecology, in addressing what Cowley (2022) terms *Haugen's problem*, we suggest treating languages as *integral to* living and the ecology. On the one hand, languages shape human experience and, on the other, they are embedded in how practices change lives and even geophysical systems.

The unifying view proposed here builds on Alexander and Stibbe's definition of the field as 'the study of the impact of language on the life-sustaining relationships among humans, other organisms and the physical environment. It is normatively orientated towards preserving relationships which sustain life' (Alexander & Stibbe 2014: 105). The normative stance has the advantage of committing ecolinguists to work for positive change. Ecolinguists can aim to change themselves, develop theories and methods, organize new practices and, ultimately, steer us towards better ways of living. Further, as elaborated in Section 4, when focused on life-sustaining relations, a second advantage emerges. One notes that all living agents are affected as practices change the ecosphere, and as languages influence *what people actually do*. Regardless of how 'languages' are construed, they inform and enable practices that presuppose (and impact on) the ecosystemic interdependency of all living systems.

To fully appreciate ecosystemic interdependency, life must be recognized to include many interlocking mechanisms on all scales, but crucially life does not reduce to the mechanistic. For example, as shown by neuroscientist Alain Berthoz, *simplex tricks* enable living systems and their parts to interact with environments and self-fabricate as they co-evolve (Cowley & Gahrn-Andersen 2022). To illustrate, the simplex trick of *inhibition* makes us abstain from acting, makes our visual system abstain from attending to noise, or reduces our neuronal excitability (with gamma-aminobutyric acids). Living is not only about doing, but also not-doing. Likewise, James Shapiro's (2011) notion of *natural innovation* explores how without genetic change molecules can self-transform (Steffensen & Cowley 2022). At all levels of organization, each living system exhibits *biological agency* or, by definition, acts to 'transduce, configure, and respond to the conditions it encounters' (Sultan, Moczek & Walsh 2022: 5). For such agents, 'novelty and stability are two sides of the same coin' in that mechanisms draw on material aspects of the 'system's functionally adaptive dynamics' (Sultan et al. 2022: 5). Building on Walsh's (2018) *Methodological Vitalism*, one can use the novelty–stability duality to pursue why 'the behaviours of living matter cannot be adequately accounted for by the sciences of non-living things' (Walsh 2018: 167). Below, we use this work to stress processes that bring simplex tricks to biological agency to enable the formation and use of biases. While not mechanistic, agents use these to exhibit resilience, adaptivity and novelty that, in this context, are seen as indicators of *vital process*.

Languages too depend on vital process as human communities weave historical products into temporal, spatial and energetic bodily flows. In the scales of history, human activity and languaging[3] bind emplacement and temporalities into global-scale changes (such as the ecological crisis) that arise as practices draw on co-actional experience. The results influence an agent and thus how and where we act, how and where we speak, how and where we breathe, and how and where we move, play or work. Thus, culturally specific constraints affect how individual acts of speaking, writing and silent thinking bundle practices into ways of acting. As they actualize practices, people collectively bind patterns and habits into familiar routines (Steffensen & Harvey 2018).

In an enlanguaged world, practices ontologically develop artefacts, social expectations, institutions and people: we engage with things and our fellows as situations prompt common experience (Blumenberg 2007). These observations answer the first part of Haugen's problem: languages 'interact' with the environment as living bodies draw on expression, timing and emplacement. Like non-humans, we use vital process to concert with others and the physical world. Given emplacement and temporalization, we draw on how a 'world' of collective values and standards bring history to human lives. Hence, our ways of acting link socially organized activity, languages and practices. In this respect, unlike other animals, we draw on languages that constrain what we do, how we act and what triggers understanding. Thus languaging, or coordinative activity in which wordings play a part (see Cowley 2014, 2019), enables collective human living: it literally integrates practices, action, population-level constraints and making/responding to perceptual hints. It emanates from a life history of places, temporalities, entities and other living human beings. Given a history of speaking and acting, durable linguistic patterns inform and consolidate an emplaced flux of experience. In literate societies, languages even evoke stable ways with wordings (i.e. using texts). This enables reflection and use of verbal expertise to enact judgements. We propose that we can unify ecolinguistics and save Haugen's vision by specifying how languages and the environment 'interact' as part of practices. In this way, Haugen's metaphor of interaction refers to how vital process links experience to emplacement, temporalities and situated judgements. This entanglement has brought forth an enlanguaged world where practices are actualized in public (see Figure 1.1).

Beyond their communicative properties, languages exert both epistemic and ontological effects. Within practices, languages contribute to binding action (Ingold 2007), perception and the imagined into physical events that arise as wordings reiterate and/or endure as patterns (e.g. 'words'). Out of such practices, epistemic and environmental effects can arise without any intent in that, as Cowley (2022: 17) notes, 'organized activity makes use of economics, technoscience, production demands, etc.' As he continues, these 'set off [...]

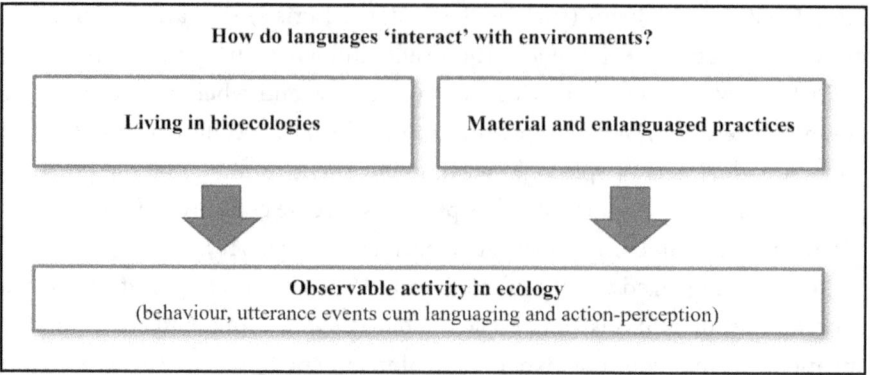

Figure 1.1 As a complex ecological phenomenon, language exerts effects on environments: observables link practices with material properties in an enlanguaged world as people mesh utterance events, wordings and action-perception.

material process that, often inadvertently, changes bioecologies and, on large scales, the ecosphere'.

Understanding how languages and languaging exert their intended and unintended influences on bioecologies and ecosystems is an important theoretical move. As outlined here – as well as in Steffensen and Fill (2014) and Steffensen (2018) – it enables the four strands of ecolinguistics to be woven together. In so doing, we invite the ecolinguistic community to begin with, not how language represents the environment, but how languages contribute to experiences, engagements and practices that affect the ecosphere.

Language and life-sustaining relations

In reframing Haugen's vision for an 'ecology of language', languages and languaging become emplaced multi-scalar activities embedded in practices. Thus, in enlanguaged worlds, humans use coordinative activity that linguists tend to model as types (e.g. 'words' or 'tones'). By emphasizing action, epistemic effects and diversity, we present languages as neither pre-given, pre-conceptual, nor self-contained (Brockmeier et al. 1999:1). Rather, languages constrain what we do: *contra* Haugen, they are *not* present 'in the mind of the user' (Haugen 1972). We thus reiterate the old objection that schools of linguistics often reify objects: we deny that languages have any autonomous status. While much is heuristically gained in idealizing their systematic properties in, say, pedagogy or editing, we reject appeal to structure sui generis (Calvet 1999). Above all, formal models leave out the coordinative dynamics of languaging. Whilst it is an observable fact that experience animates living bodies, understanding enmeshes persons, practices and social meaning with the environment. Thus, treating 'language' as a pre-given 'object' relies on, not empirical observation, but a history of institutionalized academic politics. As is well known, linguistics drew on how Saussure (1972) prioritized – or is said to have prioritized – *langue* as an object that only linguists can access and describe. This move produces a boundary object (Star & Griesemer 1989) and the organism-centred view shared by not only structuralists and functionalists, but also generative, cognitive, and even systemic-functional linguists. All tend to reduce social activity to how people draw on 'contexts' and self-contained 'signs' (*qua* forms). Like Haugen, they posit language models and analyse contextual effects such as those which ascribe a specific form/meaning to utterances, sentences, constructions, texts, discourse, etc. Oddly, a cognitivist/behaviourist doctrine – which posits that cognition centres on an organism (or mind) – is allowed to dominate even social views of linguistics. Ironically, Haugen's socially infused psychologism both enables his rich vision and, at once, prevents its realization. While allowing him to envisage language as part of the ecology, he pays the high price of adopting the doctrine that languages – not emplaced and temporalized humans – 'interact' with the environment.

What are the consequences of this linguistic reification? The short answer is: once 'language' is seen as a system that maps (or realizes) conventional forms onto (or as) content, meaning, ideas, etc., it becomes an abstraction. It reduces to a mode of representation that is separable from human living and experience. Thus, even ecolinguists ask how texts reflect and/or distort the environment (viz. how the world is 'constructed') and, typically, prioritize how things are said about issues like animal rights, global warming or threats to soils, oceans, biodiversity, etc. They focus on saying, believing, and knowing by using analytical concepts such as discourse, ideation, interpersonal function, and text. Seen as a (stable) hypostatization, language is separated from people, bioecologies and social practices. At a risk of oversimplification, we illustrate the view in Figure 1.2, where a reified entity called 'language' is shown to influence life-sustaining relations.

Given that the theoretical objects of linguistics and discourse analysis do not co-vary with life-sustaining relations, ecolinguists need to turn to a secondary mode of analysis. They evoke values and an 'ecosophy'. While also prevalent in Chinese ecolinguistics (Huang & Zhao 2021), the view is central to Arran Stibbe's

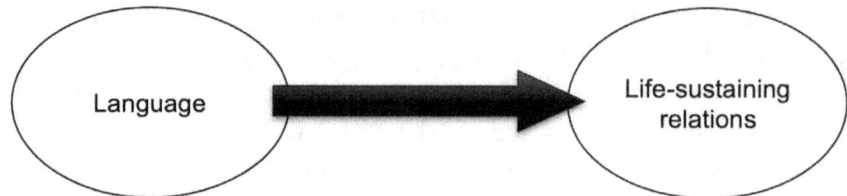

Figure 1.2 The impact of language on life-sustaining relations is seen as defining an ecolinguistic object of study.

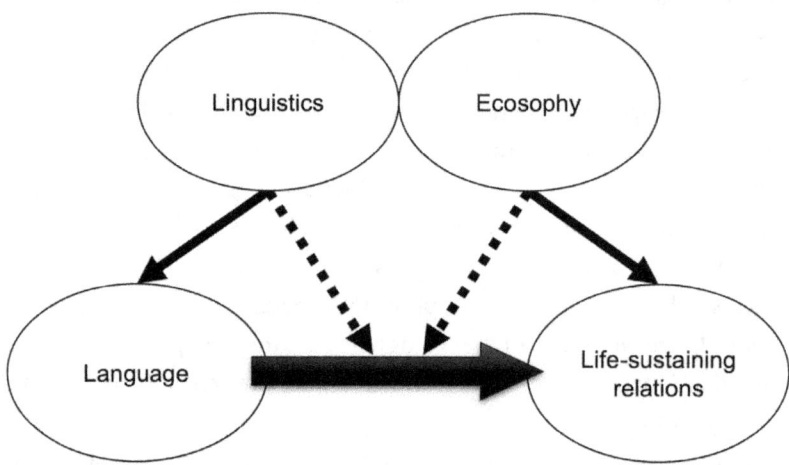

Figure 1.3 The two poles in contemporary ecolinguistics – the linguistic pole and the ecosophic pole – focus each on their domain (solid arrows). However, shown by the dotted arrows, they leave aside how language affects life-sustaining relations (i.e. the large horizontal arrow).

(2015) important research programme. He suggests 'the use of techniques of linguistic analysis to reveal the stories-we-live-by, opening them up to question and challenge from an ecological perspective' (Stibbe 2015: 9). For Stibbe, these techniques allow analytical products to be evaluated against 'a philosophy of ecological harmony' that includes 'norms, rules, postulates, value priority announcements and hypotheses concerning the state of affairs' (Næss 1995; quoted in Stibbe 2015: 12). On this view, ecosophy is 'an ethical framework that they [ecolinguists] use for evaluating the language they are analysing, whether or not it is made explicit' (Stibbe 2015: 11). By emphasizing the normative aspect, this perspective opposes a linguistic pole ('techniques of linguistic analysis') to an ecosophic pole ('philosophy of ecological harmony'). As in Figure 1.3, the two poles orient, respectively, to language and life-sustaining relations.

Since one pole is limited to language, and the other pole to evaluations of life-sustaining relations, the approach omits *how languaging and languages affect (and derive from)* life-sustaining relations. While having normative appeal, the model leaves a gaping theoretical hole. It obscures the question of *how* the living world is affected by languages, linguistic knowledge, practices and languaging. Rather than address this fundamental issue, ecolinguists tend to turn to discourses *on*, and what is said *about*, the environment: 'the field is trapped in a "paradox of aboutness": language is *about* nature, but is not *of* nature' (Steffensen & Fill 2014). Further, in highlighting how aspects of the world are 're-presented', rather than engage with experience, ecolinguists take a spectatorial view of the ecology (i.e. as separable from people). Language is viewed as a self-contained agent in a two-stage and purifying research process of 'analysis' and 'evaluation'. Due to the theoretical limitations, the approach fails to counter the toxic effects of human practices and thus to enhance life-sustaining relations.

Ecolinguistic practices

Once languages and languaging are seen as ecological phenomena – where languaging is traced to the life-sustaining relations that uphold human living – ecolinguistics can begin to develop new multifaceted, yet coherent, research practices. Such practices abandon the baggage of twentieth-century linguistic theory together with the two-stage analytical procedure that has placed narrow limits on ecolinguists. This section is dedicated to future ecolinguistic practices (as sketched in Figure 1.4). Before our outline, we emphasize, though, that practices – like 'paradigms' – cannot be designed *a priori*: they emerge and vary through academic and other work. Accordingly, our outline is intended to sketch what is enabled by ecolinguistic unification of living and languaging.

The key question guiding this section is that of how to put expertise in understanding practices to good use within the context of an ecolinguistics that counters ecological degradation. In what follows we start with two desiderata:

1. One can clarify how to use languaging (and the *Sprachspiel* of linguistic analysis) to enhance understanding through bioecological experience or awareness.

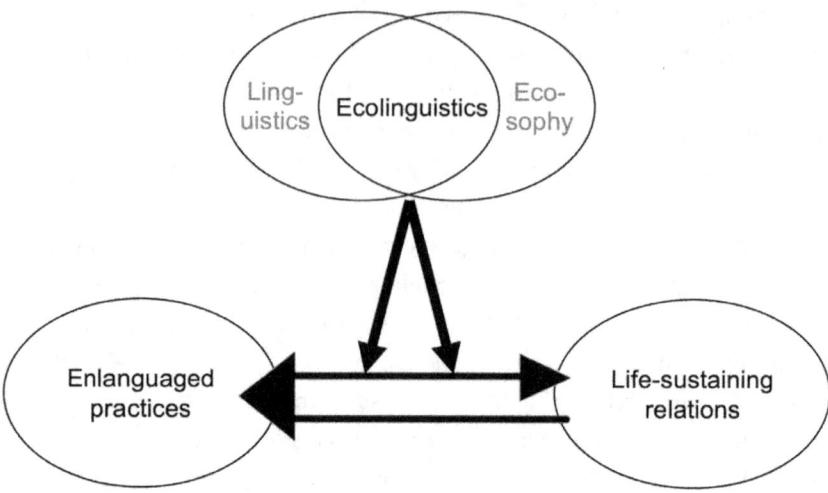

Figure 1.4 The model unites the normative orientation of ecolinguistics with a theory of languaging based in evolving life-sustaining relations. Hence, the lower part of the model connects enlanguaged practices with their impact on the life-sustaining relations. The dominance relation, shown by the 'dialectical arrow' from dialectical ecolinguistics (Bang & Døør 2007), shows that vital process constitutes and permeates languaging, practices and, reciprocally, what happens in a changing ecology. The two vertical arrows indicate the two ecolinguistic ways of seeking to enhance life-sustaining relations outlined below.

2. One can develop practical theories of how, using ecolinguistic expertise, one can work to enhance life-sustaining relations.

Feeling included in the living is part of an evolutionary heritage that appears in bioecologies as we draw on life history. A lived sense of natural inclusion attests to human emplacement. In situations, we experience particularity, set off events, observe and, at times, feel 'alive'. Human agents rely on sub-systems (e.g. neural parts) that self-regulate as vital process sets off experience. They may grant us bioecological awareness as, for example, we climb a mountain, help a friend, photograph a long-sought bird or catch a salmon – the experience connects place, an evolutionary past, experience and the workings of living bodies (including brains). Often, one draws on the bodily sub-systems that grant a person an individual voice. Citing none other than Raymond Firth, Stibbe and Alexander make just this connection:

> The human body is that region of the world which is the primary field of human experience but it is continuous with the rest of the world. [...] Voice-produced

sound has its origins in the deep experience of organic existence. In terms of living, language activity is meaningful. (Firth 1957: 24; quoted in Alexander & Stibbe 2014: 2105)

Vital process enables experience, bioecological awareness, voicing and other expressions. In an emplaced setting, it unites life history of adapting, resilience and coping with novelty. Even if the experience is often traced in careful reading of poetry, the same continuity or connectedness arises in celebrating a triumph, mourning or, perhaps, grasping a position, argument or problem. For a human agent, vital process informs lived events as one creates, identifies and transcends the familiar in ways that can seem new, true or beautiful. Having rejected the container view that meanings lie underneath, behind, or embedded in discourse or texts, humans become what Harris (1980) calls language makers. One rejects the traditions of critical discourse analysis (including ecological discourse analysis [EDA]) that seek to unearth the 'truth' behind or in a text. Rather, one acknowledges that analysis *constrains* the practice of language making. For Latour (2004b), the critical agenda uses the trick of granting disparate status to two lists of objects. Whilst the one includes discursive fetishizations to be revealed and critiqued (e.g. growth, nature, culture), the other names 'real' items like discourses and narratives. In critical practice, one takes one stance to the 'realities' (as *explananda*) while approaching the fetishes from an anti-realist stance (taking them as *explanans*). 'The whole rather poor trick that allows critique to go on,' Latour (2004b: 241) notes, 'is that there is never any *crossover between the two lists of objects*.'

Although we accept Latour's philosophical argument, we see Firth's organic existence as bringing adaptation to the events that unfold in the 'flat' ontology. While we can describe the world in terms of actants, vital process engenders leeway. In languaging, we use practices to grasp things, change our views and have insights. In text analysis too, a reader's experience can seem novel and surprising. While practice is constrained by methods, norms and conventions, emplaced experience uses gaps to trigger change and new understanding. Far from being a mode of scientific investigation, discourse analysis is a method that brings systematicity to a practice. But there is more to reading than such an approach shows. While readily illustrated by deep reading (Cobley & Siebers 2021), many kinds of text 'strike us' by appealing to bodily sub-systems (e.g. advertising that sets off desires). In disciplining how we self-regulate, the practice of discourse analysis brings control and clarity to understanding. It is a reflection such that, using experience, it can also set off bioecological effects.

In Halliday's (2003) terms, the practice draws on semogenesis, or, in Peirce's, it brings order to 'interpretants'. Vital process arises as living agents control sub-systems that self-regulate to cope with novelties while using evolution, development and experiential flow. The results shape cells, brains, individual experience of individuals and the work of teams such that, today, evolutionary biology emphasizes natural innovation (Shapiro 2011). Like reading or thinking, analysis triggers novelties that bring thoughts, feelings, and reactions to texts and, indeed, all human expression. These attest to how human agents draw on natural innovation. The insights of EDA (Alexander & Stibbe 2014) or harmonious discourse analysis (HDA; Huang & Zhao 2021) link agency with vital process and grounded, systematic and explicit practice. They rely on an emplaced agent who attends, acts and perceives while performing analytic practices. In such cases, understanding enables both analytical output (a written interpretation) and bioecological awareness (as lived experience). In principle, therefore, the results – both analytical products and experience – can be used to generate knowledge that a community can encounter and validate.

In using the practice of analysis to illustrate bioecological awareness, we stress the living human being. As one languages, emplacement and experience bring *predetermined* methods to the transformation of discursive forms. Hence, vital process serves to enable and supplement the repeated, the formalized and what is rendered systemic. In actual settings, analysis is never wholly mechanistic. While we have exemplified these aspects with discourse, the case applies to many kinds of model making. This is because biological models explore, not logical structures, but the open-ended processes of 'life itself'. In seminal work, the mathematical biologist Robert Rosen (1991) shows that, in living systems, causal entailments are always incomplete with respect to models of formal relations. Thus, understanding a model requires an analyst: it uses vital process, an agent's interpretation or, for Rosen, an 'art'.[4] While the formal theory has developed since his death (e.g. Kineman 2012), its negative thrust is generally accepted (see Baianu 2006). If one omits how living systems evolve, niches change, systems develop, and biological agents use resources and contingencies that affect the living, one can all too easily confuse a model with the modelled. One can overlook how agents feel, act and observe (or analyse) by reducing living agency to mechanisms.[5] As literate humans, many of us grasp such ideas most clearly when we link emplacement to languaging as we gain insights, puzzle, change our thinking and gain new understanding.

Having traced languaging to how agency use material and enlanguaged practices, we can now re-examine the ecolinguistic tradition. Above all, we can ask how our expertise can be used to enhance life-sustaining relations. It is with this purpose in mind that languages and discourses have typically been examined in relation to what people say about the world. Thus, as every ecolinguist knows, texts and semiotic assemblages attest to how languages partition the world. Each language has biases (Goatly 2021), discourse serves power (Penz 2017), and we can spread new and better stories (Stibbe 2015). Such findings take on new resonances when languaging is seen as part of practice. In this volume, for example, discursive knowledge is used to open conversations about the dairy industry (Moore) and in proposing collaboration with public bodies and new ways of leadering (Stibbe). Going further, one can track how languaging engages us with cows and, thus, raise bioecological awareness while raising social questions about practice (Cornips). The move links discourse and other aspects of practice to cognitive devices (Steffensen & Baggs) that can be used in many locally and globally relevant ways (Sinha and da Silva Sinha).

Given how bioecological awareness informs language making, we have much to offer to organizations that make use of communication. This is because, once seen as informing practices, languaging becomes an epistemic tool. It contributes to how practices affect agents, their development, and what they believe, know and, above all, *do*. Ecolinguistics thus becomes important to education. Not only are reading, writing, analysis and discussion practices that can raise bioecological awareness but their interconnectedness is the sine qua non of learning. Vital process further informs human skills and knowledge: languaging connects the verbal with soft powers such as emotional intelligence, communication, teamwork, creativity, docility, narrative construction and cultural sensibility (Kechagias 2011; Cowley 2024). All of these unite languaging with the self-regulation of an agent's sub-systems that shape experience and ways of using coordinated activity. They allow adaptation, coping with novelty and, at times, novelty making. Yet, as critical traditions show, human adaptivity is of most practical value when constrained by cultural history (including science). In terms that have become hackneyed, power shapes our views of things, events and even vital reasoning. In education, all can gain from tying a grasp of how we are conditioned with how, together, we can mould our conditions by using vital process. What we call 'independent' thinking is based in cultural and collective organization. Accordingly, the ecolinguistic community has much to offer the sciences, policy making, media, and, indeed, domains such as design and the arts.

Tracing languaging to vital process shows how the limits of human agency co-vary with practices. While science tends to focus on how the past can be used to shape the known, ecolinguistics stresses the narrowness of practices and awareness: much is and will remain beyond our reach. Accordingly, ecolinguists can act to select and pool expert knowledge that links our aspirations to practical theories. We can establish organized bodies that work for life-sustaining relations. In so doing, we can use what we know of languaging (and epistemic tools) to construct, sustain, select, and channel expertise between organizations and practitioners. We can strive for transdisciplinary collaboration with those whose practices contribute to changing and reimagining the future. Ultimately, we can aspire to use languaging to build an ecological epistemology.

Many would like to place life-sustaining relations at the fore of decision-making in business, policy, science, development, education, etc. Ecolinguists face the challenge of showing *how* this can be done. As a first step, expression of intent can spur the scrutiny and, at times, positive change. Indeed, bioecological awareness can spread and, in so doing, prompt others to change practices and temper destruction of the ecosphere. It can bring new ecolinguistic consciousness to fields like cognitive science and earth systems science.

Once the focus on practices is prioritized, ecolinguistics is seen to concern all who start with an ecosophy. As Steffensen and Cowley (2021: 732) argue, we can adopt Roy Rappaport's (1999: 461) view that 'if evolution, human and otherwise is to continue, humanity must think, not only about the world, but on behalf of the world of which it has become a special part and to which, therefore […] it has enormous responsibilities'. This quote epitomizes how, downplaying language about the world, we present languaging as an intrinsic aspect of the world. As human agents shape languaging and, inseparably, practices, we think and act 'on behalf of the world'. Strikingly, the formulation resonates with Guowen Huang's motto for the Center for Ecolinguistics at the South China Agricultural University: 'Think and act ecolinguistically'. In so doing, we bind practices with languaging that invites humility as we re-emplace humans within nature.

The sections of the book

As ecolinguistics has come of age over three decades, its state of the art stands between a mainstream linguistic epistemology and an ecological turn that pursues the impact of languages on life-sustaining relations (Alexander & Stibbe 2014). It is still hindered by discontinuities and lock-ins that the chapters in this volume seek to overcome (Döring & Nerlich 2005; Steffensen & Fill 2014; Steffensen & Cowley 2021). In building on our progress, we turn to how ecolinguistics currently appears and our view of its changing theoretical, methodological and empirical foundations. Accordingly, the book is organized in two parts: *Energizing Ecolinguistics* and *From Discourse to Worldly Action*.

In the first part, we highlight theoretical issues and current conceptual gaps in order to suggest implications for future ecolinguistic research. In some cases, the gaps have major epistemological repercussions as it contrasts language vs. languaging, representation vs. practices, and autonomy of language vs. entanglement of language with ecology. The second part empirically engages with these issues and shows what a change in the rationale of doing ecolinguistics entails. Here, constitutive dichotomies are rejected to bring emplaced and temporalized vitality to more-than-representational concerns (Thrift 2007). This also applies to the implications of the analytical notion of 'language' when languaging is allowed to draw on local languages and, inseparably, customs and beliefs. The theoretical shift towards focusing on the entanglement of the living not only impacts on how ecolinguistics is done but also produces insights that raise bioecological awareness. Hence, both sections are pointers to a theoretical change that can prepare ecolinguistics for future transdisciplinary challenges.

In the first chapter of part one, Leonie Cornips investigates languaging between cows and human beings. Her study of interspecies languaging brings home how a conceptual shift can alter the prospects for the field. In so doing, she refers to a multispecies turn to sociolinguistics by adopting a view where language does not separate humans from animals. In this way, she not only investigates the impact of human languaging on the environment, but also shows how a companion species (Haraway 2003) was linguistically decontextualized and socially othered. This separation is important because cow languaging offers an opportunity to reshape the human–animal relation by showing how interaction can begin to overcome any dichotomy (Haraway 2007). Cows are acknowledged as intentional, conscious, languaging animals whose articulations are construed by a human co-species. Using an autoethnographic approach, Cornips investigates contextualized cow-human languaging through events in a farming context. All interactions are video-documented and show context-specific differences in the multifacetedness of cow vocalizations. In sum, the chapter demonstrates human-cow languaging and, thus, opens up an important new area of ecolinguistic research.

In the second chapter, Sune Vork Steffensen and Edwards Baggs engage with the hyperobject (Morton 2013) of climate change. As all ecolinguists know, this is a major threat to life on earth which is hard to grasp. Global change is seen as a collective problem that sets a perceptual challenge. In this context, a new or radical ecolinguistic approach strives to reveal more than just the factual information favoured by science communication. For both, ecolinguistics lies at the intersection of culture, cognition and behaviour. In order to loosen the grip of information on thinking about language and communication, they emphasize emplacement and the need for working for climate-friendly action or lifestyles. In practical terms, they turn to temporalities that place global change in heteroscalar and homoscalar perspectives. These concepts can be used to clarify temporal and spatial dimensions of climate change that affect emplaced existence (Latour 2018). They regard the impact of languaging as direct because it cannot be reduced to using information *about* a distant ecology. Rather, climate change occurs bang *in* the middle of bioecological experience. Since languaging and climate change affect each other, ecolinguistics can look beyond its symbolic aspect. Accordingly, the authors argue that we need practical ways of using cognitive devices that change collective perception.

Stephen J. Cowley provides a theoretical perspective on gaps that exist in ecolinguistic tradition. In Chapter 3, he provides strong evidence that a conceptual shift from appeal to language-use to languaging can contribute to securing life-sustaining relations. The wor(l)dings of languaging play an essential role in material effects that unite society, individuals and the ecosphere. Negating the view that representations arise in the heads of speakers or focusing on discourses above society and ecology, he traces the interaction of society, the individual and the ecology to human entanglement with forms of life (Tsing 2021). Moreover, echoing the practice turn in the social sciences, he offers a grounded constructivism where situated and embodied practices draw on languaging. Language as a whole becomes a device that emerges at the intersections of practices and the ecology as humans participate in bioecologies. This entanglement places human-non-human-formations in lived-in places (Latour 1993, 2017) and leaves behind spectatorial views of the ecology. Thus envisaged, the role of ecolinguistics includes emplaced narratives as based on situated bioecological entanglements (Stibbe 2015). It poses fundamental challenges for current ecolinguistic research: How do humans live as parts of bioecologies? And how do non-humans and humans draw on languaging to manage practices and their effects? How could or should these entanglements be represented in the domain of institutions and politics? (Latour 2004a).

Alexander Kravchenko's chapter builds on the premise that human beings differ from other animals, because they rely on language in doing what they do. Only human beings engage in coordinations of coordinations of cooperative interactions, and by so doing, they inhabit civilizations. Even though this might be challenged by others, he uses this observation to argue that while humans have developed and enlanguaged destructive social practices, they have failed to gain wisdom in view of the current environmental degradation. If this is to be achieved, a conceptual break must allow wisdom to draw on, not philosophy alone, but its conjunction with languaging. Such a re-disciplinization treats the foundation of language as biological and as the basis whereby brains, languages and environments co-regulate. As a result, languaging is an adaptation that opens up new ecological niches. Characterizing niche construction and languaging as mutually interdependent runs counter to the scientific dichotomization of the world into nature and culture. The gains are considerable because, rather than place wisdom and language outside the ecology, they are seen as part of an ecological civilization. Hence, languaging brings inherent creativity that offers humans a means of making better use of bioecological adaptation.

The first part of the volume is closed by a chapter written by Rasmus Gahrn-Andersen. He critically engages with research in traditional ecolinguistics by laying weight on failure to clarify the relation between language and environment. Acknowledging the problematic dichotomies such as language and environment, he broaches the seldom discussed issue of sense-making in ecolinguistics. In addressing this question, he uses the work of Felix Guattari and, specifically, how the notion of enunciative assemblage can replace Saussurian ways of analysing semantic content. The move opens up new insight into expressions and their impact on meaning-making in the ecolinguistic theories of Bang and Døør (2007). Their innovative and context-dependent approach fails because it treats sense-making as an internal and mind-dependent process. In using this dichotomy, the approach remains, for Gahrn-Andersen, aligned to traditional linguistics. The problem matters because, first, many ecolinguists tend to rely on old linguistic epistemologies. Second, once one rejects the assumptions of 'internalism', one can read Bang and Døør's attempts to overcome the problem as showing that both language use and meaning-making presuppose a social and ecological context. What their internalist sense-making misses is how the social and ecological connect. Hence, their articulation of ecolinguistics overlooks views on signifying that, like that of Guattari (and many in this volume), reject the notion that language or languaging uses representations.

The volume's second part, *From Discourse to Worldly Action*, starts with Arran Stibbe's chapter on Ecolinguistics and Ethical Leadership. In considering world action, Stibbe uses the coronavirus as a starting point for reflection on the possibilities of overcoming the past pre-corona normal. In such a setting, he invokes effective use of words and stories such that ecolingusitics can contribute to ethical leadership and leadership can draw on ecolinguistics. Language arises in interactions between humans and non-humans whose bio-socio-ecological relations are informed by subcutaneous ecosophies. Hitherto, the philosophical grounding has not generated a conceptual reflection on how ethical leadership can use this normative frame. In addressing the issue, he suggests that creating stories can derive their normative grounding from life-sustaining relationships. Ecolinguists can create stories and wordings that challenge industrialized moralities, inform ethical communities of practice and enable ecological action. Such a perspective replaces essentialist views of leadership with embodied practice, languaging and, by extension, enstorying and leading. Such a narrative leadership can explicitly ground storytelling in ecosophy.

Elizabeth Oriel, Deepta Sateesh and Amal Dissanayaka's chapter also explores social and ethical consequences of enlanguaging the world. In considering the contexts of Sri Lanka and India, they address problematic relationships that arise between humans and elephants. In colonial times and through later Western styles of governance, there was a loss of ancient dialogues and ways of worlding with the land's non-human inhabitants. This essentialized idea of 'land' has proved extremely damaging to many bioecologies. Separation into nature (elephants and the surrounding land) and culture (human beings and 'their' landscape) has proved detrimental to humans and elephants alike. Sharing the land gave ways to new territorial modes of conceptualizing space that transformed multifaceted, practical relations (Latour 1993) between humans and elephants. Today, while some territories are restricted to humans, elephants are allowed, in principle, to roam in specific places. However, often there are none: the results have damaged all concerned – especially elephants. In seeking to overcome the problem, Oriel, Sateesh and Dissanayaka take a multispecies or hybrid approach (Whatmore 1998) that revives lost vocabularies to allow for the enlanguaging of the landscape (Mark et al. 2011) as a place of both elephants and humans. Ecolinguists can reinstate layers of practices as they reshape and reorganize the cohabitation of land, non-humans and human beings: rather than focus on symbolic framings, ecolinguists and new ways of telling stories can contribute much to a symbiosis of humans and non-humans.

Alison Moore explores relationality between humans and animals in the dairy industry. She highlights the industry's use of discourses about the production of milk and other dairy products. Considering languaging as essential to humans and nonhuman relations, she begins with the historical rationales for Australia's dairy history. Moore tracks the environmental damage caused by the industry in terms of greenhouse emissions, health issues (different types of cancer), social inequalities in farming environments, genetic cow-breeding and animal welfare. Moreover, she documents the detrimental impact of dairy production for all species and many bioecologies. Yet, commercial advertising of dairy products and foodstuffs uses idyllic and romantic images. Adopting a systemic-functional framework, she therefore offers eco-critical deconstruction of public relation campaigns to reveal blind spots in ways that inform conversations about human and non-human relations. Indeed, extending her ecolinguistic analysis, Moore proposes an ecocivilization in which not only are cows part of the worlding, but they contribute to multispecies sense making for dairy production.

Finally, Chris Sinha and Vera da Silva Sinha offer a way of investigating endangered languages. They take a practice-theoretical perspective by making the case for using research on endangered and local languages to benefit communities that speak the languages. Hence, protection of language or its documentation for heritage purposes should begin with attempts to understand the languaging and its linguistic life-worlds. In prioritizing ontology over epistemology, they draw on work by the anthropologist Philippe Descola (2014) which converges with ecolinguistic research. On this view, research is not *about* communities, ecology and languages, but about learning *with* communities *in* bioecologies. Sinha and da Silva Sinha frame this integrated perspective in terms of socioecological and political work where languages are living elements in the context of community practices. They criticize approaches to language protection that focus on abstraction through scientific documentation or language as a self-contained entity. The move speaks for an ecolinguistic perspective where the cultural and local aspect of languages is, at once, bio-social and grounded in local ecologies. Languages, they show, are part of living vitalities and vibrancy. Hence, languaging, as understood in ecolinguistics, becomes a theoretical starting point that has practical and theoretical implications.

Re-assembling ecolinguistics: Openings and future possibilities

The chapters in this edited volume empirically explore and provide new theoretical foundations for engaging with and doing ecolinguistics. Such an ecolinguistic approach emphasizes languaging rather than language, bioecologies rather than metaphorically conceived ecologies, and practice rather than representation. We are well aware that this might be challenging for those working in the discipline and identifying themselves as ecolinguists, but our intention here consists in productively enhancing the theoretical, methodological, and empirical scope of a discipline which has so much more to offer than just representing linguistics with an eco-prefix. Ecolinguistics is in an urgent need to be made fit for engaging with the many ecological problems lying ahead of us. Hence, this edited volume reaches out to those interested in and venturing an ecolinguistics willing to explore its relational strengths while avoiding the 'hierarchical understanding of "the human"' (Mol 2021: 1). In fact, the doings in terms of languaging, practices and the many other more-than-human engagements in the ecosphere are bioecological articulations shifting the scope away from human and linguistic exceptionalism towards a perspective that might bring a way forward that is able to deal with the shifting materialities, livingness, vitalities and dynamics of life in what we reify as *the* environment.

Each contribution in this edited volume possesses its individual and sometimes provocative and creative potential to re-assemble and engage with the changing archipelago of ecolinguistics (Steffensen & Fill 2014). So rather than concluding this introduction, we reach out and are curious as to how colleagues working in ecolinguistics and beyond are willing to get involved and attempt to deal with the research and the challenges published here. We hope that the book can become an opening for exploring the potentials and possibilities of doing ecolinguistics differently which is, obviously, up to its readers and those fellow colleagues within the terrain of what one calls ecolinguistics.

Notes

1. In the time of writing, the number of members of the International Ecolinguistics Association (IEA) has reached 1130 (http://ecolinguistics-association.org/, accessed 1 July 2023).
2. The series was launched at the South China Agricultural University in 2016, and after another two conferences organized in China (in Beijing in 2017 and in Guiyang in 2018), the ICE series moved to Europe in 2019, where ICE-4 was organized at the University of Southern Denmark, ICE-5 at the University of Liverpool and the ICE-6 at the University of Graz.
3. Languaging has a long history. While the term has been used since the sixteenth century, it has come to the fore through the work of, above others, Becker (1991), Kravchenko (2007) and Swain (2006). For an overview of the term's use, past and present, see Cowley (2019).
4. Baianu (2006) summarizes, 'Rosen's viewpoint … leads to the striking, and far-reaching, conclusion that reductionism in biology, that is the reduction of

the whole organism to the actions of its parts, or components, has quite severe limitations for understanding biological functions, or organismic/organismal physiology. His approach, therefore, stresses the importance of organization or relations between the functional parts of a whole organism over the underlying physicochemical structures of its components.'

5   For discussion of an agency perspective in evolutionary biology see Sultan, Moczek, and Walsh (2022). They trace what is here called 'vital process' to how living systems control co-regulating sub-systems in evolutionary, developmental and life-span scales.

References

Alexander, R., & Stibbe, A. (2014). 'From the Analysis of Ecological Discourse to the Ecological Analysis of Discourse'. *Language Sciences*, 41(0): 104–10.
Baianu, I. C. (2006). 'Robert Rosen's Work and Complex Systems Biology'. *Axiomathes*, 16(1–2): 25–34.
Bang, J. C., & Døør, J. (2007). Language, Ecology, and Society: A Dialectical Approach (S. V. Steffensen & J. Nash Eds.). London: Continuum.
Becker, A. L. (1991). 'Language and languaging'. *Language and Communication* 11.1/2, 33–5.
Blumenberg, H. (2007). *Zu den Sachen zurück*. Berlin: Suhrkamp.
Calvet, L. -J. (1999). *Pour une écologie des langues du monde*. Paris: Plon.
Cobley, P., & Siebers, J. (2021). 'Close Reading and Distance: Between Invariance and a Rhetoric of Embodiment'. *Language Sciences*, 84: 101359.
Cowley, S. J. (2014). 'Bio-ecology and Language: A Necessary Unity'. *Language Sciences*, 41(0): 60–70.
Cowley, S. J. (2019). 'The Return of Languaging: Toward a New Ecolinguistics'. *Chinese Semiotic Studies*, 15(4): 483–512.
Cowley, S. J. (2022). 'Ecolinguistics Reunited: Rewilding the Territory'. *Journal of World Languages*, 7(3): 405–27.
Cowley, S. J., & Gahrn-Andersen, R. (2022). 'Simplexifying: Harnessing the Power of Enlanguaged Cognition'. *Chinese Semiotic Studies*, 18(1): 97–119.
Cowley, S. J., & Markoš, A. (2019). 'Evolution, Lineages and Human Language'. *Language Sciences*, 71: 8–18.
Cowley, S. J. (2024). Ecolinguistics in Practice. In *Routledge Handbook of Applied Linguistics*, 374–385. London: Routledge.
Descola. Ph. (2014). *Beyond Nature and Culture*. Chicago: University of Chicago Press.
Døør, J., & Bang, J. C. (2000). 'Ecology, Ethics & Communication: An Essay in Ecolinguistics'. In A. V. Lindø & J. Bundsgaard (Eds.), *Dialectical Ecolinguistics: Three Essays for the Symposium 30 Years of Language and Ecology in Graz December 2000*, 53–82. Odense: Odense University.

Döring, M., & Nerlich, B. (2005). 'Assessing the Topology of Semantic Change: From Linguistic Fields to Ecolinguistics'. *Language and Logos,* 6(1): 55–68.

Fill, A. (1993). *Ökolinguistik: Eine Einführung.* Tübingen: Gunter Narr Verlag.

Fill, A. (1998). 'Ecolinguistics – State of the Art 1998'. *AAA-Arbeiten Aus Anglistik Und Amerikanistik,* 23(1): 3–16.

Fill, A. (2018). 'Introduction'. In A. Fill & H. Penz (Eds.), *Routledge Handbook of Ecolinguistics,* 1–7. New York: Routledge.

Fill, A., & Penz, H. (2018). *The Routledge Handbook of Ecolinguistics.* New York: Routledge.

Firth, J. R. (1957). *Studies in Linguistic Analysis.* Oxford: Basil Blackwell.

Gahrn-Andersen, R. (2019). 'Interactivity and Languaging: How Humans Use Existential Meaning'. *Chinese Semiotic Studies,* 15(4): 653–74.

García, O., & Wei, Li (2014). *Translanguaging: Language, Bilingualism and Education.* Basingstoke: Palgrave Macmillan.

Goatly, A. (2021). 'Ecology, Physics, Process Philosophies, Buddhism, Daoism, and Language: A Case Study of William Golding's The Inheritors and Pincher Martin'. *Journal of World Languages,* 7(1): 1–25.

Grabe, W. (2010). 'Applied Linguistics: A Twenty-First-Century Discipline'. In R. B. Kaplan (Ed.), *The Oxford Handbook of Applied Linguistics,* 34–44. Oxford: Oxford University Press.

Halliday, M. A. K. (1992). 'New Ways of Meaning: The Challenge to Applied Linguistics'. In M. Pütz (Ed.), *Thirty Years of Linguistic Evolution,* 59–95. Amsterdam: John Benjamins.

Halliday, Michael A. K. (2003 [1997]). 'Linguistics as Metaphor'. In Johnathan Webster (Ed.), *On Language and Linguistics: Vol. 3 of the Collected Works M. A. K. Halliday,* 248–70. London: Continuum.

Haraway, D. (2003). *The Companion Species Manifesto: Dogs, People, and Significant Otherness.* Chicago: Prickly Paradigm Press.

Haraway, D. (2007). *When Species Meet.* Minneapolis: University of Minnesota Press.

Harré, R., Brockmeier, J., & Mühlhäusler, P. (1999). *Greenspeak: A Study of Environmental Discourse.* Thousand Oaks, London: Sage.

Harris, R. (1980). *The Language-Makers.* Ithaca, NY: Cornell University Press.

Haugen, E. (1972). *The Ecology of Language* (Á. S. Dil Ed.). Stanford: Stanford University Press.

Huang, G., & Zhao, R. (2021). 'Harmonious Discourse Analysis: Approaching Peoples' Problems in a Chinese Context'. *Language Sciences,* 85: 101365.

Ingold, T. (2007). *Lines. A Brief History.* London: Routledge.

Kechagias, K. (2011). '"Teaching and Assessing Soft Skills", The MASS project, Thessaloniki (Neapolis)'. Downloaded from: https://www.yumpu.com/en/document/view/10974306/teaching-and-assessing-soft-skills-mass-measuring-and-/5 30 July 2021.

Kineman, J. J. (2012). 'R-theory: A Synthesis of Robert Rosen's Relational Complexity'. *Systems Research and Behavioral Science,* 29(5): 527–38.

Kramsch, C. (Ed.) (2002). *Language Acquisition and Language Socialization: Ecological Perspectives*. London: Continuum.

Kravchenko, A. V. (2007). 'Essential Properties of Language, or, Why Language Is Not a Code'. *Language Sciences*, 29(5): 650–71.

Larsen-Freeman, D., & Cameron, L. (2008). *Complex Systems and Applied Linguistics*. Oxford: Oxford University Press.

Latour, B. (1993). *We Have Never Been Modern*. Harvard: Harvard University Press.

Latour, B. (2004a). *Politics of Nature: How to Bring the Science into Democracy*. Harvard: Harvard University Press.

Latour, B. (2004b). 'Why Has Critique Run out of Steam? From Matters of Fact to Matters of Concern'. *Critical Inquiry*, 30(2): 225–48.

Latour, B. (2017). *Où atterrir? Comment s'orienter en politique*. Paris: La Découverte.

Latour, B. (2018). *An Inquiry into Modes of Existence. An Anthropology of the Moderns*. Harvard: Harvard University Press.

Mark, D., Turk, A., Burenhult, N., & Stea, D. (Eds.) (2011). *Landscape in Language. Transdisciplinary Perspectives*. Amsterdam: John Benjamins.

Mol, A. (2021). *Eating in Theory*. Durham: Duke University Press.

Morton, T. (2013). *Hyperobjects: Philosophy and Ecology after the End of the World*. Harrogate: Combined Academic Publishers.

Mühlhäusler, P. (1996). *Linguistic Ecology: Language Change and Linguistic Imperialism in the Pacific Region*. London: Routledge.

Mühlhäusler, P. (2003). *Language of Environment, Environment of Language: A Course in Ecolinguistics*. London: Battlebridge.

Naess, A. (1995). 'The Shallow and the Long Range, Deep Ecology Movement'. In A. Drengson and Y. Inoue (Eds.), *The Deep Ecology Movement: An Introductory Anthology*, 3–10. Berkeley, CA: North Atlantic Books.

Penz, H. (2017). '"Global Warming" or "Climate Change"?.' In *The Routledge Handbook of Ecolinguistics*, 277–92. London: Routledge.

Rappaport, R. A. (1999). *Ritual and Religion in the Making of Humanity*. Cambridge: Cambridge University Press.

Rosen, R. (1991). *Life Itself: A Comprehensive Inquiry into the Nature, Origin, and Fabrication of Life*. New York: Columbia University Press.

Saussure, F. d. (1972). *Cours de linguistique générale* (C. B. e. A. Sechehaye Ed. Édition critique préparée par Tullio De Mauro ed.). Paris: Payot.

Shapiro, J. A. (2011). *Evolution: A View from the 21st Century*. Upper Saddle River, NJ: Financial Times Press.

Star, S., & Griesemer, J. (1989). 'Institutional Ecology, Translations and Boundary Objects: Amateurs and Professionals in Berkeley's Museum of Vertebrate Zoology, 1907-39'. *Social Studies of Science*, 19(3): 387–420.

Steffensen, S. V. (2007). 'Language, Ecology and Society: An Introduction to Dialectical Linguistics'. In J. C. Bang, J. Døør, S. V. Steffensen, & J. Nash (Eds.), *Language, Ecology, and Society: A Dialectical Approach*, 3–31. London: Continuum.

Steffensen, S. V. (2011). 'Beyond Mind: An Extended Ecology of Languaging'. In S. J. Cowley (Ed.), *Distributed language*, 185–210. Amsterdam: John Benjamins.

Steffensen, S. V. (2018). 'The Microecological Grounding of Language: How Linguistic Symbolicity Extends and Transforms the Human Ecology'. In A. Fill & H. Penz (Eds.), *The Routledge Handbook of Ecolinguistics*, 411–23. London: Routledge.

Steffensen, S. V., & Cowley, S. J. (2021). 'Thinking on Behalf of the World: Radical Embodied Ecolinguistics'. In X. Wen & J. R. Taylor (Eds.), *The Routledge Handbook of Cognitive Linguistics*, 723–36. London: Routledge.

Steffensen, S. V., & Fill, A. (2014). 'Ecolinguistics: The State of the Art and Future Horizons'. *Language Sciences*, 41, Part A, 6–25.

Steffensen, S. V., & Harvey, M. I. (2018). 'Ecological Meaning, Linguistic Meaning, and Interactivity'. *Cognitive Semiotics*, 11(1): 1–21.

Stibbe, A. (2015). *Ecolinguistics: Language, Ecology and the Stories We Live By*. London: Routledge.

Sultan, S. E., Moczek, A. P., & Walsh, D. (2022). 'Bridging the Explanatory Gaps: What Can We Learn from a Biological Agency Perspective?' *BioEssays*, 44(1): 2100185.

Swain, M. (2006). 'Languaging, Agency and Collaboration in Advanced Second Language Learning'. In H. Byrnes (Ed.), *Advanced Language Learning: The Contributions of Halliday and Vygotsky*, 95–108. London: Continuum.

The Douglas Fir Group (2016). 'A Transdisciplinary Framework for SLA in a Multilingual World'. *The Modern Language Journal*, 100(S1): 19–47.

Thrift, N. (2007). *Non-representational Theory*. London: Routledge.

Tsing, A. (2021). *Mushroom at the End of the World: On the Possibility of Life in Capitalist Ruins*. Princeton: Princeton University Press.

Van Lier, L. (2004). *The Ecology and Semiotics of Language Learning: A Sociocultural Perspective*. Boston and Dordrecht: Kluwer Academic.

Walsh, D. M. (2018). 'Objectcy and Agency: Towards a Methodological Vitalism'. In D. J. Nicholson & J. Dupré (Eds.), *Everything Flows: Towards a Processual Philosophy of Biology*, 167–185. Oxford: Oxford University Press.

Whatmore, S. (1998). *Hybrid Geographies: Natures, Cultures, Spaces*. London: Sage.

Part One

Energizing Ecolinguistics

2

How (Dairy) Cows and Human Intertwine Languaging Practices

Leonie Cornips

Natureculture[1]

The aim of this chapter is to offer proof of principle for the animal turn in sociolinguistics, that is, for an inclusive sociolinguistics that does not use a criterion of 'language' to separate humans and non-human animals. By contrast, it takes a broad context to the study of interactions between animals, and between animals and humans (Kulick 2017). The chapter focuses on (dairy) cows or, in other terms, how cow(s) can 'take initiative in indicating directions and design'. Once this is acknowledged, it can lead to the 'disclosure of unexpected behaviors and modes of relating' (Lestel et al. 2014: 126–7). On the basis of ethnographic fieldwork, this study will pursue how two cows, with different relationships with humans, imbue interaction with meaning that, for cows and humans alike, makes sense of their social and situated context.

The Anthropocene (alternatively, Capitalocene or Chthulucene, see Latour 2018 and Haraway 2016) is increasingly used to describe the era in which we live. The name captures how human thoughts and actions are having a major impact on Earth as a living planet. As a result, we face unprecedented losses in biodiversity, damage from climate change and increased human exploitation of non-humans (Pennycook 2018: 3). Humans and human actions are like 'a major geological force' (Chakrabarty 2012) that not only changes the earth but is setting off irreversible climate change, eliminates biodiversity and is leading to mass extinction. The planetary crisis can be traced to structural power relations that are enhanced by how Eurocentric views silence both other humans and non-humans. The effect is worsened by treating the latter as inarticulate beings whose presence is merely material or natural. On these grounds, they are often shamelessly exploited (Sousa & Rocha Pessoa 2019; Deumert & Storch 2020). In the context of a planetary crisis, we should not ignore the voices of non-human animals (once more) and, especially so, those of animals whose lives are central to discussion of sustainability (Barron et al. 2020: 13).

In sociolinguistics, the epistemological commitment to the animal turn stems, above all, from challenging how humans are currently theorized as a part of natural history and the world's ecosystems (Chakrabarty 2012: 10). The move rejects the traditional distinction of 'nature' from 'culture' (Latour 2005; Haraway 2008; Braidotti & Hlavajova 2018) by denying that humans use 'language' as an abstract decontextualized system. Once the assumption is overthrown, one can treat language and environment as 'interconnected and co-constructed entities' (Döring & Zunino 2014: 35) that arise from 'a cultural organization of process that is naturalistically grounded in human biology' (Thibault 2011: 211). Thus, as part of nature, the human and other species can be theorized as natureculture. On this view, there is no simple or straightforward division between what is 'nature' and what is 'culture'. Just as with human lives, that of a dairy cow in the Dutch intensive dairy farm relies on a blurring of nature–culture distinctions (Cornips & van den Hengel 2021): a cow becomes a dairy cow through human breeding practices, compulsory pregnancies by artificial insemination, immediate calf separation after delivery and by producing more milk for humans than her calf could ever need. Hence, a decentring of humans in (socio)linguistics presents theoretical and methodological challenges to understandings, conceptualizations and theorizing of the animal Other. One can deny that whereas *nature* produces random *noise*, the human Self draws on *culture to produce* (orderly structured) language (Cornips 2019, 2022, Cornips & van den Hengel 2021, Cornips & van Koppen 2024).

In making a case for new reflections in (socio)linguistics, the chapter challenges both human exceptionalism and species hierarchy based on concepts of (human) *language* and (animal) *communication*.

In such an investigation, the main challenge becomes that of rethinking intraspecies and interspecies interactions as embodied, multimodal and sensory phenomena whose bodily mediation draws on material objects and environments. Examining the local meaning-making by the dairy cow allows sociolinguistics to critically reflect on their ideologies towards animal interactions, first, with respect to power dynamics. Second, there is a disproportionate attention to sound production as opposed to 'whole-body behaviour' which, of course, invites multimodal attention. Hence, the chapter connects to ecolinguistic research that aspires to enrich life-sustaining relations between humans and non-humans

(Alexander & Stibbe 2014). Ecolinguistics is informed by sociolinguistics, in this case, through investigation of how cow vocalizations induce humans and cows to coordinate whole-body activity. Thus, sociolinguistic research extends ecolinguistics by showing how, in cow–human relations, we can learn from study of 'their ways of languaging'. This offers a firm basis for enriching 'life-sustaining relations' between (and within) species.

In the first place, a better understanding of the non-humans 'can help humans to understand them better and build new relations with them' (Meijer 2019: 2). Further, by setting off the reflexive process one raises important interspecies issues, e.g. how to include other animals in sociolinguistics, and how to treat them respectfully as subjects who dwell in situated contexts. A reflexive fieldworker 'observes not only behaviour of performance, but also the perspective of the one who is being observed' (Lestel et al. 2014: 141). On this approach, knowledge is therefore co-produced by humans and non-human animals, objects, etc., which, together, draw on power dynamics (Van Patter & Blattner 2020) that use ancient co-evolutionary histories.

The chapter is organized in five sections. The next section discusses the need for the animal turn in sociolinguistics. In so doing, it then looks beyond the discourse focus of so much ecolinguistics. In the third section, the focus falls on the methodology used and, in the fourth I present two events in which (dairy) cows interact with humans to produce recurrent vocalizations. The fifth, and last, section discusses the analysis to offer a brief conclusion.

The state of the art: The need for an animal turn in sociolinguistics

In sociolinguistic theories, as yet, there is no widespread critical engagement with an arbitrary 'linguistic' divide between humans and non-human animals. A claim that often appears in linguistics, and especially in introductory textbooks, is '(t)he *possession of language,* perhaps more than other attributes, *distinguishes humans from other animals.* To understand *our humanity,* one must understand *the nature of language that makes us human*' (Fromkin et al. 2011: 284; my italics). Often, this is backed up with claims such as 'Language is a system that relates sounds and gestures to meanings. (….) but *their* [animals] *utterances carry no meaning*' (Fromkin et al. 2011: 304). Where one begins with such a view, a model of human language and cognition takes a deficit view of other species. As a result, "people always end up better at language than animals" (Haraway

2008: 234) for whom difference can only mean deficiency' (Kulick 2017: 373). Thus, the 7 1/2-month-old female chimpanzee Gua, with her ten-month-old son Donald, was taught to speak English for nine months (Andrews 2016) and, in explaining the lack of success, appeal was made to a laryngeal apparatus that differs from its human counterpart.

Biologists (including ethologists) offer much richer view of species-specific meaning and how vocal communication informs intraspecies interaction. On such a view the sense of 'sounds, movements, postures, touch, scents or electricity' is said to be 'construed thanks to an animal's sense organs' (Håkansson & Westander 2013: 23). A dolphin, humpback whale or orca, for example, undertakes vocal learning in its first year and, by means of whistling informs her/his mother about her/his position or, whether she/he wants to come near and rest. Every dolphin has a unique whistle for kin recognition (Håkansson & Westander 2013). Themes of humpback whale songs change over the years and are probably culturally transmitted. By contrast, the songs of orcas feature dialects that differ between groups whose unit sequencing linguists can describe and analyse as syntax (Håkansson & Westander 2013). A chicken produces about twenty-four different sounds that express various alarms (air or ground predator) and food calls (Collias 1987). Like humans, they use referential communication that, without contextual cues, elicits appropriate response in other chickens (Evans 1997: 104–5). In contrast to what was once deemed unique to humans, dogs have a 'productive, creative ability to understand novel object/action pairings' that is illustrated by Chaser, a border collie who also 'successful mastered over 1000 object referents' (Fitch 2017: 449, see Andrews 2016). Pepperberg shows that African grey parrots like Alex 'demonstrate both flexible, context-dependent interpretation of meaning (including adjectives like shape, color, material, and number), and appropriate productive usage of these abstract categories' (Fitch 2017: 449, see Andrews 2016). Neuroscientists using machine-learning systems can detect patterns in large collections of data that evoke (what we hear as) whistles, trills, twitters, grunts, hiccups and hisses of naked mole rats. At very least, this shows not only each mole rat has its own vocal signature but also that different groupings have distinct dialects (Barker et al. 2021).

This sociolinguistic study, however, differs from these studies in that its focus is on encaged animals instead of more 'wild' animals, on animal–human interspecies interaction, and on the *local* meaning-making potential of the individual non-human and human animal in its *situated context*.

2.1 Knowledge gaps in sociolinguistics

The chapter starts to fill a gap in sociolinguistic knowledge by pursuing intentional, interactional and communicative expression in animals. Since findings of biological, neurological and ethological studies do not inform sociolinguistics, anyone interested in animal communication may run into misunderstandings of animal communication in the (socio)linguistic literature (see Fromkin et al. 2011). Animals are often pictured as lacking intentionality and consciousness and, thus, as essentially different from humans (Meijer 2019). In addition, a search for language-related genes that distinguish humans from other higher primates such as chimpanzees (Fitch 2017: 455) strengthened the idea that so-called production animals have less complex expressive capacities than primates (George & Bolt 2021). These ideas about cognitive and communicative capacities (Kulick 2017) are in sharp contrast with findings from other fields of science. In the *Cambridge Declaration on Consciousness* (Low 2012), as drafted by cognitive neuroscientists, neuropharmacologists, neurophysiologists, neuroanatomists and computational neuroscientists, the neurobiological substrates of human and non-human conscious experience and behaviour are described as follows:

> Convergent evidence indicates that non-human animals have the neuroanatomical, neurochemical, and neurophysiological substrates of conscious states along with the capacity to exhibit intentional behaviors. Consequently, the weight of evidence indicates that humans are not unique in possessing the neurological substrates that generate consciousness. Non-human animals, including all mammals and birds, and many other creatures, including octopuses, also possess these neurological substrates.

The ethologist Kiley-Worthington (2017) provides details of neurobiological evidence that, like other placental mammals, humans and cows are sentient: they feel, have emotions, learn in similar ways, and acquire ecological and social knowledge. Hence, they are social, know about others' intentions, and can develop different traditions and cultures. Moreover, findings from ethological studies reveal that long-term, intensive, and systemic observation of embodied individual behaviour shows multimodal variations that are sensitive to situations and particular others. Like humans, they each have preferences and make choices (DeMello 2012; De Waal 2016; Sievers et al. 2017). Dairy cows too have stable and distinct personality characteristics, are competent learners, possess both short- and long-term memories, have individual face recognition skills, and sustain rich and socially complex lives that draw on social learning

(Marino & Allen 2017). Evidence from biology, ethology and neuroscience all concurs that the study of non-human interactions can offer a valuable and necessary input to theoretical development in sociolinguistics (Cornips 2021, Cornips & van Koppen 2024). Moreover, an important finding from ongoing research is that, in dairy cows, materiality reflects and shapes both interspecies and intraspecies interaction (Law & Mol 2008; Driessen & Heutinck 2015; Mondada 2016; Cornips & van den Hengel 2021). Hitherto, unlike biologists, sociolinguistics has not yet undertaken intensive study of how materiality permeates the sounds, bodies and movements of dairy cows. Examining whole-body activity – including sounds – of dairy cows, and mediation of embodiment by material objects provides a new perspective. Hence, it can contribute to new knowledge about language as practice, or a way of being in the world.

2.2 Why a sociolinguistic study of (dairy) cows?

The deep asymmetrical power relations between production animals and humans in industrial farming oblige sociolinguists to reflect critically on how ideologies affect our conceptions of animal interactions. Hence, *contra* Fromkin and colleagues (2011: 304), a dairy cow has a vocal meaning-making potential: she produces distinct sounds for e.g. milking delay, experiencing hunger, sexual arousal (oestrus) (Jahns et al. 1997; Jahns 2012), acknowledging the entry of a farmer/human to the barn (Cornips 2022), addressing a new-born calf and urging an older calf to stay with her or to move over to her (Padilla de la Torre et al. 2015). While sounding, she simultaneously uses gaze to claim the human's attention, holds her head and neck higher than her back, and places her ears straight out to the side, perpendicularly to the head-rump axis in a friendly manner (Fiems et al. 2018). The co-articulation of vocal and bodily expression by dairy cows thus (re)produces sociality (Tsing 2013) and social organization. The complexity makes them ripe for sociolinguistic study in that the expressions are meaningful to other cows and initiated humans (Cornips & van den Hengel 2021; Cornips 2022; Cornips & van Koppen 2024).

Even though cows have been domesticated in herds since around 10,500 BC (Marino & Allen 2017), we know less about their social behaviour than that of companion animals Yet, they have long been integrated into human work (Porcher & Schmitt 2012:40) and have adapted to close contact with humans in many farming systems (Bos et al. 2018). In historical perspective, 'documents written by veterinarians and those involved in zootechnics can be used to trace the animals' initial resistance around the eighteenth century to the shifts in dairy farming that used brutal and traumatic separation of cows from calves, and then to follow the animals' slow adaptation, through training and selection, as the relations between cows, and cows' relations with breeders, changed with the adoption of different modes of breeding' (Baratay 2015:7). In dairy cow breeding, there has been selection for skills that enable social cognition and interaction with humans (Hare et al. 2002). Stuart and colleagues (2013: 208) even argue that 'successful' long-term domestication of both human and cow have favoured human–cow understanding. Phillips (2002: 87) notes that whereas non-domesticated cattle see humans as predators and, therefore, ignore and try to stay clear, 'adequate communication [with humans/LC] is of vital importance in an intensively managed gregarious species' such as dairy cows in the Netherlands. Further, the domestication process is not unidirectional in that both dairy cows and farmers encounter related forms of oppression that are woven into the same larger power structures (Meijer 2023: 134).

2.3 Languaging

The aim is to examine whether the concept of languaging applies to dairy cows' interspecies interactions with humans in ways that can bring new light to sociolinguistics. Traditionally, two important linguistic concepts circulate in (socio)linguistics: first, many conceptualize language as a mental 'capacity' or an abstract computational system (Chomsky 2002); second, others stress a social construct in which language (in) use is interconnected with the workings of society, hence, carries social connotations of that society (Labov 1994). Both conceptualizations are limited to humans in line with the idea that grammar or language is an object, an 'existing, identifiable and singular entity (…) which we may define, interact with, or think about differently' (Demuro & Gurney 2021: 2).

However, in developing an inclusive sociolinguistics in which, like dairy cows, non-humans are taken seriously as subjects, this chapter treats the concept of languaging as a different ontological possibility, that is, one that is 'based on practices, as instances of *worlding*' (Demuro & Gurney 2021: 2). In sociolinguistics, languaging (also crossing, polylanguaging, metrolingualism, translanguaging; see Androutsopoulos 2013 for a brief overview) allows the fluid and flexible use of linguistic features. In so doing, therefore, it also disconnects fixed links between language and categories such as ethnicity, race, age, gender, sexuality and place. Hence, languaging places activity and agents, or languagers and their doings at the fore of attention. Conversely, it plays down a linguistic system and challenges any monolingual (standard) language ideology that treats 'language' as a discrete, bounded, countable and monolithic object. It thus challenges ideas based in romanticism that shaped the formation of the European nation-state.

Maturana defines languaging as connotative, as embedded in the ongoing flow of actions coordinated by individuals (see Mingers 1991: 325). It becomes embodied 'doing in the world' (Steffensen & Cowley 2021), and 'a whole-body sense-making activity that enables persons to engage with each other in forms of coaction and to integrate themselves with and to take part in social activities that may be performed either solo or together with other agents' (Thibault 2011: 215). This perspective enables an animal turn in sociolinguistics. In intraspecies and interspecies interaction in situated contexts, cows 'enact, exploit, respond to, and attune to (…) events in order to engage with others and to construct their worlds with them' (Thibault 2011: 215). Verbal action is 'obligatory' for neither human nor non-human subjects. A good example from ethnographic fieldwork is provided by Hovens (2020) who describes how he and a temporary Polish-speaking employee learn on their own how to work with a blasting machine in the noisy Finishing Department of a Dutch metal foundry. Only fifteen minutes after an experienced supervising colleague left, the blasting machine unexpectedly stopped and displayed an incomprehensible text in Dutch. While they were trying to understand, another employee walked towards the blasting machine and pressed the start button without saying a word. The machine indeed started working, and the problem – a safety measure taken by the machine itself because the employee and Hovens had moved too close – was dissolved. In the case of such action, recurrent interactions between employees, fieldworker and the blasting machine become, in the words of Maturana (see Mingers 1991) 'structurally coupled' and cooperative. Hence, learning how to operate a blasting machine in a noisy metal foundry is cooperative (non-speaking), learned in practice and based on doings that unite 'action, perception and attention' (Vallée-Tourangeau and Cowley 2013: 1). Since the 1990s, new cognitive models have widened the focus to interconnected cognitive abilities that parallel Pennycook's spatial repertoire: '(n)either agency nor language nor cognition is best understood as a property of the individual, as something located in the human mind or tied to personal action; rather it is a distributed effect of a range of interacting objects, people and places' (Pennycook 2017: 278; see also Thibault 2011; Steffensen & Cowley 2021). The distributed view makes it possible to study intraspecies and interspecies interactions of dairy cows in a range of settings. One can pursue how interaction is coordinated as cooperative action draws on simultaneous whole-body activity that emerges in time and place. These co-articulations may be sounds, gaze, movements, facial expressions (kinesics), space (proxemics) and sensory practices of meaning-making through tasting, touching, seeing, hearing, listening and smelling.

Posthuman ethnography

Since mid-2018 I have conducted multispecies ethnographic fieldwork (Hamilton & Taylor 2017; Abrell & Gruen 2020) which puts the dairy cow at the centre of a long-term and systematic observation of various kinds in situated contexts (Cornips 2019, 2022, 2024; Cornips & van den Hengel 2021). A multispecies ethnography allows no categorical divide between humans and non-humans and opens up new and unstudied communities (Buller 2015; Hodgetts & Lorimer 2015) that make dairy cows part of a sociolinguistic project. Observation highlights how cows relate to other cows, other species, the farmer(s), caretakers and their (recurrent or not) activities. Ethnography is an exemplary means for studying languaging as a situated practice, and the interrelations and interactions in the here-and-now as interactants 'intertwine practices, acting and ways of languaging' (Cowley 2024). At once, conducting ethnography is a reflexive process with full awareness of a researcher-observer whose positionality, actions and values appear in doing fieldwork, and, thus, relating to cows and farmers (Cornips 2024). The approach enables a productive analysis of the observer's interpretative role in treating 'data' as co-produced by humans, dairy cows and a situated context that enables mutual bodily resonance (Kamphof 2017).

I focus on languaging in two interactive events as a cow negotiates her environment as a material-semiotic resource by producing a meaningful world while relating to 'her' human. Hence, the cow engages 'directly with a world in which they have co-evolved' (Steffensen & Cowley 2021: 728) in ways that foreground the cow's semiotic capacities (Cornips & van den Hengel 2021; Cornips 2022; Cornips & van Koppen 2024).

The two cows live in two situations: in one, she is in a farming condition in which she has to produce milk for human consumers. In other terms, she has

Table 2.1 The two fieldwork sites in this chapter.

	LOCATION	BREED	N	BARN TYPE	MILKING	FIELD WORK (D/M,Y)
1	Small herd	*Fleckvieh, MRIJ, Lakenfelder*	7	Pasture	none	08/05, 28/05, 18/06, 4/09, 16/10, 27/11 *2021*; 30/01, 13/03, 20/04, 07/05, 03/06, 27/08, 10/09, 02/10, 20/11 *2022*; 22/01 *2023*
2	Amsterdam	*Fleckvieh*	30	Tie-stall	mobile manual milking machine	3/5, 18/7, 18/8, 19/9, 12/10, 22/10 *2019*; 4/2, 6/5, 14/5, 22/9, 15/10/, 1/12/ *2020*; 9/3/, 7/5/, 14/5, 3/4/, 16/4, 13/8 *2021*; 19/05, 23/08 **2022**

to deliver calves (or, in other terms meat). In a context such as this, the human defines himself as a farmer. In the other situation, I observe a more 'natural' small herd in which females, males and calves, live together all year round as they roam outside. These cows produce milk only for their calves (i.e. not for human consumption), and the humans have come to define themselves as caretakers and/or breeders.

The two cows are not seen as representatives of a species but, rather, as 'semiotically capable beings' whose particularity and context relate to 'their' human(s). In participating in their worlds, an ethnographer has the opportunity to gain a more thorough view of the nuances of meaning-making by the Other (Hendlin 2016: 96). The two interspecies interactions which I discuss below were collected as follows. The farmer of the tie-stall barn has regularly sent WhatsApp videos and pictures of cows interacting with him and/or with each other to help my research. One such video-recording is transcribed and analysed for this chapter (see also Cornips & van Koppen 2024). The interaction with the small herd was video-recorded by myself during field work on 27 August 2022. The 'data' consists of four separate video-recordings that were taken one after the other (see below).

Languaging in two interactive events

The actions called 'give me a cow-cookie' (see 4.1) and 'untie my neck-chain' (see 4.2) arose in shared sociability (Tsing 2013) between cows and humans. They foreground intersubjective relations between parties that allow for the formation of situated knowledge (Haraway 1988). This can arise on basis of whole-body activity and mutual body resonance (Kamphof 2017), on behalf of the ethnographer.

4.1 Living in a Small Herd: 'give me a cow-cookie'

Since spring 2021 (see Table 3.1), I have been observing and relating to a small herd in the south of the Netherlands. The herd consists of three adult females, two of whom – Janneke and Noortje – had just delivered a calf each (Ronnie and Roos, respectively). The third cow – Cato – didn't become pregnant after artificial insemination. The small herd remains outside day and night, summer and winter but they can shelter in a small shed with a roof and closed sidewalls. Probably because Cato is without her own calf, she was the first to contact the calf called Piet that I had adopted from a farmer (Cornips & Wells, subm). Indeed, she touched Piet who was then three months nose to nose on his arrival in the meadow. Due to his young age, Piet was still reliant on milk which his caretakers prepared in an outbuilding with a canopy that was located next to their living quarters. Although an iron fence prevented the herd from entering this was opened so that Piet could eat and drink. Strikingly, even when open, the rest of the herd never entered this 'human' space. When observing (27 August 2022), the two caretakers, my friend and I were busy in the 'human' space with Piet. In this space, behind the blue barrel (see Figure 2.1), the caretakers store *rundveekoeken* 'cattle-cookies' in a canopy that lies 9 metres from the fence that separates the human space from the meadow (see Figure 2.1).

As the caretaker was strolling around the blue barrel and the canopy, Noor, one of the adults vocalized. Having intuited that, perhaps, she was 'asking' for a cattle-cookie, we gave her one (not on video). In order to ascertain whether we had interpreted Noor correctly, the caretaker now deliberately strolled around the blue barrel. Once again, Noor vocalized with closed mouth while extending her head and neck towards the human space and, at once, directing her ears sideways in an upright direction (see Figure 2.2). Then,

Figure 2.1 The 'human' space with the canopy behind the blue barrel containing 'cattle-cookies', Piet and the caretaker.

Figure 2.2 Noor (right) and her youngest calf Saar (left). Noor is vocalizing with closed mouth while simultaneously showing head and neck extension, ears positioned sideways and upright, and looking in the direction of the humans.

after a pause of seven seconds, a second vocalization followed – just as if we were not responding fast enough (see Figure 2.4; and vocalization 1 and 2 in Figure 2.5). In this way, Noor managed to organize components of her current actions around visible humans by positioning herself right in the humans' line of sight (Goodwin 2000).

Figure 2.3 Noor receives a 'cattle-cookie' as the human responds to co-articulation (vocalizing, head and neck extension, ears sideways and a bit upright and looking at the humans).

As in the case described by Goodwin (2000:1499), Noor's vocalizing and gesture mutually elaborate each other within the temporal embedding of a larger action that is defined by how humans react by presenting the desired cookie (see figure 2.3). Hence, emplaced experience prompts humans to interpret Noor's co-articulations, and, just as crucially, Noor interprets our actions as we reciprocally engage directly and bodily in a situated material context (Steffensen & Cowley 2021).

In order to see whether Noor would repeat the initiative (i.e. express a wish for a cookie), the caretaker once again began to stroll around the blue barrel and the canopy. As Noor vocalized, she again stretched her head and neck forward while positioning her ears sideways. Humans and non-humans alike repeated the routine twice more (in total 5 co-articulations were collected). Whilst the first vocalization took about three seconds, the subsequent ones lasted about two seconds each. Noor received one cookie after the first two, and then one after each vocalization (four cookies in total). As a result of the 'repetition', Noor and we humans co-constructed a specific social practice, modifying, drawing on what was happening, and, crucially, reworking it on the basis of interpretations, and what was expressible (Steffensen & Cowley 2021: 730).

The spectrogram of the five vocalizations (see Figure 2.5, mid panel) shows many formants or, specifically, five in the lower part of the frequency range

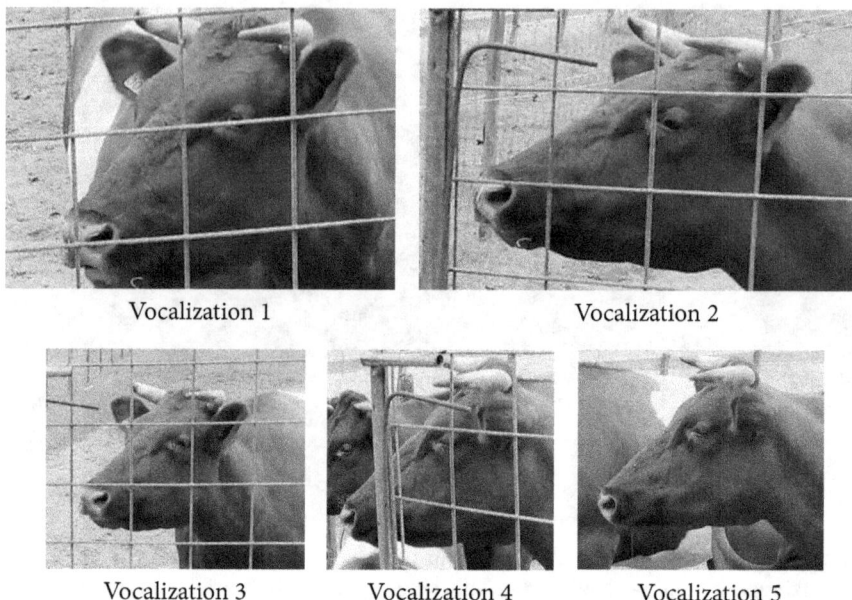

Figure 2.4 Snapshots of the five co-articulations by Noor with extending neck and head, ears sideways and a bit upright, looking at the caretaker including vocalizing.

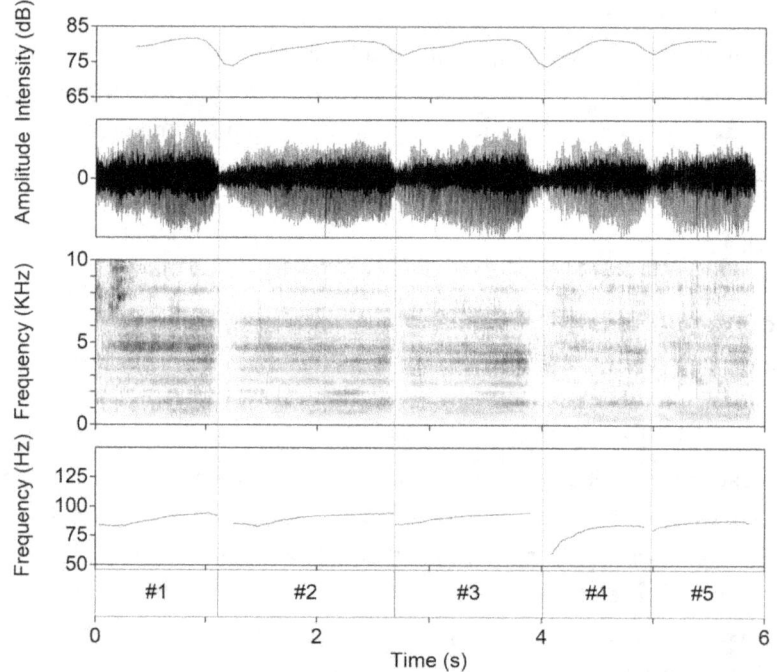

Figure 2.5 Oscillogram (top panel), spectrogram (mid panel) and fundamental frequency (pitch, bottom panel) of the five consecutive vocalizations by Noor (thanks to Vincent van Heuven).

between 0 and 3.5 kHz.[2] The first three vocalizations follow a similar pitch course (Figure 2.5, bottom panel): they start at about 90 Hz to slowly rise to 125 Hz, and then quickly fall back to 90 Hz. The fourth and fifth vocalizations deviate in showing a similar pattern but a smaller rise and a narrower range, i.e. from 90 Hz to 100, respectively 115 Hz. The first four vocalizations show a tendency to decrease slightly in length with the exception of the fifth one: call 1 – 2600 ms; call 2 – 2276 ms; call 3 – 2026 ms; call 4 – 1747 ms, and call 5 – 2057 ms.

Although all herd members, with the exception of Cato and the calves, like to eat cookies only Noor called for them. It seems, therefore, that her co-articulations cannot be attributed to the herd's shared repertoire. Since the caretakers and I, through frequent attuning to the cows, have obtained an increasing relational understanding of the individuals we continuously differentiate nuances of meaning-making for an individual cow as, over time, she becomes Other-for-a-human (Hendlin 2016: 94). Noor is highly successful in recruiting the human(s) i.e. to move to the canopy, reach for a cookie, cross 9 metres and give it to her without Noor moving into the human space. Even more importantly, the consecutive vocalizations are articulated in slightly different ways which show that, that despite interactional continuity, the slight changes can be taken as 'both significant and consequential for how participants build appropriate action' (Goodwin 2000: 1503). The slight changes have meaning potential for the humans involved. Indeed, if humans respond as we did in future encounters (i.e. by giving a cookie) this would also apply to human–non-human relations. However, it is only if relations change over time that they can be said to actualize meaning potential for the human–non-human interactional partners. Of course, the question is how (and if) they change – and how they are integral to 'whole-body activity' of a total cow–human–thing network. Thus, the question now becomes how the caretakers, Noor, and I will take this up relationally in the future. As Figure 2.5 shows, Noor's vocalizations (1 through 5) tended to become shorter over the encounter or, in other terms, she tended to reduce the length of the utterance. Further, she articulated the same pattern of rising and falling pitch but with a lower rise in her last two vocalizations compared to her first three articulations with, it seems, the same meaning. By the time she received her second cookie (third vocalization), Noor had learned in practice that humans could perceive the intent of her bodily and verbal co-articulation, that is, diving in the canopy to take a cookie, crossing the distance towards her and presenting it to her. Clearly, Noor, while relating to us, has learned from experience and reflection or, in other terms, by using the activity of languaging (Cowley 2024). As a consequence, I would suggest that, when Noor noticed that we understood her, she became 'sloppier' or reduced her vocalizing, articulating a similar rising and falling pitch-pattern but with narrower range in her last two vocalizations. The first three vocalizations may be more pronounced in that she was urging the humans to understand and to fulfil her wishes. When we did, Noor did not need to expound the meaning of her co-articulation at length. Of course, we as humans also acquired knowledge as part of the larger sequential event: Noor was indeed 'asking' for a cookie and we were able to interpret her shorter articulation much as the three fuller ones. Of course, more fieldwork is needed to establish if the subsequent 'asking' constitutes an incidental whole-body activity between the human caretakers and cow Noor, or whether it has become a routinized, hence, repeatable activity.

4.2 Living in a barn: 'You appear not to understand me'

The second interactive event took place between the farmer and a Fleckvieh cow in a tie-stall barn 1 (see Table 2.1).[3] The cow's front leg got stuck in her neck-chain when lying down (see Figure 2.6) and she could not release it by herself. On entering the barn, the cow vocalized five times, attracting attention of the farmer. Getting caught in the neck-chain happens more regularly in a tie-stall barn, and the farmer usually deals with it on entering the barn. This time, however, the farmer placed himself almost in front of the Fleckvieh cow to video-record her vocalizing as part of my research (see Figure 2.6).[4] Before the video-recording started, the cow already directed her vocalizations to the farmer, thus he started to video-record when an unfolding interaction had already started.

The farmer reports that not all cows vocalize when they find themselves in this condition because they can usually free their front leg by themselves. This cow, and interestingly also her mother, is/was among those who engage directly i.e. interact in getting the farmer to free their legs. This variation shows the importance of observing and analysing non-humans as individual 'semiotically capable beings' in their particularity and context (Hendlin 2016: 96).

In the snapshots presented in 2.6. below, the Fleckvieh cow is vocalizing while directed to, and gazing at the farmer; she has her ears sideways as her front leg is

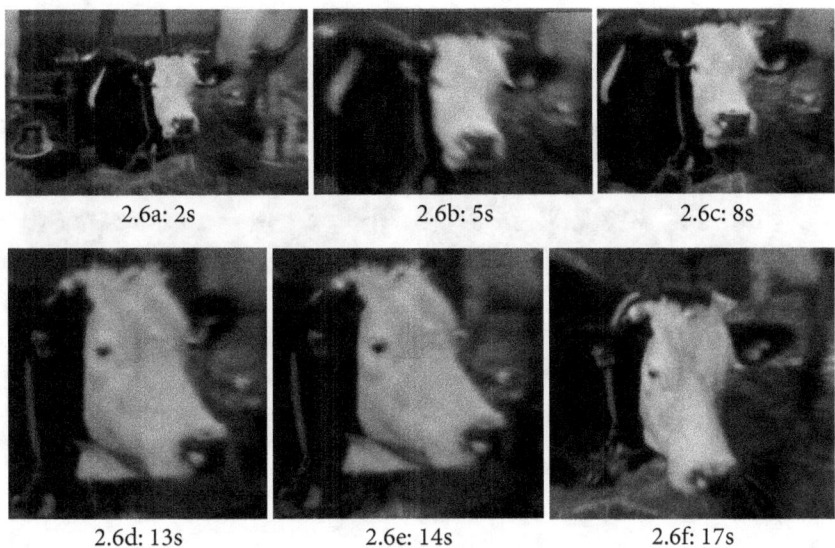

Figure 2.6 A snapshot of the five consecutive sounds in time (2s, 5s, 8s, 13s, 14s & 17s) produced by the Fleckvieh cow interacting with the filming farmer (s=second).

caught in her neck-chain. She thus catches the eye of the farmer as she vocalizes (see Figure 2.6a-f). After three vocalizations directed at the farmer without result (Figure 2.6a-c), she turns her head away, averts gaze and vocalizes twice (Figure 2.6d & 2.6e) – directing her expression sideways in space, she finishes off with her head bowed to the ground (Figure 2.6f). To her, the farmer's non-response appears as a failure because the farmer didn't, as is usual, untie her front leg straight away. The cow anticipates his non-response with averting gaze (Figure 2.6d-e) and, bowing her head down (Figure 2.6f).

The spectrogram in Figure 2.7 shows that the first three sounds directed at the farmer during the video-recording (see Figure 2.6a-c) are markedly different from the two that follow. First, the second and third vocalizations show an increase in length compared to the first, while the fourth and fifth vocalizations are relatively short: call 1 – 1112 ms; call 2 – 1584 ms; call 3 – 1350 ms; call 4 – 972 ms, and call 5 – 925 ms. The pauses between the calls (omitted from Figure 2.7) last 1845, 1823, 3635 and 1589 ms. The longest pause takes place between the third and the fourth vocalizations (3635 ms which about twice as long as the other pauses). The first two pauses, between help1 and help2 and between help2 and help3, are about the same length, while the pause between help4 and help5 is about 250 ms shorter.

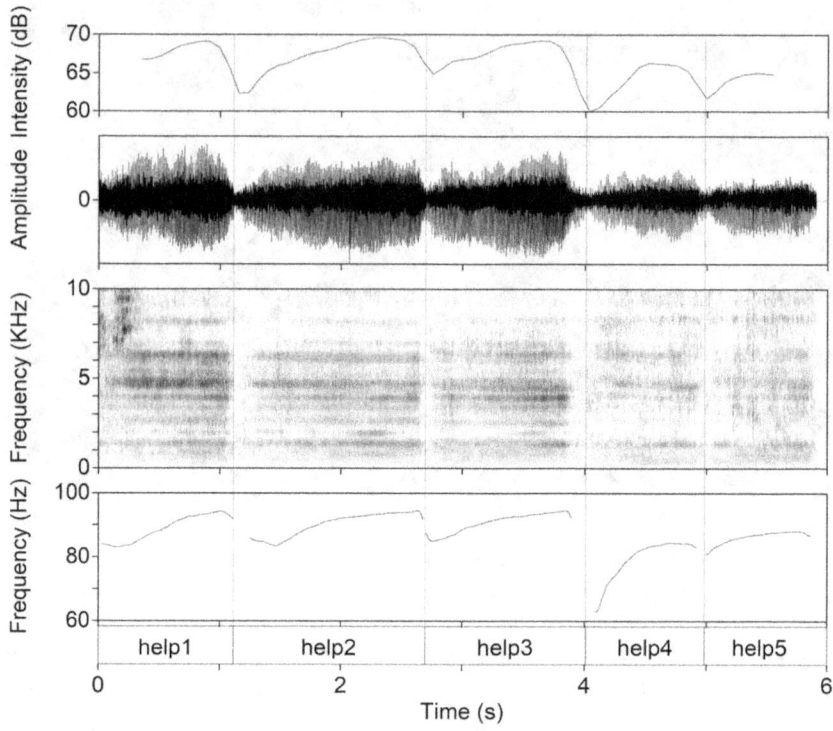

Figure 2.7 Oscillogram (top panel), spectrogram (mid panel) and fundamental frequency (pitch, bottom panel) of the five consecutive vocalizations by the Fleckvieh cow, the first three of them directed to the farmer (thanks to Vincent van Heuven).

A second contrast (also visible in Figure 2.7) arises in that the first three consecutive vocalizations are uttered in a steadily increasing intensity.[5] In Figure 2.8 below, the five intensity curves are aligned for the different durations – and are plotted on top of each other instead of next to each other: the intensity rises from the first to the third call. Note that the duration is relative in these images, so from 0 to 100 per cent of the duration of the call.

The contour for intensity over relative duration (in per cent) shows slight variation, and all three sounds directed to the farmer show an upward trend. Each sound has an increasingly higher intensity than the previous one (from low to high: help1, help2, help3), but not over the entire duration (this is especially true between 20 and 60 per cent). At the end, the intensity contours differ less and, especially so, in the last 37.5 per cent (to about 69 dB). In absolute duration help2 has a lower intensity than help3, help1 varies more (due to a slightly lower intensity around 40 per cent), but falls roughly in between (from low to high: help2, [help1], help3). The duration of the first call is short (1086 ms), the second longer (1589 ms) and the third is somewhere in between (1234 ms), but perceptibly longer than the first.

In this interaction the farmer neglects the cow's co-articulated requests – both those before the recording and the first three shown. Since the cow is not successful after three increasing ever more energetic articulations, she gives up by averting gaze, and eventually bows her head towards the ground while producing two more vocalizations with quite some lower intensity contours (helps 4 & 5 in Figure 2.8) not directed to anyone in particular. Thus, the Fleckvieh cow on the basis of her more pronounced repetition in the first three calls in relation to the non-response of the farmer anticipates that he is not going to solve her problem.

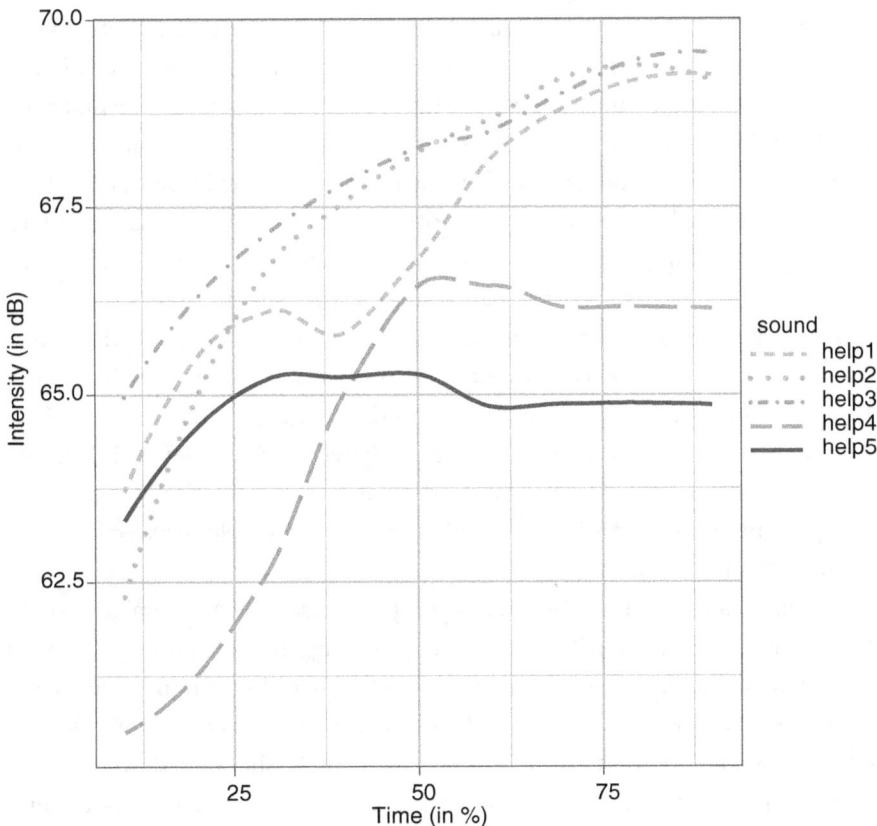

Figure 2.8 Intensity (dB) as a function of relative time (call duration, %) for five consecutive calls directed to the farmer. The first three calls show rising urgency (thanks to Etske Ooijevaar).

Reflection and conclusion

In this chapter, two interspecies interactions between a (dairy) cow and human(s) i.e. 'give a cookie' and 'untie my neck-chain' have been contrasted with respect to particulars of events in a situated context. The lens of languaging as a normal cooperative and coordinated activity in interspecies interactions enables one to show how patterns of the (dairy) cows' co-articulations influence the course of cow–human relations. These interspecies interactions in which whole bodies orient to each other in ways that are localized and emplaced such that they 'emerge, change and disappear continuously and fluidly as the interaction itself changes' (Goodwin 1986: 35) while engendering new situated knowledge(s). Both cows embed recurrent vocalizations in whole-body activities that contribute to life-sustaining relations between cows, humans, and objects like cookies, neck-chains, barns and meadows. Hence, recurrent vocalizations and human–cow relations are not fixed during interactions (Gurney & Demuro 2019: 9) but 'become meaningful through particular encounters or practices' (Barla 2021). During the ongoing interactions, both cows and humans perceive, attend and act in accordance with what is observed (Steffensen 2021: 729). In her small herd, Noor articulates more shortenings, and the same pattern of rising and falling pitch but with a lower rise in her last two vocalizations compared to her first three articulations as the human shows successful learning, namely by initiating a practice. The humans find out quickly that Noor wants a cookie by using experience to engage with her co-articulations. Equally, Noor engages with the humans' actions through whole-body activity in a shared and situated material context (Steffensen & Cowley 2021). In the barn, by contrast, the cow starts to co-articulate more energetically to establish engagement by, as she wishes, prompting the farmer to help her free her front leg from the neck-chain.

Comparison between the two languaging practices lends considerable strength to the claim that cows contribute to meaning-making. Their vocalizations directed at humans are not imitations or repetitions but, rather, alter as humans and cows coordinate, observe and perform mutual actions which the parties treat as more or less felicitous. Whereas Noor received the cookies she wanted, in the latter case, the front leg of the cow remained stuck in her neck-chain – not because the farmer didn't understand her request but because he wanted to record her whole bodily interactional efforts. Future research has to examine whether the rising pitch in the two languaging practices has the same abstract meaning. In both cases the cows make a request to the human being: 'I want something from you', or more urgently 'You have to do something for me'. The rising pitch then expresses the cow's dependencies (Cornips, ms) whereby vocalizations reach a pitch level that is significantly lower in, for instance, 'acknowledging the farmer' (Cornips 2022), and 'lying and ruminating' (Meen et al. 2015: 113).

In conclusion, in humans and cows alike learning takes place in situated collaborative activities where they engage actively with others. Like us the non-humans have expectations for to-be-achieved situated social meanings and, where results are infelicitous, perform accordingly (Ochs & Schieffelin 2011).

Notes

1. I gratefully acknowledge the support of Vincent van Heuven and Etske Ooijevaar for their phonetic analyses. Stephen J. Cowley is thanked for the constructive feedback on an earlier version of the manuscript. I also would like to thank the farmer for making fieldwork possible in his barn, for the caretakers of the small herd, i.e. Petra and Henk van de Ven, and for all their sharing knowledge about cow behaviour, and of course the cows.
2. I am very grateful to Vincent van Heuven for conducting this phonetic analysis.
3. The interaction is also described in Cornips & van Koppen (2024) but analysed only as an unsuccessful interaction from the cow's perspective.
4. The farmer sent me via WhatsApp the seventeen-second video clip featuring their interaction.
5. I am grateful to Etske Ooijevaar for conducting this phonetic analysis.

References

Abrell, E., & Gruen, L. (2020). 'Ethics and animals'. *Ethnography Working Paper. Wesleyan Animal Studies*: 1–16.

Alexander, R., & Stibbe, A. (2014). 'From the analysis of ecological discourse to the ecological analysis of discourse'. *Language Sciences*, 41, part A: 104–10.

Andrews, K. (2016). 'Animal cognition'. In E. N. Zalta (Ed.), *The Stanford encyclopedia of philosophy* (Summer 2016 Edition), Stanford University: Metaphysics Research Lab. https://plato.stanford.edu/archives/sum2016/entries/cognition-animal/.

Androutsopoulos, J. (2013). 'Networked multilingualism: Some language practices on Facebook and their implications'. *International Journal of Bilingualism*: 1–21.

Baratay, É. (2015). 'Building an animal history'. In L. M. Mackenzie & S. Posthumus (Eds.), *French thinking about animals*, 3–14. Michigan, East Lansing: Michigan State University.

Barker, A. J. et al. (2021). 'Cultural transmission of vocal dialect in the naked mole-rat'. *Science*, 371(6528): 503–7. Doi: 10.1126/science.abc6588.

Barla, J. (2021). 'Beyond reflexivity and representation: diffraction as a methodological sensitivity in science studies'. *Distinktion: Journal of Social Theory*. Doi: 10.1080/1600910X.2021.1934506.

Barron, E. S., Hartman, L., & Hagemann, F. (2020). 'From place to emplacement: the scalar politics of sustainability'. *Local Environment*. Doi: 10.1080/13549839.2020.1768518.

Bos, J, M., B. Bovenkerk, Feindt, P. H., & van Dam, Y. K. (2018). 'The quantified animal: precision livestock farming and the ethical implications of objectification'. *Food Ethics*, 2: 77–92.

Braidotti, R., & Hlavajova, M. (2018). 'Introduction'. In R. Braidotti & M. Hlavajova (Eds.), *Posthuman Glossary*, 1–14. London: Bloomsbury Academic.

Buller, H. (2015). 'Animal geographies II: methods'. *Progress in Human Geography*, 39(3): 374–84. https://doi.org/10.1177/0309132514527401.

Chakrabarty, D. (2012). 'Postcolonial studies and the challenge climate change'. *New Literary History*, 43(1): 1–18.

Chomsky, N. (2002). *On nature and language*. Cambridge: Cambridge University Press.

Collias, N. E. (1987). 'The vocal repertoire of the red junglefowl: a spectrographic classification and the code of communication'. *The Condor*, 89: 510–24.

Cornips, L. (2019). 'The final frontier: non-human animals on the linguistic research agenda'. In J. Berns & E. Tribushinina (Eds.), *Linguistic in the Netherlands, 36*, 13–19. Amsterdam: John Benjamins.

Cornips, L. (2022). 'The animal turn in postcolonial (socio)linguistics: the interspecies greeting of the dairy cow'. *Journal of Postcolonial Linguistics*, 6: 210–32.

Cornips, L. (2024). 'Getting to know the dairy cow: an inclusive and self-reflexive sociolinguistics in multispecies emotional encounters'. In C. Cutler, U. Røyneland & Z. Vrzić (Eds.), *Language activism and the role of scholars*. Cambridge: Cambridge University Press.

Cornips, L., & van den Hengel, L. (2021). 'Place-making by cows in an intensive dairy farm: a sociolinguistic approach to nonhuman animal agency'. In B. Bovenkerk & J. Keulartz (Eds.), *Animals in Our Midst: the challenges of co-existing with animals in the Anthropocene*, 177–201. Cham: Springer.

Cornips, L., & van Koppen, M. (2024). 'Multimodal dairy cow–human interaction in an intensive farming context'. *Language Sciences*. vol. 101, 101587. https://doi.org/10.1016/j.langsci.2023.101587

Cowley, S. J. (2024). 'Ecolinguistics in practice'. In *The Routledge Handbook of Applied Linguistics*, 374–385. London: Routledge.

De Waal, F. (2016). *Are we smart enough to know how smart animals are?* New York – London: WW Norton.

DeMello, M. (2012). *Animals and society. An introduction to human–animal studies*. New York: Columbia University Press.

Demuro, E., & Gurney, L. (2021). 'Languages/languaging as world-making: the ontological bases of language'. *Language Sciences*, 83(10137): 1–13.

Deumert, A., & Storch, A. (2020). 'Introduction. Colonial linguistics – then and now'. In A. Deumert, A. Storch & N. Shepherd (Eds.), *Colonial and decolonial linguistics knowledges and epistemes*, 1–21. Oxford: Oxford University Press.

Döring, M., & Zunino, F. (2014). 'NatureCultures in old and new worlds. Steps towards an ecolinguistic perspective of framing a new continent'. *Language Sciences*, 34–40.

Driessen, C., & Heutinck, L. F. M. (2015). 'Cows desiring to be milked? Milking robots and the co-evolution of ethics and technology on Dutch dairy farms'. *Agriculture and Human Values*, 32: 3–20.

Evans, C. S. (1997). 'Referential signals'. In *Perspectives in Ethology, Vol. 12: Communication*, 99–143. New York: Plenum Press.

Fiems, L, Tuyttens, F., De Sutter, R., de Graaf, S., & Sonck, B. (2018). 'Veilig omgaan met runderen'. *Instituut voor Landbouw en Visserijonderzoek (Ilvo) Mededeling*, 213: 1–48.

Fitch, W. T. (2017). 'What would Lenneberg think? Biolinguistics in the third millennium'. *Biolinguistics*, 11: 445–61.

Fromkin, V., Rodman, R., & Hyams, N. (2011). *An introduction to language*. Boston, MA: Wadsworth.

George, A. J., & Bolt, S. (2021). 'Livestock cognition: stimulating the minds of farm animals to improve welfare and productivity'. *Livestock*, Corpus ID: 237788462. Doi: 10.12968/LIVE.2021.26.4.202.

Goodwin, C. (1986). 'Gestures as a resource for the organization of mutual orientation'. *Semiotica*, 62(1/2): 29–49.

Goodwin, C. (2000). 'Action and embodiment within situated human interaction'. *Journal of Pragmatics*, 32: 1489–522.

Gurney, L., & Demuro, E. (2019). 'Tracing new ground, from language to languaging, and from languaging to assemblages: rethinking languaging through the multilingual and ontological turns'. *International Journal of Multilingualism*, 1–20. Doi: 10.1080/14790718.2019.1689982.

Håkansson, G., & Westander, J. (2013). *Communication in humans and other animals*. Amsterdam: Benjamins.

Hamilton, L., & Taylor, N. (2017). *Ethnography after humanism. Power, politics and method in multi-species research*. London: Palgrave Macmillan.

Haraway, D. (1988). 'Situated knowledges: the science question in feminism and the privilege of partial perspective'. *Feminist Studies, Inc.*, 14(3): 575–99.

Haraway, D. (2008). *When Species Meet*. Minneapolis, London: University of Minnesota Press.

Haraway, D. (2016). *Staying with the trouble: making kin in the Chthulucene*. Durham: Duke University Press.

Hare, B., Brown, M., Williamson, C., & Tomasello, M. (2002). 'The domestication of social cognition in dogs'. *Science*, 298: 1634–6.

Hendlin, Y. H. (2016). 'Multiplicity and Welt'. *Sign System Studies*, 44(1/2): 94–110.

Hodgetts, T., & Lorimer, J. (2015). 'Methodologies for animals geographies: cultures, communication and genomics'. *Cultural Geographies*, 22(2): 285–95.

Hovens, D. (2020). 'Workplace learning through human–machine interaction in a transient multilingual blue-collar work environment'. *Journal of linguistic anthropology*, 30(3): 369–88.

Jahns, G. (2012). 'Computational intelligence to recognize animal vocalization and diagnose animal health status'. In C. Moewes & A. Nürnberger (Eds.), *Computational intelligence in intelligent data analysis*, 239–49. Berlin: Springer.

Jahns, G. et al. (1997). 'Sound analysis to recognize different animals'. *IFAC Proceedings Mathematical and Control Applications in Agriculture and Horticulture*. Hannover, Germany.

Kamphof, I. (2017). 'Gereedschap voor nieuwsgierigheid. Over lichamelijke resonantie tussen mens en kip'. *Wijsgerig*, 57(1): 34–41.

Kiley-Worthington, M. (2017). 'The mental homologies of mammals. Towards an understanding of another mammals world view'. *Animals*, 7(87). Doi:10.3390/ani7120087.

Kulick, D. (2017). 'Human–animal communication'. *Annual Review of Anthropology*, 46: 357–78.

Labov, W. (1994). *Principles of linguistic change. Volume 1: Internal Factors*. Oxford/Cambridge, MA: Blackwell.

Latour, B. (2005). *Reassembling the social: an introduction to actor-network-theory*. New York: Oxford University Press.

Latour, B. (2018). *Down to earth: politics in the new climatic regime*. London: Polity Press.

Law, J., & Mol, A. (2008). 'The actor-enacted: Cumbrian sheep in 2001'. In C. Knappett & L. Malafouris (Eds.), *Material agency: towards a non-Anthropocentric approach*, 57–78. Cham: Springer.

Lestel, D., Bussolini, J., & Chrulew, M. (2014). 'The phenomenology of animal life'. *Environmental Humanities*, 5: 125–48.

Low, P. (2012). The Cambridge Declaration on Consciousness. Proceedings of the Francis Crick Memorial Conference, Churchill College, Cambridge University, July 7 2012, pp 1–2.

Marino, L., & Allen, K. (2017). 'The psychology of cows'. *Animal Behavior and Cognition*, 4(4): 474–98.

Meen, G. H., Schellekens, M. A., Slegers, M. H. M., Leenders, N. L. G., van Erp-van der Kooij, E., & Noldus, L. P. J. J. (2015), 'Sound analysis in dairy cattle vocalisation as a potential welfare monitor'. *Computers and Electronics in Agriculture*, 118: 111–15.

Meijer, E. (2019). *When animals speak. Toward an interspecies democracy*. New York: New York University Press.

Meijer, E. (2023). 'Speaking about farming. Embodied deliberation and resistance of cows and farmers in the Netherlands'. In J. Dugnoille & E. Vander Meer (Eds.), *Animals matter: resistance and transformation in animal commodification*, 132–54. Leiden/Boston: Brill.

Mingers, J. (1991). 'The cognitive theories of Maturana and Varela'. *Systems Practice*, 4(4): 319–38.

Mondada, L. (2016). 'Challenges of multimodality: language and the body in social interaction'. *Journal of Sociolinguistics*, 20(3): 336–66.

Ochs, E., & Schieffelin, B. (2011). 'The theory of language socialization'. In A. Duranti, E. Ochs & B. Schieffelin (Eds.), *The handbook of language socialization*, 1–21. Oxford: Blackwell.

Padilla de la Torre, M., Briefer, E. F., Reader, T., & McElligott, A. (2015). 'Acoustic analysis of cattle (Bos taurus) mother-offspring contact calls from a source-filter theory perspective'. *Applied Animal Behaviour Science*, 163: 58–68.

Phillips, C. (2002). *Cattle behaviour and welfare*. second edition. Malden: Blackwell.

Pennycook, A. (2017). 'Translanguaging and semiotic assemblages'. *International Journal of Multilingualism*, 14(3): 269–82.

Pennycook, A. (2018). *Posthumanist applied linguistics*. London/New York: Routledge.

Porcher, J., & Schmitt, T. (2012). 'Dairy cows: workers in the shadows?' *Society & Animals*, 20: 39–60.

Sievers, C., Wild, M., & Gruber, T. (2017). 'Intentionality and flexibility in animal communication'. In K. Andrews & J. Beck (Eds.), *The Routledge handbook for the philosophy of animal minds*, 333–43. London: Routledge.

Sousa, L. P. de Q., & Pessao, R. R. (2019). 'Humans, nonhuman others, matter and language. A discussion from posthumanism and decolonial perspectives'. *Trabalhos em Linguistica Aplicada*, 58(2): 520–43.

Steffensen, S. V., & Cowley, S. J. (2021). 'Thinking on behalf of the world: radical embodied ecolinguistics'. In W. Xu & J.R. Taylor (Eds.), *The Routledge handbook of cognitive linguistics*, 723–36. New York.

Stuart, D., Schewe, R. L. & Gunderson, R. (2013). 'Extending social theory to farm animals: addressing alienating in the dairy sector. *Sociologica ruralis*'. *Journal of the European Society for Rural Sociology* 53(2): 201–22.

Thibault, P. J. (2011). 'First-order languaging dynamics and second-order language: the distributed view'. *Ecological Psychology*, 23(3): 210–45.

Tsing, A. (2013). 'More-than-human sociality'. In K. Hastrup (Ed.), *Anthropology and Nature*, 27–42. New York: Routledge.

Vallée-Tourangeau, F., & Cowley, S. J. (2013). 'Human thinking beyond the brain'. In S.J. Cowley & F. Vallée-Tourangeau (Eds.), *Cognition beyond the brain computation, interactivity and human artifice*, 1–12. London: Springer-Verlag.

Van Patter, L. E., & Blattner, C. (2020). 'Advancing ethical principles for non-invasive, respectful research with nonhuman animal participants'. *Society & Animals*, 28: 171–90.

Ecolinguistics and the Cognitive Ecology of Global Warming

Sune Vork Steffensen and Edward Baggs

Introduction

The tragic view of human-caused climate change

Over the last twenty years or so, social psychologists have often commented on the link between human nature and human-caused climate change. Many have drawn pessimistic conclusions. The pessimistic position is summed up well in a sentence that appears in an opinion piece that was published in *The Washington Post* in 2009: 'To a psychologist, climate change looks as if it was designed to be ignored' (cited in Atkinson & Jacquet 2022). This sentence expresses a tragic view of human nature and human-caused climate change (Johnson & Levin 2009). According to the tragic view, we know that climate change is happening, and we know that we caused it, but we are simply psychologically incapable of changing our behaviour. Human nature made us this way. We are hopeless spectators to our own doom.

A number of review articles have focused on alleged psychological biases and blindspots that are hypothesized to act as barriers to effective behaviour change (e.g. Gifford 2011; Clayton et al. 2015). These psychological barriers are proposed as potential explanations for why individuals often fail to respond to the reality of climate change by changing their behaviour, even though they may accept the reality of human-caused climate change as a propositional fact. Commonly suggested psychological barriers include the difficulty of prioritizing events that are remote in time and space, the propensity to favour self-interest over the common good, a lack of perceived control over the problem (the 'drop in the bucket' effect), and denial and rationalization linked to cognitive dissonance (Atkinson & Jacquet 2022).

The tragic view of human nature and climate change is, on the surface, compelling. But it is based on an unreasonably narrow view of human decision making. The tragic view relies on a narrow understanding of human behaviour as the output of internal, mental processes. The tragic view assumes that our behaviour is something that we, as individual bodies, are entirely in charge of. This ignores the existence of cultural, social and environmental constraints. Atkinson and Jaquet caution against the tragic view. They write that 'the most tractable barriers to tackling climate change are not found in human biology, but in human culture' (2022: 625). We agree with this. We believe that psychological work on behaviour change in the context of human-caused climate change should begin not with a catalogue of alleged psychological biases, but with the study of how cultural phenomena constrain groups' and individuals' behaviour vis-à-vis each other and the environment. Culture, on this view, is a population-level pattern that manifests itself in situated behaviour and in the human shaping of the environment.

These remarks are of relevance to the ecolinguist because not only are culture and behaviour interdependent; both are also interdependent with language. Accordingly, the ecolinguist is in a decisive position to contribute to the study of how culture, cognition and behaviour intersect in ways that shape conditions for the living. The ecolinguistic position allows for the scrutiny of human-caused climate change.

Along these lines, we discuss three real-world examples of cultural practices that have implications for our understanding of our place in nature. All three examples involve practices that depend on the weaving of cognitive devices into individual perceptual experience. We use the term 'cognitive device' as a theoretically neutral term to denote a very broad family of ways of augmenting perception and thought. A cognitive device, in our terms, is a culturally mediated schema or artefact that allows for the augmentation of individual thought. We intend the term to denote both linguistic and symbolic structures, as well as external artefacts and representations.[1]

In what follows, we focus on a subset of cognitive devices, namely on a set of devices that augment human perception of the environment, enabling individuals to perceive climate change as a meaningful domain of concern, rather than as a distant, purely theoretical threat. The three examples illustrate different ways that climate change can be transposed into the scale of perceptual experience. We will suggest that the three examples begin to erode the tragic view of human nature and climate change.

The tragic view is itself based on a defective cognitive device, namely an overly individualized and intellectualized framing of human behaviour. In contrast, the examples illustrate three different cognitive devices that place human behaviour back in its natural context. In the second half of the chapter we will discuss some possible implications for ecolinguistics. We will elaborate on our proposal that ecolinguistics is concerned with a class of cognitive devices at the interface between culture and cognition. Finally, we include an epilogue where we respond to a concern that we have failed to adequately counter the tragic view.

Two assumptions of temporality and perception

Before turning to the examples, we first briefly want to make explicit two assumptions that inform our analysis. The first assumption pertains to time and temporality. The word 'culture', as it is generally used, denotes processes that occur on at least two different temporal scales. First, 'culture' refers to activity that occurs at the scale of behaviour. Human behaviour is shaped by the individual's history of learning, from the language the person speaks to the culturally transmitted skills they have learned. A person who has learned to throw pottery on a wheel is exhibiting a cultural behaviour (cf. Malafouris & Koukouti 2022). Second, 'culture' refers to processes at the scale of populations. Here, 'culture' refers to patterns that exceed the timespan of behaviour. Culture in this sense typically plays out on timescales of months, years and decades. The practice of making pottery on a wheel is part of the cultural heritage of particular populations of humans, developed piecemeal over many generations. The difference between culture at the scale of behaviour and culture at the scale of populations is thus a difference in timescales. Moreover, the scale of behaviour and the scale of population are themselves, in turn, embedded within larger-timescale processes. Both the individual potter and the larger institution of pottery making have arisen within a larger material world that has developed on timescales of centuries, millennia and geological epochs. On this background, we face a challenge that has been convincingly formulated by Brian MacWhinney: 'Our challenge is to understand how forces with very different time scales mesh together in the current moment' (MacWhinney 2005).

To meet this challenge, we need a detailed ecological model of the interconnections of the timescales of the material universe, culture and behaviour. Such a model has been presented by Uryu, Steffensen and Kramsch

(2014), with more recent updates in Steffensen and Pedersen (2014) and Loaiza, Trasmundi and Steffensen (2020). Rather than rehearse the arguments presented in these articles, we will point to one important implication of the model, namely a distinction between homoscalar and heteroscalar descriptions and analyses.[2] A homoscalar approach focuses on temporal connections that pertain to a single timescale. Examples include action–perception coordination on a behavioural scale (e.g. when baseball players solve the 'outfielder problem' [Anderson 2014: 184f.]) and intercultural differences on a cultural scale (e.g. differences in social forms of greeting, such as British handshakes, Thai wai bows and French cheek kissing). A heteroscalar description, in contrast, focuses on how human activities are constrained by multiple timescales. For instance, when coordinating our behaviour during the preparation of a meal, we mesh embodied activities (e.g. handing a knife to another person), cultural patterns (e.g. customs about how to prepare specific food items) and socio-economic conditions (e.g. cooking food items that are imported from another hemisphere, shipped in vessels powered by the burning of fossil fuels). By acknowledging the complex organization that connects situated cooking activities to a socio-economic network of district heating plants, farmers, butchers, shipping agents, sailors and supermarkets, we describe cooking behaviour as vastly heteroscalar. On the heteroscalar view, behaviour does not pertain only to individual agents, but also to distributed behavioural systems embedded in vast cognitive ecologies (Hutchins 1995a, 2010).

This framework of timescales allows us to reconsider the connection between culture, behaviour and climate change. The challenge is how we come to understand the interconnection between climate change, which is vastly heteroscalar, and human perception which is attuned to the homoscalar results of its actions. In other words, how do we overcome the phenomenological barrier that prevents us from perceiving the heteroscalar consequences of our own actions? Here, culture comes to the fore. Culture too is vastly heteroscalar, but at the same time it meshes with our behaviour. Our working hypothesis is that culture equips the homoscalar agent (i.e. the individual person) with cognitive devices that enable that person to perceive the longer-timescale process of climate change. Cognitive devices are thus cultural snippets that enable us to perceive climate change – not merely with our bare eyes, not even merely with 'the eyes in the head on a body supported by the ground' (Gibson 1979: xiii), but with eyes in a head on a body that is cognitively augmented through its history of enculturation.

The second assumption pertains to perception. In this context we rely on the ecological theory of perception developed by James Gibson (1966, 1979). Gibson's theory is based on a rejection of the classical theory of perception according to which the structure of the external world is not directly accessible to an agent but must be inferred via impoverished sensory stimulation. According to the classical theory, the stable phenomenal existence of the world is a consequence of our mental activity: sense impressions are pointillistic, but the world seems to be stable because we impose a stable, subjective interpretation onto the fleeting impressions. Gibson argued that the apparent existence of a stable world is not due to our mentally positing such a stable world, but is due to the fact that the stable world exists and that our perceptual systems have evolved in order to sample information that specifies the structure of that stable world. On Gibson's account, visual perception is possible because light is richly structured at any arbitrary point of observation in a natural environment. We learn to navigate our environment by exploiting invariances in the changing patterns of light that our visual system samples as we move around. For Gibson, then, visual perception is dependent on the movement of the observer:

> Perceiving is a registering of certain definite dimensions of invariance in the stimulus flux together with definite parameters of disturbance. The invariants are invariants of structure, and the disturbances are disturbances of structure. (Gibson 1979: 238)

Gibson did not himself write about the perception of climate change. His theory, however, provides an explanation for why climate change eludes the basic processes of perceptual knowledge. The reason why we cannot directly perceive climate change is that the lifespan of an average human being is too short to pick up the relevant variance in the stimulus flux. Given that 'invariants of structure do not exist except in relation to variants' (Gibson 1979: 79), we can predict that invariants will simply not be noticeable if the change is sufficiently slow.

Gibson's theory might, then, at first impression, be taken as evidence in support of the tragic view of human nature: Climate change is happening on the wrong timescale for our perceptual systems to be able to detect it directly. But this conclusion need not necessarily follow. Climate change eludes direct perception by the perceptual systems of an individual perceiver. But climate change has nevertheless been detected! The reality of climate change has been detected through extended perceptual means, namely through measuring instruments, through symbolic representations of historic temperature recordings and the like. These tools of scientific practice are, in our terms, examples of cognitive devices. These cognitive devices can reconcile the two temporal scales – the temporal scale of perceptual experience and the temporal scale of climate change – by transposing the one into the other. The term 'transposition' is familiar from music where it denotes the practice of performing the same piece of music in different keys. In music, a transposition works when a set of invariants (namely the relative frequencies of tones) are maintained across a variance in key. Likewise, in the domain of perception, a transposition requires that indetectable environmental invariants become perceivable.

A transposition can function in two different ways: (i) long, slow changes can be compressed in such a way that it plays out on a timescale that fits the perceptual systems of an observer; (ii) the sensoria of the perceiver can be extended in ways that allow the person to detect changes on a timescale longer than their individual lifetime.

The former is uncontroversial. For instance, the long process of temperature variation can be compressed into a homoscalar representation, such as a chart plotting average atmospheric temperature on the y-axis against year on the x-axis. The latter, in contrast, requires a bit more explanation. Thus, prima facie, such a temporal extension of the sensorium seems impossible. How can we observe something beyond our own lifetime? Gibson hints at this problem when he juxtaposes his theory to the 'stimulus-sequence theory of perception' and the 'snapshot theory of perception' (Gibson 1979: 236). Both rely on comparisons between single states of perceived reality, and if one accepts that, a temporal extension would merely imply that one compares a current perceptual input with a record of a past input.[3] However, Gibson rejects this view in favour of the ecological view that 'the apprehension of persistence is a simple act of invariance detection' (Gibson 1979: 236).

Gibson was concerned with invariance detection as an achievement of the individual perceiver. An important point here, however, is that humans have developed methods of invariance detection that go beyond the individual perceiver. Human groups, through cultural innovations and cognitive devices such as graphs and scientific instruments, are sometimes able to detect invariants even in situations where no single organism can do so on its own. Hutchins (1995a), for instance, describes how a group of navigators perceive their position vis-à-vis a nautical map, by measuring the angle between the ship's movement and a set of static landmarks. Such a group can be distributed over time (Hollan, Hutchins & Kirsh 2000), so that the invariance detection of the group is transformed into an invariance detection of one member of the group who exploits the perception of past events of invariance detection. This observer thus relies on the sensoria and observations of past observers. This temporal extension requires, however, that the invariance is converted into a structure that is sufficiently stable across distributed perceptual events. This point is important in an ecolinguistic context because language can contribute to such structural stability (for an elaboration on the connection between Gibson and Hutchins, see Baggs and Steffensen [2023]).

With these theoretical remarks on homoscalarity, heteroscalarity and the transposition of events into a perceivable timescale, we can now turn to our three case studies.

Case study 1: The climate spiral

In measuring climate change, climate scientists rely on the collection of longitudinal data. This practice has given rise to the well-known figures with time on the x-axis and a measurement of a variable (temperature, atmospheric CO_2 concentration, etc.) on the y-axis. Such graphs aim to capture longitudinal change within a single static representation, as in Figures 3.1 and 3.2.

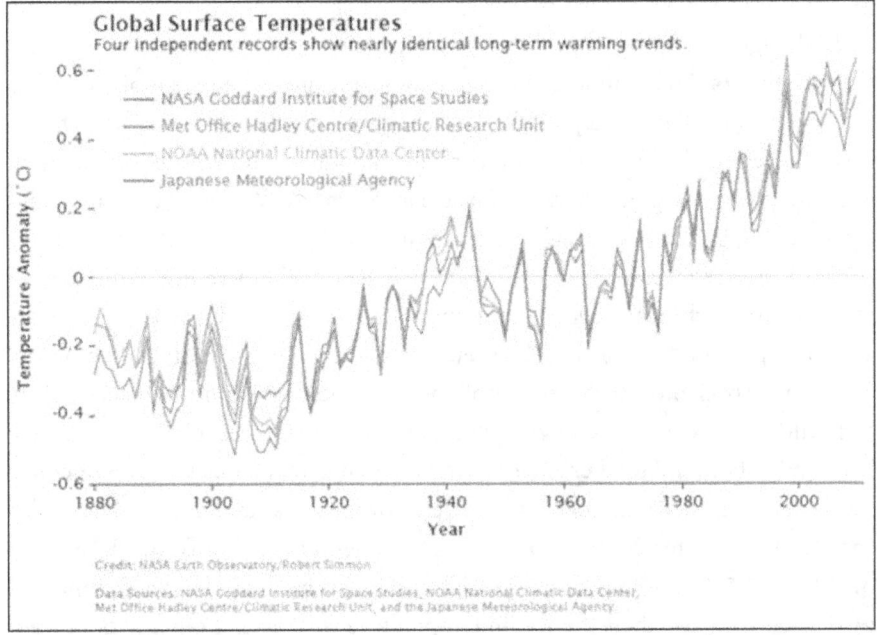

Figure 3.1 Global Surface Temperature, 1880–2013. Time is an invariant on the x-axis, and temperature is an invariant on the y-axis. The lines indicate temperature anomalies (i.e. the difference between a given temperature and a baseline reference value, which is the value of the pre-industrial year of 1850). The figure is from NASA (https://climate.nasa.gov/news/468/global-temperature-records-in-close-agreement/; retrieved 25 October 2022).

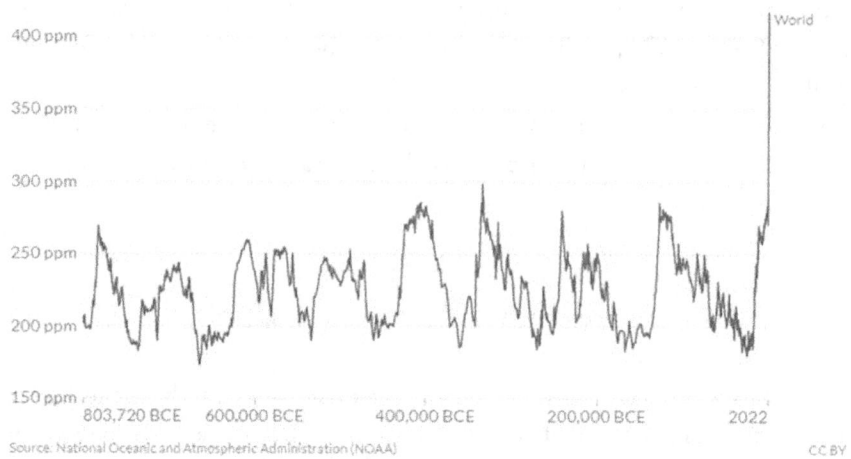

Figure 3.2 Global atmospheric CO_2 concentration. Time is an invariant on the x-axis, and CO_2 concentration is an invariant on the y-axis (the figure is from Ritchie, Roser, & Rosado, 2020).

Both figures convey important scientific data. Our concern here is with the question of what happens, in psychological terms, when we look at figures like these. Both figures depict changes that are difficult to reconcile with our direct experience of feeling the atmosphere via our bodies. Figure 3.1 shows an increasing trend in global average surface temperature. We know that this trend is happening. But as individuals we do not personally experience the atmosphere in this way. We all have first-hand experience with temperature, but rarely in terms of the technical concept of 'temperature anomaly'. Likewise, the figure does not provide any easily interpretable baseline. In isolation, a fluctuation between −0.6°C and +0.6°C may not sound terribly alarming, because it does not reflect the relevant ecological vulnerabilities and thresholds. The mistake is to understand the total change of 1.2°C as being analogous to a cup of coffee being 91.2°C rather than 90°C, or the outdoor temperature being 28.2°C rather than 27°C. A better comparison is body temperature rising from the normal 37.5°C to 38.7°C, not for a few days, but permanently. Accordingly, if 'climate' is associated with 'weather', the rise in temperature will prompt other actions than if it is associated with 'a complex system of the same kind as my body'. Likewise, Figure 3.2 signals an abrupt and unprecedented change, and while an educated audience may be able to conceptualize the implications of such changes in CO_2 concentration, these implications are again beyond the perceptual realm and thus not something that meshes easily with our day-to-day behaviour.

Static, two-dimensional plots such as those shown above are, however, not the only representational format available for presenting historic climate data. Other data visualizations make use of more dynamic representational devices. One of the most widely reproduced of such visualizations is Ed Hawkins' 'climate spiral' (Hawkins, Fæhn & Fuglestvedt 2019) which is depicted in Figure 3.3.

It is interesting to compare the experience of watching the climate spiral to the experience of looking at the static figure depicted in Figure 3.1. The reader is invited to look up the climate spiral animation and conduct this comparison for themselves. If the reader's experience is consistent with ours, then the animation will be experienced as emotionally more compelling than the static images. Why might this be? We can identify at least four cognitive devices that have been employed in the construction of the spiral animation. Each of these devices exploits features of our cognitive and perceptual systems.

First, and most obviously, the visualization exploits the GIF architecture, which allows for multiple frames to be displayed as an animated sequence.

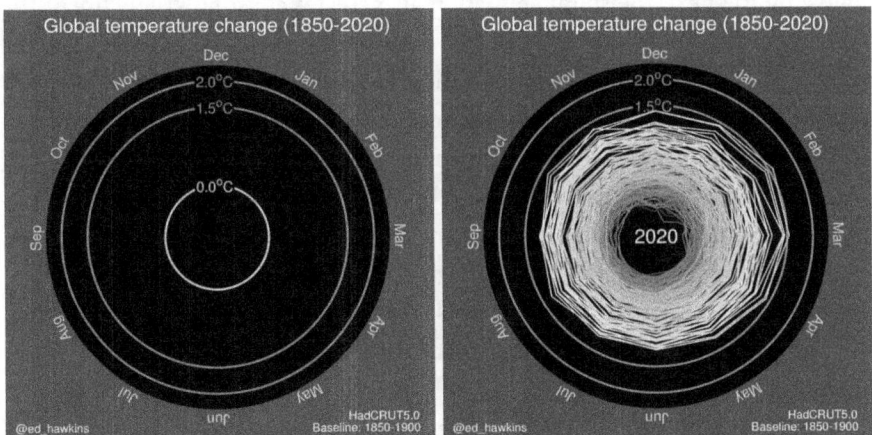

Figure 3.3 The climate spiral. 3a (left) depicts the climate spiral at the start of the 17 seconds cycle; 3b (right) at the end. The spiralling line depicts the temperature anomaly from 1850 to 2020. Each turn of the temperature line is the equivalent of one year, going from January (at one o'clock) to December (at twelve o'clock). Temperature anomaly is indicated by the distance of the temperature line to the 0.0°C baseline which is initially given by a white circle in 3a. The two red circles represent temperature anomalies of 1.5°C and 2.0°C. The colour of the temperature line changes as a function of time (not temperature), starting from dark blue in 1850 and ends with yellow in 2020. Each additional layer of time is placed in front of the previous layer. This article relies on the version found on: https://cpb-eu-w2.wpmucdn.com/blogs.reading.ac.uk/dist/3/187/files/2021/01/spiral_2020_large.gif; accessed 8 November 2022.

The animation thus compresses 170 years of temperature development into a 17-second GIF. In contrast, in Figure 3.1, temperature increase is plotted spatially against a static representation of time (either as an increase in the distance from the x-axis or as a positive gradient of the line). Something important is lost in the static representation in Figure 3.1. In the static figure, time is only represented spatially. This is a familiar convention. But the static format erases the event structure of the temperature increase. In reality, the change occurs over time, unfolding from a known present into a not-yet-known future. The static representation erases this unfolding structure. It presents the whole 170-year sequence as a single piece of scientific knowledge. The animation also preserves the unfolding structure by transposing time onto a spatial format (the clock-like representation of measurements for each of the months within a year). But it preserves aspects of the invariant temporal format of the sequence being represented. Thus, to find out where things are going to end up, we must watch until the end of the animation.

Second, in addition to maintaining the temporal event structure of one year following the next, the spiral animation also creates a lasting visible trace. The movement of the climate spiral is outwards from the centre, and each turn is superimposed on the previous turns. The data is real-world data and is therefore noisy. The line spirals unevenly, sometimes crossing over itself where the average temperature for a given month happens to be lower than for the same month in previous years. The presence of the trace means that, by the time one has watched to the end of the animation, one is presented with the exact same data as is presented in the static figure in Figure 3.1. A clever feature of the design of the animation is that it manages to preserve the temporal event structure while still, in the end, preserving the complete visualization of the data in one frame (Figure 3.3b).

The third cognitive device is, we suspect, not a deliberate part of the animation's design, but is nevertheless interesting from a perceptual standpoint. The spatial representation of the spiral, with increasing temperature being represented as the distance of the line from the centre, combined with the fact that the line superposes itself as the animation progresses, yields the impression that the line is coming out towards the observer. The effect is similar to what Gibson described as a looming effect (1979: 167). Gibson investigated this effect using a shadow-casting apparatus that created an expanding form on a screen. Gibson conducted experiments with various animal species, observing their reactions to this looming display. Gibson wrote that 'there seemed to be a direct perception of an event that could be described as approach-of-something'. Looming, he suggested, 'specifies impending collision, and the rate of magnification is proportional to the imminence of the collision' (Gibson 1979: 167). In the case of the spiral animation, as the warming polygon magnifies, it takes up more of the screen of the device on which you are viewing the animation. This in turn makes it appear as if the animation is looming out towards the viewer. In other words, the looming effect conveys a perceptual experience of climate warming at the verge of colliding with the observer. Deliberately or by coincidence, the animators have found a way to exploit a basic feature of our perceptual system. Something looming towards us is intrinsically meaningful.

Finally, a salient element in the spiral is the colour of the line. It draws on a heat map rhetoric where a gradient is indicated by a colour scale that goes from dark blue over light blue, green, yellow, and orange to bright red. However, in spite of the fact that the line borrows its colour scheme from heat maps, the colours do not correspond to temperature, but to temporality: the blue end of the spectrum is 'early' and the 'yellow' end is late.[4] This design feature of the spiral is obviously a rhetorical device: time is not a continuum with two extremes, and there are no invariants that dictate the rate of change in colour. In principle, the line could go from dark blue to green or to orange or to red; the choice of 'yellow' to denote the present point in time is a rhetorical choice that makes the change in colours a message about the temperature approaching the critical limits indicated by the two red circles. Interestingly, as this change in colour is the only aspect of the model that does not pertain to perceptual invariants, it is open to different interpretations which hinge on whether one interprets 'yellow' as far-away-from-blue or as not-yet-red:

> Although it may be tempting to use the analogy that temperatures are 'spiraling out of control,' as some media stories did, an alternative (and more positive) message is rather that decision-makers and society can still take control and choose to avoid danger. (Hawkins et al. 2019)

In summary, the climate spiral renders climate change visible through the use of four cognitive devices that draw on both perceptual and symbolic contrivances in order to present the viewer with an emotionally engaging depiction of what is in fact the same scientific knowledge as is presented in a more emotionless format by the static plot in Figure 3.1.

The spiral animation does, however, remain firmly within the scientific mode of knowledge representation. The animated representation may be more compelling than the static representation, but both are merely representations.

Both representations present facts but provide no guidance on how to reconcile those facts with our lives at the behavioural scale. The spiral, like the static graph, presents merely abstract knowledge. This is not the case for our second case study.

Case study 2: Lytton, British Columbia

In June 2021, a wildfire swept through the town of Lytton in British Columbia, burning and destroying most of the town's buildings. The fire occurred after three consecutive days on which the local weather station registered record highs in atmospheric temperature. The peak temperature was recorded the day before the fire, 29 June 2021, at 49.6ºC – the highest temperature ever recorded in Canada at the time of writing. The immediate cause of the fire remains unknown (Transport Safety Board of Canada 2021).

This event is interesting for our purposes because it is a real-world example of an event that was caused by global warming, and for which we have some contemporary evidence of how people responded to that event. Of particular interest is the narrative framing that was used to interpret the causes of the fire (Stibbe 2015). A narrative framing is a cognitive device for organizing knowledge about some domain of interest. For a catastrophic event, deciding on a narrative framing to identify the causes of that event is a decision charged with significance. In Lytton, two competing narratives were distinguishable. One narrative was concerned with the proximate cause of the fire; the other narrative was concerned with more distant causal factors.

In the immediate aftermath of the fire, the homoscalar proximate-cause narrative was prevalent in media articles. Some residents blamed the train that runs through the town for causing the initial spark. One contemporary news report carries the headline, 'Cause of Lytton, B.C., wildfire not yet known, resident saw train brake then smoke rise' (https://globalnews.ca/news/7998818/lytton-bc-wildfire-train-brake-smoke/). Canada's Transportation Safety Board opened an investigation into the allegation that the wildfire was sparked by a train. The investigation ultimately found no evidence to link the fire with the passing train (Transport Safety Board of Canada 2021).

Whatever its origin, the spark was only the proximate cause of the fire. Another way of framing the question of what caused the fire is to ask what caused the hot and dry conditions in the days preceding the fire. This second kind of framing invokes a heteroscalar distal-cause narrative. The town had experienced a prolonged period of extreme heat and drought. A distal-cause narrative framing that was observed in the aftermath of the wildfire sought to explain the fire not only in terms of the proximate cause, but also in terms of a more long-term event, namely anthropogenic climate change. The BBC interviewed Patrick Michell, chief of Kanaka Bar Indian Band and a resident of Lytton. Michell said, 'It wasn't a train that burned my house down. It was a by-product of climate change. Heat, drought, wind, created conditions in our town that required one spark. And that spark occurred and we lost our town' (https://www.bbc.com/news/av/world-us-canada-59227915).

Choices of narrative framings are not neutral. A homoscalar framing seeks only to identify a proximate cause. Residents used this framing when seeking to apportion blame on the train operator. The second framing is a heteroscalar framing. It reconciles an event that has occurred on the scale of perceptual experience with larger-scale changes in the Earth's atmosphere, caused by decades and centuries of human activity. The heteroscalar framing depends on a cognitive device that transposes depictions of both abstract events and concrete events into the same narrative format (here a BBC feature, but the same device underlies much climate sci-fi literature).

The Lytton case study is consistent with the tragic view of human-caused climate change, as outlined above. The narrative framing of the wildfire as being the result of human-caused climate change may help to place the event in global context, and it may have played a role for the residents as they grieved for their lost town. But narrative framing alone could not prevent the wildfire from happening.

Case study 3: Andean agriculture

Our final case study is more optimistic. It concerns a community that has used its existing systems of knowledge to guide adaptive behaviour change in response to climatic changes in the local ecosystem. The example is taken from Postigo's (2014) study of how rural populations perceive climatic change in the Andean Tropics.

In any location on Earth, there occur periodic temperature changes as a function of the Earth's rotation and its position relative to the sun. Such periodic cycles occur on a diurnal scale (days are warmer than nights) and on an annual scale (summer is warmer than winter). Until the start of the Holocene, some

11,700 years ago, the Earth also experienced periodic cycles of glaciation, each cycle taking around 100,000 years to complete.

Temperature thus varies as a function of time. However, in mountainous regions with large differences in elevation, temperature also varies as a function of altitude. This is because climate in high elevations is colder than at sea level. This difference gives rise to elevational zonation (Patterson, Stotz, Solari, Fitzpatrick & Pacheco 1998) where patterns of flora and fauna vary with elevation.

We use these comments on altitude and temperature to discuss one of Postigo's examples from the Andes:

> Some peasants perceived that the altitudinal range of pests is expanding as they follow rising temperatures to higher elevations. In the community of Pampahuasi (Cusco), previously unknown pests are attacking the crops. Moreover, in Yanque Hurin Saya, broad beans were attacked by 'chocolate spot' – *Botrytis fabae Sardiña*. Prior to this attack, the peasants from Yanque Hurin Saya had only seen this pest at lower elevations. They attributed the pest's range expansion to increased temperatures at higher elevations. (Postigo 2014: 390)

This passage demonstrates three things: (i) the Yanque Hurin Saya peasants have a linguistic category called 'chocolate spot' which refers to a disease that affect broad beans and which is caused by a fungus (*Botrytis fabae Sardiña*); (ii) the peasants have prior experiences with this phenomenon from elevation zone X only; (iii) the peasants now observe the same phenomenon in elevation zone X+1. Given that an increase in elevation coincides with a decrease in temperature along the entire elevation gradient, an upward change in the elevation zone of a specific species is an indicator of rising temperatures.

The Andean community, thus, has established a long-term cultural classification system of agricultural products as well as of the pests and diseases that affect them. Within an agrarian culture, such classifications are shared among social groups engaged in pastoral activities, and they are extended to newcomers into the groups. Since the agrarian 'community of practice' (Lave & Wenger 1991) is composed by overlapping generations, the specific cultural categorizations are inherited within emplaced lineages. Thus, a specific pattern of place-language co-evolution is established, which allows for the transposition between the change in the elevation zone of chocolate spots and the increase in temperature. Consequently, in this specific place-language co-evolution, climate change is observable, even if no observer has direct experience with the prevalence of chocolate spots beyond their own lifetime. It is sufficient that the intergenerational community of practice has the necessary cultural practices of ascertaining the elevation zones of beans and chocolate spots.

The example demonstrates how a group can engage in distributed perception over time, to the degree that the perceptual act is stabilised through cognitive devices, including what Goodwin (1994) refers to as 'discursive practices'. Indigenous naming practices thus scaffold the 'professional vision' (Goodwin 1994) of situated agents, which becomes an important shaper of behaviour. This is in contrast to the universalist Linnaean taxonomy that sought to provide a pure classification scheme from a disinterested, detached viewpoint, *sub specie aeternitatis*. With professional vision, scaffolded by discursive practices, agricultural communities exploit cognitive devices that help them keep track of the prevalence of pests, simply because a change in prevalence can be observed by any observer who is part of such a community of practice.

A similar example is the change in precipitation patterns as observed by one of Postigo's observers:

> The rainy season has shortened in its duration; it used to start in October/November – for sowing season – and last until April/May; now the onset of rainy season is December/January and ends in March/April. Rain has become irregular – it used to rain a constant amount, but now it rains heavily – like pouring rain for one or two days and then it is dry for several days. (Postigo 2014: 389; the author's translation from Spanish)

In this example, the temporal transposition works through a well-established class of cognitive device, namely (lunisolar) calendars that function as invariant measures onto which changes in ecological phenomena can be mapped. In this example, the informant relies on a colonial remedy (the Gregorian calendar), but prior to its introduction in the Andes, Indigenous technologies had the same function. Thus, rather than treating the onset of the rainy season as an ecological origin, the calendar allows one to perceive changes in this onset in relation to the solar year.

Cognitive devices include naming practices and conventions for segmenting temporal cycles. They depend on a community that maintains and contextualizes such practices by allowing children and adolescents to 'utilize different linguistic resources for participating in linguistic practices' (Dufva, Aro & Suni 2014). These linguaform cognitive devices acquire a transpositional function in that they allow for making longitudinal comparisons of the time and place of ecological phenomena. They thus function as a cultural memory system (Sutton 2010) that allows human agents to transpose ecosystemic changes onto a stable sociocultural background (calendars) or a stable environmental background (elevation).

Not only do these cognitive devices allow the Andean communities to register climate change. The also function as means for adapting the agricultural practices to the changed climatic realities. Thus, as Postigo (2014: 392) reports, 'actions taken by the majority of peasants to cope with climatic events rely on local knowledge of environmental and biological signals. These signals improve peasants' abilities to forecast weather or to anticipate seasonal changes'. Postigo mentions the example of bird nesting: 'if *Vanellus chilensis* Molina *(leque leque)* nests are at high elevations it means that it will be a rainy year; however, if the nest is at lower elevations, the year will be dry' (Postigo 2014: 392f.). While Postigo focuses on how the interpretation of constellations, wind directions, time of flowering and animal behaviour guides behaviour, our focus is on how cognitive devices pertaining to a community of practice allow for this guidance. Thus, by having access to meaningful linguistic and cultural ways of categorizing ecological events, the Andean communities are in a better position for adapting to climate change. This insight emphasizes the ecolinguistic concern for linguistic diversity, since the extinction of language does not merely imply a loss of communicative tools or identity markers, but crucially the disappearance of a class of cognitive devices that aid Indigenous communities in making their way in a local environment impacted by exogenous climate changes.

An ecolinguistics of cognitive devices

In the previous section, we discussed the perception of climate change. We selected climate change as our case because it is of vital significance, both for ecolinguistics and for the wider politics of survival, but we maintain that the approach sketched above has wider implications than for this area alone. Likewise, we focused on perception as a starting point for understanding how language impacts on human behaviour. In this section, we will abstract from these two foci and discuss what our case studies imply for ecolinguistics more broadly. In the first subsection we elaborate on what the preoccupation with cognitive devices amount to in an ecolinguistic context. In the second subsection, we call for an ecolinguistic research agenda for scrutinizing how language and culture, via cognitive devices, impact on human behaviour in ways that have long-reaching environmental consequences.

Cognitive devices and linguaculture

Why are cognitive devices relevant to ecolinguistics? Ecolinguistics is concerned with how language plays a role in ecological processes pertaining to 'life-sustaining relationships' (Alexander & Stibbe 2014). The premise of this preoccupation is that language has consequences for the non-symbolic, material environment. Since language is a distinctly human activity, the link between language and the environment is human beings.

The human body, in other words, is the intermediary between language and environment. But how does language impact on embodied human behaviour? To respond to that question, we need to turn our attention to cognition, understood as that which allows for flexible, adaptive responses to environmental events. For language to have environmental consequences, it has to impact on human cognition which in turn will shape behaviour, which in turn will impact on the environment. This argument underlies our interest in linguistically moulded cognitive devices. We believe that the class of cognitive devices are exactly what ecolinguistics is concerned about in its quest to understand the interrelationship between language and environmental conditions for life.

But what is a cognitive device? A cognitive device is a heteroscalar achievement that transposes otherwise invisible, distant or non-local phenomena into the present situation of living agents. Although situated agents rely on 'embodied capacities for perception and action' (Chemero 2009: 150), we focus here on cognitive devices that transpose the perceivable, rather than devices that transpose the act-upon-able. In an ecolinguistic context, the main question is how linguistic phenomena interact with perception in ways that transform how human beings perceive the world.

While some features of human perception are cross-culturally invariant (such as the looming effect discussed in relation to the climate spiral), other features depend on culturally salient features of the environment. Thus, what functions as a cognitive device for a given community depends on the cultural dynamics of the population of which the agent is a member, as well as on the specificities of the environment. Accordingly, even if the perceptual dynamics between the perceiving organism and its environment are invariant, as argued by Gibson (1979), there will be a degree of cultural variability in the visual perception of the environment, because perception is intertwined with action and behaviour in an environment, and ecologically embedded action and behaviour depend on cultural variables (e.g. how one makes a living, how one exploits different cosmologies to understand one's surroundings, or indeed how one understands the environment in which one lives).

To illustrate how cognitive devices overlay direct perception with culturally variable perceptual models, we will turn to linguistic anthropology and the study of cattle perception in pastoral cultures. As shown by Petrollino (2022), ethnographers and anthropologists have known for decades that the perceptual terminology in pastoral cultures escapes the Western hue-brightness-saturation model of colour perception. In some communities, according to Magnus (1880), members 'cannot name green and blue, and think it highly amusing that there should be names for these colors' (quoted in Petrollino 2022: 3). In a study on the Southwest Ethiopian Hamar people, Petrollino (2022: 19) describes how 'cattle appearance is mapped onto other domains of visual perception: the fact that abstract geometric patterns and designs are described in terms of cattle appearance strongly supports the view of a cattle model as a general framework which pastoralists apply in their visual experience of the world'.

While anthropological studies emphasize the heteroscalar dimension of cattle perception, that is, how the cognitive device of classifying cattle appearance has grown out of a cultural setting rich in interaction with cattle, K. David Harrison (2010: 26–35) demonstrates the homoscalar importance of such devices. Reporting from his studies among the Tuvan, Tofa and Todzhu nomads in Siberia, Harrison highlights the function of such rich terminologies. He argues that they allow reindeer herders to keep track of hundreds of animals, sometimes herding them as a herd, at other times singling one out for specific consideration: 'By learning the [reindeer categorization] labels, they also acquire for free a great deal of extra information about how reindeer are best classified, utilized, and domesticated' (Harrison 2010: 28). For instance, when speakers of Todzhu identify a single reindeer in a large herd with the term *döngür*, they do more than compress the lexical information of 'male domesticated reindeer from second fall to third fall; first mating season; may be castrated or not, but even if not, will probably not be allowed to mate' (Harrison 2010: 29). Crucially, they use this information in guiding their interactions with the herd, including how they regulate the reindeers' mating behaviour in accordance with their own interests.

Thus, in slowly evolving cultural settings, a linguacultural classification is a behavioural resource for solving the tasks at hand. In effect, when the linguistic resources are attuned to specific bio-ecological circumstances, they extend the sensorium of the agents. They co-constitute a stabilised sensoric apparatus that sensitises speakers to varieties in fauna and flora, which in turn allow them to perceive subtle changes in their environment, as well as more abrupt changes as those experienced by the Andean peasants. Thus, given these linguacultural cognitive devices, human agents are capable of observing climate change as it is instantiated in the Umwelt. Accordingly, when languages stop being used (such as when the Siberian herders are forced to speak Russian), these cognitive devices become defunct.

Arguably, the link between linguistic diversity, behavioural diversity and bio-ecological diversity depends on how cognitive devices integrate in behaviour as human agents make use of natural resources for their survival. This diversity is currently shrinking. As Levisen (2019: 84) points out:

> [P]ostcolonial-semantic studies in color and visuality have shown how European color-based visual semantic systems have been imported and imposed on many speakers, and that many languages of the world have been semantically and visually 'Europeanized' in recent times as a consequence of colonialism and globalization.

Both globalization and urbanization constitute a drive towards human monoculture and monolingualism. For that reason, we are currently part of a global experiment where we test how a narrow set of linguacultural cognitive devices are used to funnel behaviour across very diverse bio-ecological settings ranging from polar to equatorial, from insular to continental, from coastal to inland, from riparian to desert. The results of this experiment do not look too promising.

Implications for ecolinguistics

In this subsection we ask what the kind of work presented in this chapter may imply for the field of ecolinguistics. We do so in two tempi: First we emphasize the continuities between our approach and the main tradition of ecolinguistics, and then we point to some discontinuities. The tradition with which we engage in a dialogue is Arran Stibbe's version of ecolinguistics, as presented in his *Ecolinguistics: Language, Ecology and the Stories We Live By* (Stibbe 2015).

Basically we see our approach and Stibbe's as convergent. Our research interest is in how human behaviour is shaped by cognitive devices which include linguistically constituted classification systems (such as the Andean knowledge about elevation zones, or the Todzhu classification of reindeers). In a similar vein, when Stibbe evokes '*stories-we-live-by*' (Stibbe 2015: 186), he connects a class of devices ('stories') and human activity ('we live'). Indeed, Stibbe's 'eight forms that stories take' (Stibbe 2015: 186) index mechanisms that would probably qualify as cognitive devices in our terminology (perhaps with a slight degree of reconceptualization and reassessment).

The two main differences between Stibbe's approach and ours are, first, that we do not restrict cognitive devices to be merely linguistic or narrative structures. Designing the climate spiral to achieve a looming effect is irreducible to a linguistic or a symbolic achievement, and only in the most abstract sense can it be taken as a story. Accordingly, while ecolinguistics should indeed study narrative framing devices, such as those comprehensively discussed by Stibbe, we argue that it should include a broader class of cognitive devices. That said, we have no reason to assume that Stibbe would disagree with us on this question, as he makes no claim that the stories-we-live-by are all there is to understand from an ecolinguistics point of view.

The second difference is more substantial. Stibbe follows Lakoff and Johnson (1980) in focusing 'at the level of conceptual system' (Stibbe 2015: 186) which is alleged to exist in the minds of individuals. This focus prompts Stibbe to adopt a version of Social Representation Theory (not unlike Moloney et al. [2014]), which is based on the post-structuralist assumption that values, ideas and practices exist as symbolic forms ('representations') shared by members of a given social group. In contrast, we build on the ecological (or 'radical embodied', cf. Steffensen and Cowley [2021]) tradition of William James, James Gibson, Harry Heft and Anthony Chemero. While this tradition's implications for the language sciences are yet to be spelled out in detail, a key difference lies in the theoretical status it ascribes to symbolic and linguistic phenomena. Thus, as it rejects representational models of mind and cognition, it aspires to trace linguistic meaning directly to ecological meaning (i.e. an organism's perception of itself in relation to other organisms and its environment), without positing a domain of symbolic linguistic meaning (Steffensen & Harvey 2018).

A cognitive device is thus a material or behavioural prompt that scaffolds or funnels behaviour. On this view, cognitive devices are inherently heteroscalar: they are created or designed in the past, upheld over time, and function through their impact on later behaviour (cf. Hollan et al. 2000). Thus, they involve at least a timescale of becoming distinct from a timescale of functioning. As we observed in the case studies, some cognitive devices are inherently linguistic. In these cases, cognitive devices functions as linguistic techniques that exploit the fact that language has both a heteroscalar and a homoscalar side. On the one hand, language exhibits heteroscalarity in that it allows us to exploit the historical products of human practices over millennia. When I speak, I both use my tongue, which is mine, and my mother tongue, which is my mother's and my ancestors. In that way, language depends on the merging of biological agency and sociocultural patterns (Steffensen & Harvey 2018). On the other hand, language exhibits homoscalarity in that it is tightly coupled to embodied action–perception cycles. When coordinating with other agents, we can use symbolic nudges – 'wait here', 'hand me the salt, please', 'look out', 'wanna go for a swim?' – that are integrated with our current activities. Accordingly, when we imbue given activities with linguistic and symbolic structures, these activities become heteroscalar. This peculiar form of human agency is the bedrock of ecosocial practices, that is, a community's habituated ways of constraining agents' engagement in and with a shared environment.

The main difference between our conceptualization of ecolinguistics and the one found in many publications in the field (for an overview, see Fill and Penz [2018)]; Steffensen & Fill [2014]) lies in our insistence that lived activities are at the heart of ecolinguistics. While we may be able to extract ecosophic positions from media representations and other texts – and evaluate their worldviews by comparing them to our own ecosophies – we have no way of approaching the question, how do such texts shape behaviour? The reason is that ecolinguistics has adopted its linguistic toolbox from twentieth-century linguistic methodologies, which in turn rests upon the view that the foundational function of language is to transmute mental representations into publicly shareable (vocal or graphic) meaning-bearing symbolic structures. Building on early structural assumptions about the immanence of language (e.g. Hjelmslev 1961), such methods are adapted to the investigation of linguistic structures (texts, sentences, etc.). However, if one is concerned with the question of how language plays a role in the life-sustaining relations between humans, other species and the environment, then one's object of study is not textual. Rather, one is studying a conglomerate of textual and non-textual elements. Accordingly, it makes no sense to rely fully on methods for textual analysis.

When we propose an ecolinguistics for cognitive devices, the reason is not that we propose a 'cognitive turn' in ecolinguistics. The reason is that we subscribe to the notion of ecolinguistics as the study of how life and language intermingle. Putting life centre-stage is a pivotal concern of ecolinguistics, but we can only do so if we in fact pursue a research agenda that examines life itself, and not merely language *about* life.

Conclusions

It is a well-established truth that the climate crisis is driven by human behaviour. But what drives human behaviour? Why do we act as we do? This chapter has proposed that these questions are key questions in ecolinguistics, and indeed that we need an ecolinguistic vantage point to answer the behavioural question, because language is a powerful force that shapes behaviour in strangely under-theorized ways. In this way, the ecolinguistic agenda of investigating how ecological problems depend on linguistically co-constituted behaviour has two theoretical sub-themes. On the one hand, ecolinguistics is concerned with what grants language such transformative powers; on the other hand, it sets out to understand the species-specific kind of cognition that has endowed *Homo sapiens* with the ability to obliterate the planet and the stupidity not to abstain from it. To pursue an ecolinguistic agenda, then, the first question is 'what is language?' and the second question is 'what is human cognition?' The two questions merge in an attempt to understand human behaviour that undermines the conditions of life on Earth.

In this chapter, we have made a modest attempt at outlining how ecolinguistics could pursue a research agenda along these lines. Our starting point was that on the tragic view of anthropogenic climate change, behaviour is the result of internal, mental processes. On this view, action is the materialization of thought. As argued by Steffensen (2018), this cognitive model has also won a foothold in ecolinguistics where climate-destructive behaviours are often traced to values, discourses and similar mental constructs. Such views pivot on the assumption that human thinking is a sort of computational processing of mental symbols, and that such symbols can be externalized by coding them into sound sequences or their written counterparts. Thus, by identifying discourses as patterns in externalized language activity, one can assume that one has indeed identified patterns that also exist in the pre-externalized reality of human thinking. By adopting such a viewpoint, ecolinguistics has established a theoretical model where both language and behaviour are traced to the same underlying mental structure. Accordingly, by analysing language, the ecolinguist can characterize the same structure that also causes behaviour.

To counter the tragic view, we followed Steffensen and Cowley's (2021) proposal and adopted an alternative model of cognition, namely the radical embodied cognition view, where 'mental gymnastics' (Chemero 2009) is rejected in favour of an 'epistemic stance [that] uses a methodological imperative that traces what people think, say, and do to a multi-scalar history of dynamic coordination' (Steffensen & Cowley 2021: 728). Whereas the mentalist model relies on language primarily having a representational function as a tool for describing reality, the radical embodied view assumes that language functions as a population-level constraint that shapes multiscalar coordination dynamics between human beings in specific environments. On that view, the question is less about how we depict or describe climate issues. The issue, rather, is how language partakes in behaviour, that is, how our everyday decision making – leaving the car in the driveway in favour of the bicycle or public transportation, or abstaining from flying on holiday – depends on sociocultural and linguistic constraints.

We pursued this perspective by considering a central theme in ecolinguistics, namely climate change. We demonstrated how linguistic and symbolic structures functioned as cognitive devices that allow human agents to perceive climate change. This analysis hinges on a view of human behaviour as multiscalar, that is, its conditions and consequences play out on multiple timescales. As events on some timescales escape our situated perception, cognitive devices function through the transposition of either observed events or of perception. Either events that are so slow that they escape our perception are compressed into a rate of change that we can pick up, or our sensorium is socially extended in a way that resembles Hutchins's description of distributed cognition (Hutchins 1995a, 1995b, 2014).

Our three case studies elicited quite different cognitive devices. Those involved in the climate spiral depend on transposing perceptual invariants (e.g. by preserving event structures across timescales or creating the cognitive experience of a looming impact), whereas those involved in the Lytton case depend on narrative framings. In the latter case, our understanding of such cognitive devices come very close to Stibbe's (2015) view on stories-we-live-by. Finally, in the Andean example, we examined how Andean peasants relied on cultural classification systems that allow contemporary members of this agrarian culture to perceive changes that were otherwise too slow to be observed. In this example, we close in on linguistic anthropology, and we foresee that there is a rich dialogue for future ecolinguists in this tradition.

Epilogue: Does it matter?

We end this chapter with a short epilogue prompted by a colleague who, blind to the authors' identities, challenged the whole endeavour. He wrote:

My own view is that the paper has missed its target. The take on Gibson, while interesting, seems quite irrelevant. This is because [the] issue at stake, I believe, is the absolutely enormous, indeed incalculable, influence of the fossil fuel lobby on all areas of social, cultural and intellectual activity and it is therefore necessary to 'follow the money' in all these areas. [...] I believe this position [presented in this chapter] is not going to help and is, in all probability a damaging distraction. Human-made climate change is largely the product of capitalist development and it is these economic interests, with all the power at their disposal (including corrupting influences on academic research), which I would say is the main issue.

Is there something to be gained from our perspective, or is our chapter a damaging distraction? Basically, we agree with this colleague that the climate crisis is a result of the development of capitalism. As such, yes, perhaps we may have wasted our time, and our readers' time, by writing this chapter. Indeed, this whole book may be a waste of time. Ecolinguistics may be a waste of time. Academia may be a waste of time. Perhaps everything is a waste of time but direct revolutionary action aiming at overthrowing capitalism.

In noting our colleague's self-contradiction (why do they waste their time by engaging in a scholarly exchange of opinions when capitalism still prevails?), we are sympathetic to the Marxist position hinted at by our colleague and unfolded, inter alia, by Søren Mau (2023). But we still believe that there is a deeper raison d'être for the kind of work presented here, also as seen from a Marxist position. The key premise of Marxism is the fact that human beings are biologically underdetermined. There is no 'natural' way of being a human being, for which reason human metabolism cannot be isolated from sociopolitical processes (including subsumption, violence and compulsion). Accordingly, the critical project starts from a Marxist anthropology that strives to understand the human condition that has allowed capitalism to drive a wedge between humanity and nature. Understanding capitalism is insufficient to the Marxist project. We also need to understand those constituents of human nature that allow for both capitalism and the post-capitalist modes of production. We have not managed to get the full picture in this chapter, but we believe that our starting point is valid and valuable, also for our colleague's legitimate political project. Indeed, capitalism is ubiquitous. But so are language and perceivable structures in the environment. We would argue that the project of replacing capitalism with a more sustainable system is in part the project of replacing the cognitive devices of capitalism – devices that are built on the assumption of a separation between humanity and nature – with better devices that are built on ecological thinking.

Notes

1. Our notion of a cognitive device is related to Cecilia Heyes's notion of a cognitive gadget – i.e. a culturally acquired cognitive mechanism (Heyes 2018). Whereas Heyes's cognitive gadgets are internal to the individual, our notion of a cognitive device is more general and includes material structures that are found in the shared environment (Baggs, Raja & Anderson 2019).
2. The perspective on organism-environment relations in terms of homoscalarity and heteroscalarity relies on collaborative work done together with Christian M. Johannessen.
3. For instance, the *United States Geological Survey* (USGS) has run the *Repeat Photography Project* since 1997; the project juxtaposes historic photographs of glaciers with contemporary ones. See: https://www.nps.gov/glac/learn/nature/glacier-repeat-photos.htm (accessed 25 October 2022).
4. In the spiral, red is reserved for the two circumpolar lines that indicate temperature anomalies of 1.5°C and 2.0°C.

References

Alexander, R., & Stibbe, A. (2014). 'From the analysis of ecological discourse to the ecological analysis of discourse'. *Language Sciences*, 41(0): 104–10.

Anderson, M. L. (2014). *After Phrenology: Neural Reuse and the Interactive Brain*. Cambridge, MA: MIT Press.

Atkinson, Q. D., & Jacquet, J. (2022). 'Challenging the idea that humans are not designed to solve climate change'. *Perspectives on Psychological Science*, 17(3): 619–30.

Baggs, E., Raja, V., & Anderson, M. L. (2019). 'Culture in the world shapes culture in the head (and vice versa)'. *Behavioral and Brain Sciences*, 42: e172.

Baggs, E., & Steffensen, S. V. (2023). 'Perception and problem solving'. In M. Segundo-Ortin, M. Heras-Escribano & V. Raja (Eds.), *Places, Sociality, and Ecological Psychology: Essays in Honor of Harry Heft*. London: Routledge.

Chemero, A. (2009). *Radical Embodied Cognitive Science*. Cambridge, MA: MIT Press.

Clayton, S., Devine-Wright, P., Stern, P., Whitmarsh, L., Carrico, A., Steg, L., & Bonnes, M. (2015). 'Psychological research and global climate change'. *Nature Climate Change*, 5(7): 640–6.

Dufva, H., Aro, M., & Suni, M. (2014). 'Language learning as appropriation: How linguistic resources are recycled and regenerated'. In P. Lintunen, M. S. Peltola & M.-L. Varila (Eds.), *AFinLA-e Soveltavan kielitieteen tutkimuksia 2014 / n:o 6*, 20–31.

Fill, A., & Penz, H. (2018). *The Routledge Handbook of Ecolinguistics*. New York, NY: Routledge.

Gibson, J. J. (1966). *The Senses Considered as Perceptual Systems.* London: George Allen & Unwin.

Gibson, J. J. (1979). *The Ecological Approach to Visual Perception.* Boston: Houghton Mifflin.

Gifford, R. (2011). 'The dragons of inaction: Psychological barriers that limit climate change mitigation and adaptation'. *American Psychologist May–June*, 66(4): 290–302.

Goodwin, C. (1994). 'Professional vision'. *American Anthropologist*, 96(3): 606–33. doi:10.1525/aa.1994.96.3.02a00100.

Harrison, K. D. (2010). *When Languages Die: The Extinction of the World's Languages and the Erosion of Human Knowledge.* Oxford: Oxford University Press.

Hawkins, E., Fæhn, T., & Fuglestvedt, J. (2019). 'The climate spiral demonstrates the power of sharing creative ideas'. *Bulletin of the American Meteorological Society*, 100(5): 753–56. doi:10.1175/bams-d-18-0228.1.

Heyes, C. M. (2018). *Cognitive Gadgets: The Cultural Evolution of Thinking.* Cambridge, MA: The Belknap Press of Harvard University Press.

Hjelmslev, L. (1961). *Prolegomena to a Theory of Language.* Madison: University of Wisconsin Press.

Hollan, J., Hutchins, E., & Kirsh, D. (2000). 'Distributed cognition: toward a new foundation for human-computer interaction research'. *ACM Transactions on Computer-Human Interaction (TOCHI)*, 7(2): 174–96.

Hutchins, E. (1995a). *Cognition in the Wild.* Cambridge, MA: The MIT press.

Hutchins, E. (1995b). 'How a cockpit remembers its speeds'. *Cognitive Science*, 19(3): 265–88.

Hutchins, E. (2010). 'Cognitive ecology'. *Topics in Cognitive Science*, 2(4): 705–15.

Hutchins, E. (2014). 'The cultural ecosystem of human cognition'. *Philosophical Psychology*, 27(1): 34–49.

Johnson, D., & Levin, S. (2009). 'The tragedy of cognition: Psychological biases and environmental inaction'. *Current Science*, 97(11): 1593–603. Retrieved from http://www.jstor.org/stable/24107300.

Lakoff, G., & Johnson, M. (1980). *Metaphors We Live By.* Chicago: University of Chicago Press.

Lave, J., & Wenger, E. (1991). *Situated Learning: Legitimate Peripheral Participation.* Cambridge: Cambridge University Press.

Levisen, C. (2019). '"Brightness" in color linguistics: New light from Danish visual semantics'. In I. Raffaelli, D. Katunar & B. Kerovec (Eds.), *Lexicalization Patterns in Color Naming: A Cross-linguistic Perspective*, 83–105. Amsterdam: John Benjamins Publishing Company.

Loaiza, J. M., Trasmundi, S. B., & Steffensen, S. V. (2020). 'Multiscalar Temporality in Human Behaviour: A Case Study of Constraint Interdependence in Psychotherapy'. *Frontiers in Psychology*, 11(1685): 1685. doi:10.3389/fpsyg.2020.01685.

MacWhinney, B. (2005). 'The emergence of linguistic form in time'. *Connection Science*, 17(3–4): 191–211.

Magnus, H. (1880). *Untersuchungen über den Farbensinn der Naturvölker: mit einem chromo-lithographischen Fragebogen* (Vol. 7). Jena: Verlag von Gustav Fischer.

Malafouris, L., & Koukouti, M. -D. (2022). 'Where the touching is touched: The role of haptic attentive unity in the dialogue between maker and material'. *Multimodality & Society*, 2(3): 265–87.

Mau, S. (2023). *Mute Compulsion: A Marxist Theory of the Economic Power of Capital*. London: Verso.

Moloney, G., Leviston, Z., Lynam, T., Price, J., Stone-Jovicich, S., & Blair, D. (2014). 'Using social representations theory to make sense of climate change: What scientists and nonscientists in Australia think'. *Ecology and Society*, 19(3): 19.

Patterson, B. D., Stotz, D. F., Solari, S., Fitzpatrick, J. W., & Pacheco, V. (1998). Contrasting patterns of elevational zonation for birds and mammals in the Andes of southeastern Peru'. *Journal of Biogeography*, 25(3): 593–607.

Petrollino, S. (2022). 'The Hamar cattle model: The semantics of appearance in a pastoral linguaculture'. *Language Sciences*, 89: 101448.

Postigo, J. C. (2014). 'Perception and resilience of Andean populations facing climate change'. *Journal of Ethnobiology*, 34(3): 383–400. doi:10.2993/0278-0771-34.3.383.

Ritchie, H., Roser, M., & Rosado, P. (2020). 'CO_2 and Greenhouse Gas Emissions'. *Our World in Data*. Retrieved from https://ourworldindata.org/co2-and-other-greenhouse-gas-emissions.

Steffensen, S. V. (2018). 'The microecological grounding of language: How linguistic symbolicity extends and transforms the human ecology'. In A. Fill & H. Penz (Eds.), *The Routledge Handbook of Ecolinguistics*, 411–23. London: Routledge.

Steffensen, S. V., & Cowley, S. J. (2021). 'Thinking on behalf of the world: Radical embodied ecolinguistics'. In X. Wen & J. R. Taylor (Eds.), *The Routledge Handbook of Cognitive Linguistics*, 723–36. London: Routledge.

Steffensen, S. V., & Fill, A. (2014). 'Ecolinguistics: The state of the art and future horizons'. *Language Sciences*, 41, Part A, 6–25. doi:10.1016/j.langsci.2013.08.003.

Steffensen, S. V., & Harvey, M. I. (2018). 'Ecological meaning, linguistic meaning, and interactivity'. *Cognitive Semiotics*, 11(1): 1–21.

Steffensen, S. V., & Pedersen, S. B. (2014). 'Temporal dynamics in human interaction'. *Cybernetics & Human Knowing*, 21(1–2): 80–97.

Stibbe, A. (2015). *Ecolinguistics: Language, Ecology and the Stories We Live By*. London: Routledge.

Sutton, J. (2010). 'Exograms and interdisciplinarity: History, the extended mind, and the civilizing process'. In R. Menary (Ed.), *The Extended Mind*, 189–225. Cambridge, MA: MIT Press.

Transport Safety Board of Canada (2021). 'Rail transportation safety investigation R21V0143'. Retrieved from https://www.tsb.gc.ca/eng/enquetes-investigations/rail/2021/r21v0143/r21v0143.html#.

Uryu, M., Steffensen, S. V., & Kramsch, C. (2014). 'The ecology of intercultural interaction: Timescales, temporal ranges and identity dynamics'. *Language Sciences*, 41, Part A, 41–59. doi:10.1016/j.langsci.2013.08.006.

4

Regeneration: From Language Use to Languaging

Stephen J. Cowley

Introduction

Economics, marketization and technoscience have enabled dominant institutions to promise prosperous lifestyles. Yet, the physical logic of growthism (Halliday 2003a) offers little to most humans and, worse, decimates the earth's life systems. Using junk media, greenwash and post academic facts, not only institutions but also regulators and corporations favour models and policy that pay little attention to the plight of life on earth. Debates are all too often dominated by anonymous parties who emphasize complexity, science and risk. So, how can we sustain biodiversity based on, perhaps, four billion years of evolution? Can we slow, or even reverse, the toxic effects of growthism? The chapter argues that, as one step, we can gain by tracing knowledge, media and institutions to how people happen, or *languaging*. A turn to languaging is, some suggest, a strong 'starting point [… in] response to the ecological crisis' (Zhou 2021: 464). Indeed, conceptual innovation is necessary in working to enhance life-sustaining relationships. In seeking regeneration, I trace languaging to vital process[1] and, in humans, semogenesis. The move can alter beliefs, build hopes and engage in positive action. Ecolinguists can bring new awareness to understanding and, in time, give shape to a new theory of practices. Thus, as Stibbe suggests (2021), we gain new stories to live by.

Ecolinguistics began with a vision of pursuing 'interactions between any given language and its environment' (Haugen 2001: 325). In the past fifty years, much has been achieved as, above all, toxic effects have been traced to how ecosystems are destroyed as a side effect of classism and growthism (Halliday 2003a). In this work, many use what Fill (1998) calls 'non-metaphorical' analysis of environmental discourse. However, in an analytical approach, one cannot avoid a spectatorial attitude – one that linguists trace to Saussure's dream of a new science. Countering, many demand practical ways of working for 'life-sustaining relationships of humans, other species and the physical environment' (Alexander & Stibbe 2014: 105). Yet, if one relies on analysis, one cannot clarify *how* this can be done. In filling the gap, Cowley (2021a) asks *how* languages affect eco-systems: in response, he stresses that 'interactions' work through people because, as living beings, we engage in languaging. Humans draw on wordings (and, thus, languages) as part of coordinative activity (e.g. looking, feeling, hearing) that transforms living bodies. Once conceptualized as languaging, its effects can be tracked to their source in *semogenesis* (Halliday 2003b). As is explained below, semogenesis informs practices. It is emplaced human activity that links embodiment, action and wordings. In turning from 'language use' to 'languaging' situated wordings are taken to be reciprocally coupled with coordinative activity (see Cowley 2019, 2021c; Steffensen & Cowley 2021). Hence, *language use*, *words* and *discourse* are linguistic metaphors (Halliday 2003b) that anchor aspects of talk (e.g. wordings) in alphabets, ideographs, digits, computer programs and so on. As abstract entities, like societies or markets, viewed from the 'outside', they appear as what Saussure (2011) calls 'objects', As a result, while rooted in coordinative activity, languaging enables groups to build spectatorial models. Even the environment can become 'a remote object of observation and prediction' (Bogdan 1997: 104). Yet, while models matter, the ecolinguist's first concern is with life-sustaining relations and, therefore, changing how people understand, act, speak, hear as they contribute to human practices.

Overview

Ecolinguists aspire to bring change to actual living systems. Yet, where one starts with language use, one turns to analysis and critique of discourse about the environment. One faces Haugen's problem (Cowley 2021a) or, simply, how languages can *do* anything at all. In Haugen's terms, *how do languages interact with the environment?* Cowley's two-part solution is to argue, first, that languaging builds on natural innovation and semogenesis; hence languages work through coordinative activity and ways with wordings. Second, languaging occurs as people actualize practices that exert material effects on the living (for good and ill). Languages thus affect the environment, not through 'interactions', but as intended and unintended effects cascade through living, languaging and our limited ability to understand, regulate and control social practices (or praxis).

Before defending the turn to languaging, I specify reliance based on appeal to language use. Having done so, I trace languaging to semogenesis and how vital process pervades the ecosphere. On one hand, I stress that both languaging and semogenesis are emplaced and, on the other, that they are embedded in practices. The move brings two *desiderata* for a regenerated ecolinguistics. First, we can strive for bioecological awareness, or a sense of being included in the living. Second, we can use the results to change attitudes and organize in order to alter practices. Accordingly, returning to Haugen, I suggest that putting the spectatorial in its place can help ecolinguists to develop a theory of practices that can be used to achieve outreach. In working for life-sustaining relations, the mechanisms of marketization, technoscience and economics cannot be allowed to dominate the future of life on earth.

Ecolinguistics: a practical turn

Human engagement is increasingly influential on life-sustaining relations between living beings (Stibbe 2021). Yet, surveys report that ecolinguistics (e.g. Fill 1998; Steffensen & Fill 2014; Zhou 2021) deal with analytical methods and concepts like *discourse, grammar* and *language use*. This is because Haugen (2001) and Halliday (2003a), fathers of the field, highlight how societies use linguistic systems and features and, in the latter case, how experience is construed. Leaving aside practice and living systems, they attribute social reality to *languages* and *discourse*. Perhaps, they were mesmerized by Chomsky's view that language [*sic*] is a capacity to 'synthesize or predict' the 'sentences of a natural language' (Joseph et al. 2001: 126). Rejecting biologism (not mind), Haugen, Halliday, Hymes (1973) and others ascribe synthesis to how *language use* draws on *context* and *interaction*. Haugen's American descriptivism, like Halliday's systemic-functional model, focuses on forms, meanings and discourse. Having influenced language policy and social critique, the work's diminishing returns depend on (a) reliance on analysis of structure; (b) methodological individualism; and (c) ascribing linguistic form to a 'something' (e.g. meaning/reality) that is distinct from people and particulars.

The structuralist posits that 'forms' (*signes*) constitute a language-system. Where the picture is used by linguists or ecolinguists, they commit to: (1) methods of *analysis* which, typically (2) map forms onto *functions/meanings*.

Often, these are traced (3) in *discourse* or a level above the sentence. The premises peel away from living beings, coordinative activity and practices. What is conceived of as 'language' is treated as self-contained or autonomous. While the approach offers much to describing functions and meanings, it omits how autonomous systems emerge, function or, indeed, alter the effects they exert on the living world. Yet, for ecolinguists, the issues are pressing. How can discourse, and 'language use', be life damaging or, indeed, aid life-sustaining relationships? Without bodies, effects and practices there is a gaping hole. Everything depends on what 'we' know as users of language systems. As knowledge is undefined, appeal to discourse and 'language use' leaves unasked who 'we' are and, thus, the role of persons, agents and living bodies. Often, appeal is made to a putative device that (allegedly) produces and/or construes linguistic products. On such a view 'language' takes on agency and people reduce to performers who rely on mind or, perhaps, habitus. Consequently, structuralism encourages both methodological individualism and the optimistic view that communication leads to mutual understanding based on the *abstracta* of 'language' (i.e. how 'knowers' of a language-system use forms).

If *abstracta* can be understood as having meanings, one assumes a methodological individualism. For the purposes of analysis, one posits that the relevant decision-making is organism-centred and predictable. Indeed, without it, meaning/function would be externally imposed. Thus, any appeal to form hints at inner process or, at least, constructs that the folk attribute to a concept of mind. This is because, once perception is ascribed to sense-impressions, form (linguistic or not) can only be cognitive. Thus, while some, like Chomsky (1965) ascribe generative powers to a mind/brain, others resist this move without challenging its logic. They ascribe 'language use' to brains, context and interaction. Taking such a view, Haugen overtly places languages 'in the minds of their users' (Haugen 2001 [1972]: 57). More cautiously, Halliday tracks 'acts of communication' (Halliday 2004: vii) which enable 'language use' to draw on what, as clarified below, is called semogenesis (Halliday 2003b). While guarded about mind, he stresses that, in social contexts, individuals (and brains) make communicative use of a social semiotic. Remarkably, there is no argument that speaks for an ecology of language (Lechevral 2009) and Haugen's work must be seen as a sketch or, at best, a wide vision (Eliasson 2015). Even Halliday's challenge to growthism and classism rests on little more than a cluster of concepts and an applicable method. Famously, Fill (1998) called the former metaphorical and, by juxtaposition, deemed environmental discourse 'non-metaphorical'. One can therefore object that the whole tradition abstracts 'language' away from acting, knowing and people who engage in practices.

Spectatorial views present models of hidden and theoretical objects that are available to public scrutiny. This applies, for example, to discourse about the environment. Where subject to analysis, one can make claims about facts, beliefs and positions that constitute an abstract object. In short, discourse about the environment can shape non-metaphorical discourse about the environment. Cyclically, this can be used in discourse that describes, contests, or extends discursive themes, positions and procedures. The resulting twists and turns, unsurprisingly, prompt ecolinguistic approaches to diverge. In their state of the art, therefore, Steffensen & Fill (2014) find four main camps: the symbolic, natural, cognitive and social-cultural. These address discourse as language use, as referring to nature, as emerging and as historical. Within each camp, divisions abound. As an 'umbrella term', Fill & Penz (2018) apply *ecolinguistics* to approaches where 'language' reflects what, oddly, they call a 'convironment' (Fill 2001). It informs a loop of language about language use (or discourse). Indeed, this is Haugen's difficulty too. When one builds on linguistic premises, one cannot ask, let alone explain, how languages 'interact' with the environment (or convironment). They don't and they can't – if languages are autonomous. Thus, the tradition offers little in terms of *working* for life-sustaining relations. Ecolinguists have everything to gain by escaping from discursive loop and acknowledging our embedding in practices. In breaking the circle one sees the limits of analysis, the weakness of methodological individualism, and the narrowness of the spectatorial. Instead, one can start with observed effects of *languaging* and, at once, how it constitutes experience. By tracing this to living, and vital process, ecolinguistics regenerates.

Languaging

In aspiring to reunite ecolinguistics, Steffensen and Fill (2014) identify the challenge to the field. They echo Halliday's (2003a) view that language, forms and functions are, in one sense, metaphorical. Hence, the terms are targets whose source is practical activity, or what Halliday also calls 'languaging'. Rather than posit an autonomous domain, one can ask how bodies coordinate as they draw on wordings and an embedding in practices. Languaging unites how agents self-coordinate as they think, look and/or listen/speak while pursuing cultural concerns. As people engage in practices, their languaging is bodily, social and practical which, as experienced, re-evokes life history. As Maturana (1978) insists, languaging enables observing (see Kravchenko 2011) and, thus, human hearing, understanding and feeling. As coordinative activity, it prompts human use of bias, belief, affect and, yes, spectatorial knowledge. People can deal with these because, habitually, we treat aspects of languaging as repeatable: we orient to accents, tones and, above all, *wordings*. Although these latter repeatable events can be standardized as types ('words') they always re-render and re-elaborate the already considered. For this reason, a focus on repeating is insufficient to show how wordings (and other repeatables) inform activity. In practice, wordings often act as nonce events. The structuralist's error is to start with, not emplacement, but analysis. While wordings *are* pictured and used as types, their embedding in practices is animated by bodies, semogenesis (see below) and, ultimately, coordinative activity. In humans, as in non-humans, meaning/function engages arises in engaging with what is here, now. A person is conditioned by a social reality that appears in an enlanguaged world. Indeed, a flow of experience grants languaging a constitutive role in what we become and, thus, how we engage in practices.

Today *languaging* is prominent in applied linguistics where, without reference to its history (Niu & Li 2017), the term is said to have been 'invented' to describe second language meaning-making (e.g. Swain & Watanbe 2013). More recently, it has been traced to semiotic assemblages and practices (e.g. Pennycook 2020). In attempting a general review, Cowley (2019) highlights its pre-modern underpinnings, the work of Becker (1991) and Maturana's cognitive biology (see Kravchenko 2011). Recently, Luz Seiberth (2021) traces languaging to the naturalist philosophy of Wilfred Sellars. Given such diversity, use of languaging is, first, an escape from the trammels of linguistics. Given pre-modern origins, it also can free one from methodological individualism and, by implication, any mind/society divide. Emblematically, for Mulcaster (1582), languaging arises in a schoolboy's use of the vernacular to render aloud his grasp of a classic text. The schoolboy uses *natural wit* to make up a translation – semogenesis meshes activity with a flow of wordings. The role of wit reverberates over the centuries as languaging is used of, say, bad poetry, the declamations of prophets, the strangeness of school children's talk and how, before chiselling into prose, text writes itself. Since languaging is intuitive and coordinative, while indexing conventional meanings (as 'words'), wordings bring an emplaced sense for each party to events. Influentially, Becker (1991) stresses how languaging unites the particular, the cultural and the connotative. In so doing, he ties languaging to threads in Wittgenstein, Heidegger and, in biology, Maturana. Importantly, the latter traces coordinative activity to how structural coupling, which occurs in all species, bundle wordings (the patterns of a 'consensual domain') as acts of languaging. The results thus unite two orders, each, as Love (2017) reminds us, irreducible to the other. Coordinative activity is irreducible to the wordings that we so readily repeat just as, conversely, their generality defies reduction to a history of lived particulars (or 'learning'). This symbiosis of systems makes languaging an epistemic tool that can be used to engage with, critique and change practices.

Although Sellars uses *languagings* sparingly, the concept groups a naturalistic view that avoids both coherentism and the Myth of the Given (Sellars 1956).[2] As for Maturana, Love and Kravchenko, *languagings* unite wordings with lived events. Given a concern with ontology, Sellars traces them to, not perception, but direct or empirical relations. In an English-speaking world, where a triangle is red, one can see it as *red* (under standard conditions). In other conditions, of course, one can see the same triangle as *looking red* (while knowing it is green). Thus (what I call) wordings unite emplacement with how they function as generals: as we actualize practices, we use places (and memories) to engender a particular sense (e.g. *Karen*'s red hair). Given empirical relations, generals sustain spectatorial models, warrant claims, and, thus, populate a space of reasons. For Sellars (1979), languagings transcend experiential flux. In Mulcaster's terms, this *is* natural wit: further, while often public, languagings can be overt, covert and even hidden (see Seiberth 2021). Even when wordings are unspoken, they allow action and understanding to bind as rapid bodily expression/sensation. Where, as in paradigm cases, they use linguistic embodiment (Cowley 2014b), one can investigate them by using multimodal methods (see Thibault 2020). Further, even if languaging is sometimes used in a restricted sense, by tracing it to coordinative activity, one invokes all applications of overt and covert wordings.

In spite of differences in use, most concur that languaging is activity that embodies understanding of wordings. Although some highlight the face-to-face (Kravchenko 2011; Thibault 2021), like Love (2017), others ascribe languaging to *all activities* that draw on wordings. On this view, also taken here, we inhabit an enlanguaged world where perceivings, happenings and persons are inseparable from covert languagings. We attend to things, events and individuals. In ascribing this to a history of appropriation, most adopt a constructivist logic (see Raimondi 2019; Kravchenko 2011). Humans, like non-humans, use the structural coupling and coordinative activity by engaging in social activity that informs agency. Over a life span, humans use practices to stabilize ways of acting, observing and drawing on wordings as they perceive, act, feel and come to know (and believe). As a result, languaging spreads as it shapes practices and semiotic assemblages, cognitive activity, and thus human use of distributed agency (e.g. Pennycook 2020). Languaging binds *how* we speak and move as wordings (and ways of doing things with wordings) prompt us to manage social and bodily coordination. Languaging, in brief, is multi-scalar in that it combines how one understands, speaks or attends to the other, how one actively perceives what is said/meant and, at once, uses the coordinative in both recall and pre-reflective experience. Perception with action in the scale of doings and sayings co-occur with what, drawing on neuroscience, is known as *percaction* (Berthoz 2012; Cowley & Gahrn-Andersen 2022). As we speak and act (in scales measured by seconds), we monitor their unfolding and while using percaction to modulate facial expression, movement and voice dynamics. The rhythms of percaction shape events around syllabic bursts in public displays that attest to pre-reflective experience. Interpersonal coordinative activity serves to co-regulate events and pick up on (or attribute) purport/import. Hence, together and alone, we actualize practices as we orient to others by accommodating, linking repeated patterns to feelings, attitudes and, above all, using social meaning (Eckert & Labov 2017). We draw on voices, emplaced others and, at once, both set off and suffer semogenesis.

Languaging enables languages to constrain how a living being engages in practices. Haugen's problem, as noted, lies in overplaying 'interaction'. In fact, languages and varieties of languages connect coordinated activity with the environment. We make use of practices, wordings and events that are bidirectionally managed through coordinative activity – we orient to the sense of second-order cultural constructs (Love 2017). As a result, generals permeate how we understand, perceive things and entertain thoughts (as we monitor events). Thus, as we pick up on coordinative activity, we engender pre-reflective experience. Although lacking causal power, verbal patterns use coordinative activity to re-evoke experience, talk, practices, rituals, books, technology techniques, etc. The brain supports synthesis such that, in an enlanguaged world, one can see a triangle that looks green but *is* red (Sellars 1956). This might occur in an experiment when, for example, a person observes an object under non-standard conditions. For Sellars, we must reject sense impressions: in the terms proposed here, vital process prompts going on or, as Halliday (2003a) suggests, we are moved by semogenesis (and agential bodily sub-systems).

Semogenesis

Human expression, verbal, vocal and of many other kinds, can be described by signs and, thus, in Halliday's (2003a) terms, semogenesis. Even taking a selfie on Table Mountain can, and has been, traced to a synthetic process (Johannesen

& Boeriis 2021). At such times, semogenesis arises as parties use equipment in practices that highlight a momentary end point that, by definition, commands attention. Whether in taking a selfie or saying something, the result may satisfy/disappoint and, thus, set off a cycle of repetition or, indeed, learning. While technology makes this especially clear, semogenesis first appears in early development. In even this case, it draws on practices and, thus how, often shared, experience informs both an individual's specious present and a *here*. Typically, the results nudge the use of wordings, devices and other cultural constructs and institutions. Hence, semogenesis has a constitutive role in both doing things and, inseparably, influencing others.

Halliday (2004) finds the roots of semogenesis in his son's first act of communication. This arose at twelve days [sic] when Nigel had been crying miserably. As his mother undressed him for his bath, she noticed 'an unpleasant boil in the crook of his arm'. Calling Halliday, she said, 'Come here … look at this.' Nigel *stopped crying*: his inhibition was communicative. His tears stopped and did not restart. For Halliday, he 'knew his mother had found out what was wrong, and that was what mattered' (Halliday 2004: viii). Nigel goes beyond the information given and gains some distance from his pain. He inhibits and, by so doing, coordinates with his parents' perceiving, acting and, thus, construals of experience. Even if Halliday overinterprets, semogenesis brings soothing. Parties change the pre-reflective as, in rapid scales, percation serves to co-regulate movement, gaze and prosody. Next, therefore, I make the case that most (or all) activity that can be described by signs draws on coordinative activity. Indeed, as is shown by Cornips (this vol.), the propensity appears even in languaging with cows.

While I trace semogenesis to vital process, Halliday (2003a) uses the concept to describe how higher order meaning links the material (i.e. biology cum physics) with what he views as the functional systems of a language. He posits a system network to realize language use or, specifically, its metafunctions. By fiat, the systems work *in* a brain or, loosely, as inner powers. Language use unites the time dimensions of evolution, development and action. These amalgamate in the moment as circumstances rebound into the conditions of existence (where 'material' includes 'life'). The brain links the semiotic to a parallel material domain. For Halliday, while the roots of semogenesis are out of reach, it enables the making of texts and/or, more generally, language use. He thus leaves aside events and particulars to ask how a general sense (e.g. of *red*) or 'meaning' informs experience.

In languaging, multi-scalar events merge in a moment. While the brain's role is necessary, it functions as emplaced parties, often together, draw on sub-systems as they engage in practices. Importantly, Nigel's case shows that emplacement matters to human babies. While there are many ways of construing vital process, the twelve-day-old Nigel (or, more precisely, his sub-systems) attune to emplaced particulars. As he feels pain, he shows sensitivity to emplaced voices and norms of an enlanguaged world. Unbeknown to him, his family orients to concerns and general meanings ('look at this') and concerns that bind circumstances, experience and a mother's projections. Hence, semogenesis is constitutive of events. More generally, it changes children over time as they develop relationships, learn ways of engaging with things and, later, come to talk. Much depends on the percactional or, how the pre-reflective shifts as, prompted by *this now*, we move and feel. While the percactional directs concern about either a baby or a selfie, semogenesis also affects wordings as we read, think, speak or write. Emplacement thus informs practices like seeing the colour of a triangle or how, in language games (Wittgenstein 1957), the said (and thought) informs judgements as movements index rules and meanings. While we also use definitions, we begin by agreeing, momentarily at least, on who someone 'is' or what counts as a 'tree.' Given semogenesis, things and people come with meanings attached (Gahrn-Andersen 2021). In time, we come to conceive how practices link the spectatorial, devices and organizations.

The semogenic role of percaction can be heard in feeling while vocalizing. For example, Cowley (2014b) tracks how an adult daughter uses voice dynamics to coordinate with her mother's *ah bene*. In orienting to percactional aspects of her mother's voice, the daughter senses that things are awry. She directly picks up voice dynamics and, reworking them, tries to stop the flow. Percaction unites how they do being [sic] as, in the now, distributed agency shapes a little world.³ Although her intent fails, her audible social meaning sets off feelingful response. The mother overrides the hint, redoubles her complaint, and confirms her daughter's intuition. The 750 milliseconds show (1) semogenic events have public meaning potential (and invite overinterpretation); (2) living bodies manage emplaced languaging (here, across parties); and (3) distributed agency enable people to link felt experience, social reality and practices. Just as in the selfie, but without technology, co-regulated percaction integrates coordinative activity with moves that appear as 'signs' (viz. saying 'oh good').

Semogenesis draws on bodies (and, at times devices like a camera) in ways that serve to modulate multi-scalar action, percaction and response. Crucially, distributed agency enables people to shape events as neural sub-systems set off syntheses that punctuate *how* practices unfold: Parties use each other's displays of judging/inhibiting as, in slower scales, they more explicitly act to coordinate what they do and say. In an enlanguaged world, especially if organized around routine practices, similar powers inform judgements about facts that can be framed by a spectatorial view. Action and percaction connect social meaning, collective history and judgements in domains where ways of reaching outcomes, and outcomes reached, can be stabilized as warranted or not. Ways of life enable rule-following and acting without understanding. Hence, languaging becomes a phenomenon that can be described *as* 'language use' even if, at root, it remains emplaced, social coordinative activity.

Bioecological awareness and attitudes

Languaging involves more than appears from a spectatorial stance. In rejecting individualism, one sees that *language use* blinds us to semogenesis. In solving Haugen's problem, one finds that natural wit, or understanding, shapes experience as, in time, aspects of a world become familiar. Conversely, the familiar and its *abstracta* take on potential to affect awareness, observations, and how we actualize practices. As part of what Bateson (1979) calls *creatura*, humans use semogenesis, and wordings to link activity, material effects and natural innovation. In history, social reality self-constructs within an ecosphere (Kauffman 2000). This domain transcends geophysical states and ecosystems even if, of course, certain aspects align with what spectatorial models describe. However, normative ecolinguistics is mainly concerned with the ecosphere, or roughly, a planetary ensemble of niches, habitats and places. Whilst claims about the domain are sometimes valid (i.e. align with established knowledge), it is just as striking that percaction in the ecosphere sets off bioecological awareness. Observers use pre-reflective experience and natural inclusion (see Rayner 2018) because the world, so-to-speak, participates in us. Hence, bioecological awareness may also be familiar from, say, gardening, climbing mountains or looking at the stars. Yet, once traced to semogenesis, it becomes coordinative activity whereby vital process draws on evolutionary history. It brings the pre-reflective sense of *here* to how, in a moment, we reach symbiosis between covert (or overt) wordings and whole-body expression.

Bioecology applies to cases like observing the life of an ancient oak. Originally, Clements & Shelford (1939) used the term in capturing the complexity of animal-plant-life formations in a pond. Such places, as they note, draw on human interdependencies (Cowley 2014a). Given what Sellars calls direct relations, we engage in bioecologies as actors (e.g. who move), observers (who perceive) and holobionts (who teem with life). Semogenesis and the material affect experience, moving and, thus, languaging. It is because the results shape observing and, by extension, thought that post-Humean appeal to sense-impressions is mistaken. In positing the Given, they overplay the brain (or mind) and blind us to how living beings change the parameters that inform distributed agency. In our lineage, place is important – we care about how *here* feels for us/me. Moreover, like every bioecology, every utterance is unique and, at times, alters the adjacent possible (Kauffman 2000). Once one grasps how observation is entangled with wordings that make up worlds, we extend bioecological awareness. We also grasp that places, as observed from within enlanguaged worlds, bring understanding and an impetus to moral sensibility. Far from tracing right and wrong to 'language', we see that responsibility arises in response to emplaced events that include/evoke other beings. Over the lifespan, we come to embody a history of percaction, observing, and pre-reflective experience. Bioecological awareness grounds new narratives, new attitudes and can be used to develop citizen-based science (Finke 2019). It also ensures that life-sustaining relations are entangled with human concerns for ecosocial equity.

Bioecological awareness also bears on more complex issues. It affects our views of abstracta like the environment, the climate catastrophe and human/non-human well-being. Indeed, as included in a here, attitudes can become explicit and, in certain settings, shape an ecosophy. One can ask, say, how marketing uses 'green' signs to mislead consumers (see Stöckl & Molnar 2018) and, in scrutinizing public discourse, use bioecological awareness to judge the effects as good and ill. Such results shape ethical attitudes, knowledge and expertise. Once traced to what is shared with non-humans, one can reject identity politics and, thus, individualism, universalism and voluntarism (Cobley 2016; Cowley 2021b). Given the smallness of observer worlds, we gain humility and, like Deely (2015), see the limitations of knowledge based on data, models and laws (Cowley 2021c). Bioecological awareness helps us to put mechanistic science in its place. As for Bateson (1979), Markoš et al (2009), Sultan et al. (2022) and many others, we need to pay due consideration to vital process and, indeed, new stories (Stibbe 2015) that put expertise to work. Given emplacement, for example, marketization and growthism can seem logically incompatible with experience of embodiment, change and human becoming.

Towards an ecolinguistic theory of practices

Practices arise as human activity that draws on how agency is distributed. Given the role of languaging, one can aspire to develop a theory of practices (Li 2017).

Such a theory can aspire to address both how practices are possible and, crucially for ecolinguistics, how the results impact on humans and non-humans alike. As we have already seen, living systems rely on vital process and how entanglement with humans enhances life-sustaining relations. By contrast, 'language' unzips the verbal from semogenesis and practice to invite loops of discourse about discourse. Interestingly, the rich descriptions of *practice theory* (Schatzki 2016) face problems like those of linguistics: they tend to reduce practice-knowledge to 'use' of resources (viz. equipment, routines and what people do/say). In a famous example, Latour (1996) illustrates going to purchase a postage stamp at a post office. His account stresses distributed agency that allows humans and non-humans (e.g. the grille at the counter) to inform the practice. Human actors act as if accessing sub-systems and selecting menus by speaking and acting or, in Latour's metaphors, they localize and globalize. As a result practices can be described in terms of a 'flat ontology' (Latour 1998; Schatzki 2016). While this has the advantage of distributing agency, it leaves out how this occurs and, above all, how practices are possible. Such models focus on the regular – and variation is often irrelevant to many concerned – at the price of ignoring how they are actualized. They leave aside social settings and the living bodies and, thus, how vital process and semogenesis set off intended and unintended effects. Further, they leave aside how languaging can bring understanding through experiential modulations both in what happens and, just as crucially, in favouring future change.

There are problems with reducing practices to how knowledge, routines and equipment are used. For example, Knudsen (2023) shows that, since 'flat ontologies' mask how change appears, trends develop and pattern emerges, they fail as social and political critique – or challenges to power. Second, as with the case buying a stamp, they adopt a methodological individualism (Knudsen 2023) where 'participants' perform independently of history, contingencies and particulars. In response, we can use the solution to Haugen's problem: just as with languaging, practices and their effects draw on vital process and semogenesis. Just as with taking a selfie or talking to your mother, practices are both emplaced and world-involving. However, the main benefits of the ecolinguistic approach arise from, not these observations, but its normative orientation. Rather than simply describe how practices emerge, one can pursue their role in favouring/damaging life-sustaining relations. One can investigate emplacement, actual effects and use observations to propose change in cases where practices have demonstrably toxic effects. Although a full-blown theory of practices will encompass evolution, history, development, etc., an ecolinguistics of languaging can suffice to offer a true-to-life view of agency and, with this, promote active responses to cases that have life-sustaining/negating effects.

In order to avoid opposition of structure to agency, practice theory distributes these between humans and non-humans. Humans become performers in language games or, as in Latour (1998), actors who localize and globalize. Accordingly, humans become largely automatic and, viewed close up, the case parallels appeal to 'language use'. Of course, this is an idealization. However the case of baby Nigel is construed, it shows how semogenesis and voices enact soothing experience. At twelve days, the baby acts within an assemblage or social whole that includes a mother, a bath, a baby with a boil on his arm and, nearby, a father. Within the assemblage, Nigel draws on activity and voices to cease crying in his 'first act of communication'. As a social actor, vital process prompts the parties to actualize practices – semogenesis is an orchestrated social response to pain and voices. Hence languaging informs events that shape what Bakhtin calls appropriation (Dufva, 2024). The baby will use vital process to understand pain and the (limited) powers of his parents as well as responses that they are likely to judge more or less appropriate. Hence, a true-to-life view of agency demands a theory of practices that allows semogenesis and, above all, an account of how vital process enables parties to self-construct.

An ecolinguistic theory of practices thus has much to offer education. Not only can one critique overemphasis on transmission, learning and technology but self-actualizing can be traced to soft skills like teamwork, emotional sensitivity, co-creativity and communication (Cowley, 2024). Just as importantly, it brings new weight to noticings, reportings, co-perceivings and even overinterpretation. An ecolinguistic theory of practices stresses the emplacement of learning, appropriation and how affect shapes living entanglement. Further, just as ecolinguistics offers much to education, the classroom can be used to shape bioecological awareness. Although this can also draw on working in a garden, much is gained by, say recognizing biodiversity, noting soil depletion, reading poetry or, indeed, grasping the toxic effects of growthism on humans/non-humans. Given the importance of emplacement, educational theory and practice are at odds with global forces like markets and technoscience. In China, history is used to bring bioecological concerns, harmonious discourse analysis (see Huang & Zhou 2021) and ancient values of balance and change. In Europe, concepts like translanguaging (e.g. Li 2018) enable distributed agency to shape new identity-practices based on new forms of appropriation. Elsewhere, even technology is shown to enable human becoming (see Zheng et al. 2019). Just as centrally, one can challenge reduction of reading to brain-based skills. Not only do such models serve political ends (Cobey & Siebers 2021) but they omit embodiment, ignore how reading changes over time and place (Benne 2021) and, bizarrely, suppress imagination (Trasmundi et al. 2021).

Atomistic views of 'language' ignore how semogenesis contributes to distributed agency. Conversely, a theory of practices can begin to clarify why such models still dominate education. In part, they reflect written language bias and, in part, they are pragmatic. Not only is learning to read based on a language stance (i.e. treating arrangements of symbols as 'language') but the resulting phenomena serve many kinds of skilled action (Dufva, 2024). However, this is no defence for an atomistic view that works against creativity and social learning. Further, as Goatly (2021) shows, many are biased by grammatical and discursive features of English and related languages. These condition a picture of a world that consists in little things that grant human mastery of passive nature. Worse, for monolinguals, this can seem inevitable (or 'natural'). Unlike speakers of, say, Blackfoot (a language of the first nation Nitsitapii), they may demean the pre-reflective and overlook the ubiquity of process. Indeed, English and related languages favour a naïve realism where 'objects' correspond to words, phrases. Not only is this aligned to Newton's mechanistic world but, perhaps, it throws some light on why we are hypnotized by computation and rarely ask how such devices affect creativity, social learning, intellectual habits, or entanglement with the living.

An ecolinguistic theory of practices can be used to track intended and unintended effects. This may be especially important where 'politics' is dominated by debates for and against (discursive) realities. Hermine Penz (2018) illustrates such a case in a study which contrasts the use of *climate change* and *global warming*, respectively. For all the many differences, her conclusion pulls no punches: 'Media representations (of environmental issues as of other topics) do not present facts but reflect (and negotiate) power relations' (Penz 2018: 281). In illustrating the importance of issue, she stresses that *representations* shape 'knowledge and discourses between individuals and communities' (Boykoff 2007: 478; cited Penz 281). But what does appeal to representations show? For those who allow that facts *can* exist through, and/or independently of media, Penz merely reaffirms their discursive framing. Public debates about global warming/climate change use icons, narratives and media that are influenced by marketization, technoscience, politics, etc. Yet, for readers of this chapter, this is old news. A theory of practices can be used to reach beyond ideational questions to address, not just how to use beliefs, but also how to document effects of practices in ways that support life-sustaining relations.

Non-trivially, increasing concentrations of CO_2 are killing billions of non-humans and, today, threaten whole human communities. This is because 'measures of indoor CO_2 at more than 1000 parts per million are noxious' and, crucially, the claim is warranted. Penz would say, of course, that the 'fact' and rhetoric are representations of sociopolitical interests and attitudes. Just so. It is because of the power to re-evoke that it is so important that they use warranted judgements. A theory of practices can bring the normative to observed effects, warranted ideas of reality, and, as a result, motivate change in practices. In so doing, it can trace effects to how distributed agency enhances, or extinguishes, vital process. Hence, ecolinguists can pursue how languages, and ways of languaging, bear on claims, models and expertise that impacts on life-sustaining relations. For example, challenging paradigm-based normal science, Zellmer et al. (2006) advocate an approach to ecosystems that unites use of objective measures, models and narratives. Such work, I submit, can change our practices and promote an agency perspective on living (see Sultan et al. 2022). More practically, Jepson et al. (2018) use rewilding to link 'biophysical, institutional and political characteristics of place' with 'the agendas, worldviews and action philosophies of the practitioner groups involved' (2018: 1–2). The needs of a place (hence, not just discourse) unite ecosystemic issues, discourse and bio-ecological well-being. Philosophically, subjectivity and narrative add to science or, alternatively, 'different logical types that can play a positive role in the evaluation of any scientific project' (Harries-Jones 2016: 286). Stories change who 'we' are – both, for others (human and non-human) and ourselves. An ecolinguistic theory of practices thus promises to improve ourselves both with reference to the effects of practices and how they are actualized. Then, using explicit commitment to life-sustaining relations, we can demand that practices, and science, be anchored to new political and moral imperatives.

Regeneration

In turning to languaging, ecolinguistics regenerates as a transdisciplinary field that aims to enrich life-sustaining relations. So, what is regeneration? A reader may picture how, after encountering a cat, a lizard can regrow its tail. Just as for humans, a lizard's agency depends on, not a 'thing', but an assemblage constituted by a niche, a lineage and the organism's sub-systems. In parallel, a regenerated ecolinguistics cannot rely on the things of 'language'. Following Standen et al. (2014), it can be compared to how, like a 400-million-year-old tetrapod, a Polypetrus fish regenerates archaic skeletal features. The fish *makes up* bodily forms by using coordinative activity (moving on land) to ensure terrestrial survival. Drawing on its ancient lineage, it fish changes posture, gait and, thus, brings latent plasticity to skeletal development.[4] Especially in times of stress, regeneration uses adaptations that are enabled by the past. My case is that the potential for ecolinguistics – and for a theory of practices – lies in how, as Mulcaster (1582) saw, we can coordinate while rendering understanding aloud.

To be sure linguistic change does not rival the timescales of evolution. Yet, I stress that normative realm of discourse uses ancient adaptations for semogenesis, coordinative activity and vital process. Coming up with the new is common to a twelve-day-old child and an experiment within the life-span of a fish. Coordinative activity (that may or may not draw on wordings) transcends the mechanical. Hence, Chomsky was correct that, as a trait, human language enables creative synthesis. Yet, by starting with languaging, one privileges, not the brain, but semogenesis and distributed agency. As Nigel shows, a communicative act leads to soothing that meshes effects of the boil, parental voices and neural sub-systems: synthesis uses sensibility, semogenesis and wordings. Halliday's semiotic meshwork draws on vital process as a complex of social systems enable bodies to actualize practices. Once traced to semogenesis, they enable us to draw on appropriation while engaging with others who bring similar biases to the meshwork that orchestrates how we feel, think, believe and act. Hence sensibility grants sense to places, coordinative activity and pasts as, with time, we come to gauge what appears rightly said. Each person has some responsibility for knowing and, thus, its ecological effects – we each use the ecosphere rather as does a Polypetrus that, for a while, walks the shoreline. Like the fish, we build a life history on coordinative activity that is informed by the lost worlds of others.

Unlike the fish, we integrate wordings with percaction as we modulate projections, movements, inhibition, prosody and gaze. Given practical outcomes, they can be controlled and linked to expertise and even scientific models (or warranted claims). Rebalancing the ecosphere is apractical matter, one of recognizing our ignorance, and of linking scientific knowledge with human and non-human demands. As with rewilding, vital process can be co-opted to serve life-sustaining relations. Yet, a theory of practices also has social consequences. Ecolinguists will have to address how stories they tell and actions they take bear on ecosocial equity. Both equity and inequity arise as intended and unintended consequences of how practices are organized. They arise as distributed agency and semogenesis in draw on life-sustaining relations over which we can exert some control. One can oppose mechanistic and market biases by working together, pooling sound knowledge, and striving for outreach that links linguistic knowhow and practices to the understanding of local and distal communities. Humans too matter in enriching life-sustaining relations by linking bioecological awareness with formal, functional and statistical tools and a more fully developed theory of practices.

Ecolinguistic expertise can be built in seeking to change practices generally, in our own bioecologies, and in human communities. In rejecting 'language', their actualization is traced to coordinative activity, languages and languaging. *Contra* Haugen, we rely on, not interactions, but how humanity draws on the humanity of others and, through vital process, evolutionary history. In coming to terms with this, we must be humble about our knowledge, skills and powers. As ecolinguists, we can raise bioecological awareness, change attitudes, frame new understanding and, using explicit values, build theories. We can show how and why, in challenging economics, technoscience and marketization, languaging has a vital role. We need to find ways of using practices to steer growth that serves life-sustaining relations. In order to enrich local bioecologies, as ecolinguists, we need to defend ecosocial equity together with economists, engineers, artists and all who aspire to rebalance the ecosphere.

Notes

1. Vital process described agency perspective in evolutionary biology (see Sultan et al. 2022; Steffensen et al., this vol.) where living systems use co-regulating sub-systems in evolutionary, developmental and life-span scales; the view treats life as its own designer (Markoš et al. 2009).
2. For Simonelli (2023), this includes 'any conception of knowledge of some aspect of reality as simply given to us, and intelligible only as given in this way'.
3. Cowley (2014b) notes that her musicality includes unexpected falling tone draws on a socially marked lengthening of [bː] (in bene) that prefigures a 'decisive' fall of half an octave (on *bene*). Not only does she reach a full standard deviation below her norm (152 Hz) but her speech rate *matches* her mother's: whereas he rate is 240 ms per syllable, the daughter's is 250 ms.
4. This classic morphological change is genetically enabled (not determined). In challenging neo-Darwinian doctrine, Sultan et al. (2022) argue that, at times, ecological and phenotypic change lead to selection of genes – not the contrary. In parallel, languaging shapes changes in 'language use', languages and how persons and practices are constituted.

References

Alexander, Richard, & Stibbe, Arran (2014). 'From the analysis of ecological discourse to the ecological analysis of discourse'. *Language sciences*, 41: 104–10.

Bateson, Gregory (1979). *Mind and Nature: A Necessary Unity*. New York: Dutton.

Becker, Alton (1991). 'Language and languaging'. *Language & Communication*, 11(1): 33–5.

Benne, Christian (2021). 'Tolle lege. Embodied reading and the "scene of reading"'. *Language Sciences*, 84: 1–8.

Berthoz, Alain (2012). *Simplexity: Simplifying Principles for a Complex World* (trans. by G. Weiss). Cambridge, MA: Harvard University Press.

Bogdan, Radu (1997). *Interpreting Minds: The Evolution of a Practice*. Cambridge, MA: MIT Press.

Boykoff, M. T. (2007). 'The cultural politics of climate change discourse in UK tabloids'. *Political Geography*, 27: 549–69.

Chomsky, Noam (1965). *Aspects of a Theory of Syntax*. Cambridge, MA: MIT Press.

Clements, Frederic, & Shelford, Victor (1939). *Bio-ecology*. New York: John Wiley.

Cobley, Paul (2016). *Cultural Implications of Biosemiotics*. Dordrecht: Springer.

Cobley, Paul, & Siebers, Johan (2021). 'Close reading and distance: Between invariance and a rhetoric of embodiment'. *Language Sciences*, 84: 101359.

Cornips, Leonie. this vol. How (Dairy) Cows and Human Intertwine Languaging Practices: Recurrent Vocalizations Are Not the Same.

Cowley, Stephen J. (2014a). 'Bio-ecology and language: A necessary unity'. *Language Sciences*, 41(1): 60–70.

Cowley, Stephen J. (2014b). 'Linguistic embodiment and verbal constraints: Human cognition and the scales of time'. *Frontiers in Psychology*, 5: 1085.

Cowley, Stephen J. (2019). 'The return of languaging'. *Chinese Semiotic Studies*, 15(4): 483–512.

Cowley, Stephen J. (2021a). 'Ecolinguistics reunited: Rewilding the territory'. *Journal of World Languages*, 7(3): 405–27.

Cowley, Stephen J. (2021b). 'For an actional ethics: Making better sense of science'. In S. Booth & C. Mounsey (Eds.), *Reconsidering Extinction in Terms of the History of Global Bioethics*, 205-21. London: Routledge.

Cowley, Stephen J. (2021c). 'Biosemiotics and ecolinguistics: Two tales of scientific objectification'. *Rivista Italiana di Filosophia del Linguaggio*, 15(2): 176–98.

Cowley, Stephen J. (2024). 'Ecolinguistics in practice'. In *The Routledge Handbook of Applied Linguistics*, 374–85. London: Routledge.

Cowley, Stephen J., & Gahrn-Andersen, Rasmus (2022). 'Simplexifying: Harnessing the power of enlanguaged cognition'. *Chinese Semiotic Studies*, 18(1): 97–119.

Deely, John (2015). 'What semiotics is'. *Language and Semiotic Studies*, 1/1. Available at:http://lass.suda.edu.cn/_upload/article/files/be/0d/3283c81f44fa822b29066a72fe9f/5a0fc96d-e6d9-406b-b9c6-64d22d8cec64.pdf downloaded 15 June 2022.

Dufva, Hannele (2024). From 'psycholinguistics' to the study of distributed sense-making: Psychological reality revisited. *Language Sciences, 103*, 101627. https://doi.org/https://doi.org/10.1016/j.langsci.2024.101627.

Eckert, Penelope, & Labov, William (2017). 'Phonetics, phonology and social meaning'. *Journal of Sociolinguistics*, 21(4): 467-96.

Eliasson, Stig (2015). 'The birth of language ecology: Interdisciplinary influences in Einar Haugen's "The ecology of language"'. *Language Sciences*, 50: 78-92.

Fill, Alwin (1998). 'Ecolinguistics: State of the art'. *Arbeiten aus Anglistik und Amerikanistik*, 23(1): 3-16.

Fill, Alwin (2001). 'Language and ecology: Ecolinguistic perspectives for 2000 and beyond, Applied Linguistics for the 21st Century'. *AILA Review*, 14: 60-75.

Fill, Alwin, & Penz, Hermine (Eds.) (2018). *The Routledge Handbook of Ecolinguistics*. London: Routledge.

Finke, Peter (2019). 'Linguistics at the end of the Baconian Age; or: Five Essentials of Ecolinguistics'. In S. V. Steffensen (Ed.), The Aalpiri Papers: Two Critical Reflections on Contemporary Ecolinguistics. Odense: University of Southern Denmark.

Gahrn-Andersen, R. (2021). 'Conceptual attaching in perception and practice-based behavior'. *Lingua*, 249: 102960.

Goatly, Andrew (2021). 'Ecology, physics, process philosophies, Buddhism, Daoism, and language: A case study of William Golding's *The Inheritors* and *Pincher Martin*'. *Journal of World Languages*, 7(1): 1-25.

Halliday, Michael A. K. (2003a [1990]). 'New ways of meaning: The challenge to applied linguistics'. In Johnathan Webster (Ed.), *On Language and Linguistics: Vol. 3 of the Collected Works M. A. K. Halliday*, 139-76. London: Continuum.

Halliday, Michael A. K. (2003b [1997]). 'Linguistics as metaphor'. In Johnathan Webster (Ed.), *On Language and Linguistics: Vol. 3 of the Collected Works M. A. K. Halliday*, 248-70. London: Continuum.

Halliday, Michael A. K. (2004). *The Language of Early Childhood* (Johnathan Webster Ed.). London: Continuum.

Harries-Jones, Peter (2016). *Upside-down Gods: Gregory Bateson's World of Difference*. Fordham: Fordham University Press.

Haugen, Einar (2001). 'The ecology of language'. In A. Fill & P. Mühlhäusler (Eds.), *The Ecolinguistics Reader. Language, Ecology and Environment*, 57-66. London: Continuum. [originally, 1972].

Huang, Guowen, & Zhao, Ruiha (2021). 'Harmonious discourse analysis: Approaching peoples' problems in a Chinese context'. *Language Sciences*, 85: 101365.

Hymes, Dell (1973). 'Speech and language: On the origins and foundations of inequality among speakers'. *Daedalus*, 102(3): 59-85.

Jepson, Paul, Schepers, Frans, & Helmer, Wouter (2018). 'Governing with nature: A European perspective on putting rewilding principles into practice'. *Philosophical Transactions of the Royal Society B: Biological Sciences*, 373(1761): 20170434.

Johannessen, Christian, & Boeriis, Morten (2021). 'Accelerating semogenesis: An ecosocial approach to photography'. *Visual Communication*, 20(4): 527-51.

Joseph, John. E., Nigel, Love, & Taylor, Talbot. J. (2001). *Landmarks in Linguistic Thought II: The Western Tradition in the Twentieth Century* (Vol. 2). London: Routledge.

Kauffman, Stuart (2000). *Investigations*. Oxford: Oxford University Press.

Knudsen, Ståle (2023). 'Critical realism in political ecology: An argument against flat ontology'. *Journal of Political Ecology*. Available at: https://www.researchgate.net/profile/Stale-Knudsen/publication/367524781_Critical_realism_in_political_ecology_An_argument_against_flat_ontology/links/6413228166f8522c38ad4550/Critical-realism-in-political-ecology-An-argument-against-flat-ontology.pdf. Accessed 4 September 2023.

Kravchenko, Alexander (2011). 'How Humberto Maturana's biology of cognition can revive the language sciences'. *Constructivist Foundations*, 6(3): 352–62.

Lakoff, George (2014). *The All New Don't Think of an Elephant!: Know Your Values and Frame the Debate*. White River Junction, VT: Chelsea Green Publishing.

Latour, Bruno (1996). 'On interobjectivity'. *Mind, Culture, and Activity*, 3(4): 228–45.

Lechevrel, Nadine (2009). 'The intertwined histories of ecolinguistics and the ecological approach of language. Historical and theoretical aspects of a research paradigm'. In *Symposium on Ecolinguistics – Ecology of Science*. University of Southern Denmark.

Li, Wei (2017). 'Translanguaging as a practical theory of language'. *Applied Linguistics*, 39(1): 9–30.

Love, Nigel (2017).' On languaging and languages'. *Language Sciences*, 61: 113–47.

Markoš, Anton, Grygar, Filip, Hajnal, László, Kleisner, Karel, Kratochvíl, Zdenek, & Neubauer, Zdenek (2009). *Life as Its Own Designer*. London: Springer.

Maturana, Humberto (1978). 'Biology of language: The epistemology of reality'. In G. Miller & E. Lenneberg (Eds.), *Psychology and Biology of Language and Thought*, 27-63. New York: Academic Press.

Mulcaster, Richard (1582). *The First Part of the Elementarie Vvich Entreateth Chefelie of the Right Writing of Our English Tung*. Ann Arbor, MI; Oxford: Text creation partnership 2005–10 (EEBOTCP Phase 1). https://quod.lib.umich.edu/e/eebo/A07881.0001.001?view=toc.

Niu, Ruijing, & Li, Lijia (2017). 'A review of studies on languaging and second language learning (2006–2017)'. *Theory and Practice in Language Studies*, 7(12): 1222–8.

Pennycook, Alistair (2020). 'Translingual entanglements of English'. *World Englishes*, 39(2): 222–35.

Penz, Hermine (2018). 'Global warming or climate change'. In Alwin Fill & Herminze Penz (Eds.), *The Routledge Handbook of Ecolinguistics*, 277–92. London: Routledge.

Raimondi, Vincenzo (2019). 'The bio-logic of languaging and its epistemological background'. *Language Sciences*, 71: 19–26.

Rayner, Alan (2018). 'Natural inclusion: A new understanding of the evolutionary kinship of all life on earth'. In Janet McIntyre-Mills, Norma Romm & Yvonne Corcoran-Nantes (Eds.), *Balancing Individualism and Collectivism*, 461–70. London: Springer.

Saussure, Ferdinand De (2011). *Course in General Linguistics*. New York: Columbia University Press.

Schatzki, Thomas (2016). 'Practice theory as flat ontology'. In G. Spaargaren, D. Weenink, and M. Lamers (Eds.), *Practice Theory and Research: Exploring the Dynamics of Social Life*, 28–42. London; New-York: Routledge.

Seiberth, Luz Christopher (2021). 'The transcendental role of languagings in Sellars' account of intentionality'. *Rivista Italiana di Filosofia del Linguaggio*, 15(2): 19–48.

Sellars, Wilfred (1956). 'Empiricism and the philosophy of mind'. *Minnesota Studies in the Philosophy of Science*, 1(19): 253–329.

Sellars, Wilfred (1979). 'After meaning'. In W. Sellars (Ed.), *Naturalism and Ontology*, 120–54. Altascadero, CA: Ridgeview Publishing.

Simon, Herbert (1968). 'The future of information processing technology'. *Management Science*, 14(9): 619–24.

Simonelli, Ryan (2023) Sellars's two worlds. Available at: https://www.academia.edu/99511622/Sellarss_Two_Worlds. Accessed 4 September 2023.

Standen, Emily, Trina, Du, & Larsson, Hans (2014). 'Developmental plasticity and the origin of tetrapods'. *Nature*, 513: 54–8.

Steffensen, Sune Vork, & Cowley, Stephen J. (2021). 'Thinking on behalf of the world: Radical embodied ecolinguistics'. In Wen Xu & John R. Taylor (Eds.), *Routledge Handbook of Cognitive linguistics*, 723-36. London: Routledge.

Steffensen, Sune Vork, & Fill, Alwin (2014). 'Ecolinguistics: The state of the art and future horizons'. *Language Sciences*, 41: 6–25.

Steffensen, Sune Vork, Döring, Martin, & Cowley, Stephen J. (this vol.) Ecolinguistics: Living and languaging united.

Stibbe, Arran (2015). *Ecolinguistics: Language, Ecology and the Stories We Live By*. London: Routledge.

Stibbe, Arran (2021). 'Ecolinguistics as a transdisciplinary movement and a way of life'. *Crossing Borders, Making Connections: Interdisciplinarity in Linguistics*, 71–88.

Stöckl, Hartmutt, & Molnar, Sonya (2018). 'Eco-advertising: The linguistics and semiotics of green(-washed) persuasion'. In Alwin Fill & Herminze Penz (Eds.), *The Routledge Handbook of Ecolinguistics*, 261-76. London: Routledge.

Sultan, Susan, Moczek, Aqrmin, & Walsh, Denis (2022). 'Bridging the explanatory gaps: What can we learn from a biological agency perspective?' *BioEssays*, 44(1): 2100185. doi:https://doi.org/10.1002/bies.202100.

Swain, Merril, & Watanabe, Yuko (2013). 'Languaging: Collaborative dialogue as a source of second language learning'. In Carole Chappelle (Ed.), *The Encyclopedia of Applied Linguistics*, 3218–25. London: Wiley.

Thibault, Paul J. (2020). *Distributed Languaging, Affective Dynamics, and the Human Ecology volume I: The Sense-Making Body*. London: Routledge.

Trasmundi, Sarah, Kokkola, Lynne, Schilhab, Theresa, & Mangen, Anne (2021). 'A distributed perspective on reading: Implications for education'. *Language Sciences*, 84: 101367.

Wittgenstein, Ludwig (1957). *Philosophical Investigations* (second edition). London: Blackwell.

Zellmer, A. J., Allen, T. F., & Kesseboehmer, K. (2006). 'The nature of ecological complexity: A protocol for building the narrative'. *Ecological Complexity*, 3(3): 171–82.

Zheng, Dongping, Hu, Ying, & Banov, Ivan (2019). 'A multiscalar coordination of languaging'. *Chinese Semiotic Studies*, 15(4): 561–87.

Zhou, Wenjuan (2021). 'Ecolinguistics: A half-century overview'. *Journal of World Languages*, 7(3): 461–86.

5

The Epistemological Conundrum of Language: Humans as Ecologically Special and Ecologically Destructive

Alexander Kravchenko

The unasked questions

Humans have minds, they can think, and they know. They know things about things, they know how to do things, and they know why things are the way they are, because they are a very special biological species, *Homo sapiens*. They are social and have cultures based on commonly shared practices, including science and high technology in literate cultures; together, these characterize the stage of their development and the way of life, or civilization – something other species don't have. One would think that to build a civilization is to make sure that its members enjoy the benefits of living in harmony with Mother Nature as the giver of life to everything living. For humans, however, it has not been the case, and the effect of modern cultures on the environment has been devastating.

The advent of the Industrial Revolution in the eighteenth century made possible by the ingenious human mind armed with science, marked the beginning of an era of the ever-growing conflict between human animals and the rest of the world as their natural habitat. By the mid-twentieth century, industrially developed countries succeeded, unwittingly, in large-scale poisoning of the air we breathe and the water we drink – the essential parts of our environment which we share with all other forms of life on our planet. As if this were not enough, nuclear power was added as a permanent threat to life itself, and the existing stockpiles of nuclear weapons are enough to annihilate every living thing on Earth many times over. Burning with a desire to generate ever more power for the industries so they could churn out more things that we believe would continue making our life better and better, proponents of the 'peaceful atom' advocate for the construction of new power plants, having learned nothing from the lessons of the Three Mile Island, Chernobyl, Fukushima and many other nuclear disasters of various scales. Armed with powerful technologies, humans seem to stop at nothing in their urge to consume more and more, and, by making literally everything disposable, they sacrifice nature itself for their fleeting whims. Forests disappear, rivers change their natural course, oceans suffocate on plastic waste, landfills claim more and more land while deserts grow, and entire species become extinct at an accelerating rate as humans triumphantly carry the banner of civilization over the globe. As observed by Hummer (1985: 28), 'animal life from insects to higher mammals abounds on our planet, though in nearly every respect it is threatened by human maladaptation to the environment and our lack of understanding of its fragile interrelationships'.

This gruesome reality makes one wonder, asking disturbing questions. Why don't humans, as a biological species, live up to their name, 'wise man'? What is it to be 'wise', and what makes us wise if we agree that the word is not a misnomer, and we are, indeed, vastly different from all other species? Is our being 'wise' a generous gift from Mother Nature to her beloved children, or is it a great power that implies responsibility for its use before the rest of the world? If the latter, do we show maturity and good judgement, or do we act like little children playing with fire? Finally, what do we, as humans, know about the nature of humanness, that is, why we are what we are and do what we do? In keeping with established academic tradition, questions like these belong to the domain of philosophy rather than the language sciences, and they are usually not asked by linguists because they do not seem to bear directly on language as the subject of linguistic research. I intend to break this tradition for several reasons.

First, there may be no philosophy without language – or, for that matter, any science at all because 'it is impossible to disassociate language from science or science from language' (Lavoisier 1789, 3d paragraph). The belief that the job of 'true' science is to study objects which exist in reality independent of what we, intentional subjects, think of them, in order to discover universal truths about the independently existing world and then 'express' them in language, is the foundation of philosophical realism as the mainstream epistemological paradigm. However, as was shown by Harris (2005), science itself is a construct of language because scientists impose their language on what they assume is there to be named by that language. Through operations of distinction made in language, scientists-as-observers specify entities which, once distinguished, become things with the properties that the operation of distinction specifies: reality is 'the domain of things [...] specified by the operations of the observer' (Maturana 1978: 54), and objectivity is 'observer-dependent' (Maturana 1985).

Second, the human mind, our ability to think is not something pre-given that comes conveniently packed in a nicely wrapped package with a label 'Human baby' on it. Taking the human ability for abstract thought as a given, a property of the brain as the result of our species-specific evolution, scientists are not eager to ask an obvious question: 'What makes our biological species so uniquely different from all other higher animals with a central nervous system, such as the primates, for example?' Even when they do ask it and come up with an expected answer, 'Language', the answer is typically defined by the unquestioned belief in the instrumental function of language propagated by linguists, philosophers and cognitive scientists, when language is viewed as a means of packaging our thoughts and rendering them public (Evans 2015: 3). Thus, language appears to be the product of human intelligence, and this is a common delusion:

> Since we usually regard language as no more than the means by which we express our thoughts, it seems natural to think that language should issue from intelligence, rather than vice versa. It seemed equally obvious, to naive observers, that the earth was the center of the universe, and the sun, moon, and planets all went around it.
>
> When it comes to mind, intelligence, and language, we're just about where people were with regard to the universe, say a thousand years ago. (Bickerton 2009: 58)

But do we have to stay so far behind in our understanding of the nature of our unprecedented mental powers and continue to believe that it is just the kind of brain we humans have that makes us *Homo sapiens*, 'wise man'? Certainly not, if we stop flowing with the stream of orthodox thinking about language and approach it biologically[1] (Maturana 1978; Givón 2002; Cowley 2014; Raimondi 2019; Kravchenko 2021). Among other things, such an approach means viewing the properties of the human brain as the result of its co-evolution with language (Deacon 1997), because 'language and brain adapted to each other' (Schoenemann 2009: 180). 'The evolution of language must have taken place during the evolution of humans [...] as arguably the most important part of that evolution' (Bickerton 2014: 83).

Third, although modern civilization is to a great extent defined by, and depends on, knowledge as power, and we efficiently use it to transform the world, we don't really know what knowledge is nor what it is to know (Maturana & Varela 1987). Because of the properties specified by the operation of distinction, 'knowledge' is perceived as a thing that exists in reality as the domain of things, with all the inevitable implications. The dire consequences of knowledge reification are, probably, most obvious in modern education which has been steadily losing its value in the public eye (Kravchenko & Payunena 2017).

This told, I suggest a single simple answer to the questions above: 'We are where we are in this world, and we continue to look at it as a means to accommodate our incessantly growing insatiable needs because *we don't know or understand much about our own species*.' To clarify, we take too much of the so-called scientific knowledge for granted, especially when it is honoured by time and authority. We are not too willing to get out of the rut made in the winding road to 'wisdom' by generations of knowledge seekers, because we rely on 'sound' reason that tells us to follow the path trodden by many before us, for surely our predecessors couldn't have been all wrong in choosing to continue on the well-established course. And the established course in the study of human uniqueness in the world of the living has been, and still is, from brain/mind to language/communication.

Whence the sapience?

In the humanistic paradigm, humanity is seen as a dominating force because of the human cognitive ability for abstract thought (Sagsan & Medeni 2012). This ability is believed to have emerged with the evolution of the human brain which is larger in relation to body size than the brains of many other mammals, and it is generally acknowledged that humans are by far more intelligent than other mammals because they have bigger and better brains. However, there is no universal definition of intelligence or procedure to measure it, and it is not quite clear to what evolutionary factors humans owe their outstanding intelligence (Roth & Dicke 2005; Willemet 2013).

There are two competing approaches to explaining human intellectual supremacy, based on the idea of (dis)continuity between animal and human behavioural capacities. Proponents of the continuity model argue that not only is human physiology not radically different from the physiology of mammals (Rachels 1990), but that specifically human cognitive powers are not unique as many of them are displayed by non-human animals (Hummer 1985; Savage-Rumbaugh & Lewin 1994; Pepperberg 2002; Call 2006, inter alia), and there is 'continuity in mentality between the last common ancestor and us' (Sherwood, Sibiaul & Zawidzky 2008: 447). Human greater mental capacities are tied to the increased information processing capacities of the enlarged human brain (Gibson 2002; Schoenemann 2009; Clowry 2014), and the measure of biological intelligence is the complexity of the neural (micro)circuitry of the cerebral cortex (Hofman 2003, 2014). However, the computer metaphor is not very helpful in understanding and explaining human mental functions, because the brain is not a computer (Lamb 1999). As for the complexity of the neural (micro)circuitry of the cerebral cortex as the measure of biological intelligence, a question remains how this complexity came about and to what evolutionary factors it might be attributed. Various explanations found in the literature (Humphrey 1976; Clutton-Brock & Harvey 1980; Milton 1981; Schaik, Isler & Burkart 2012, inter alia) are not supported by empirical evidence and remain what they are – just hypotheses.

The Darwinian view (the evolutionary continuity of cognitive development) is questioned by those who see major qualitative behavioural and mental dissimilarities, or even gaps, that separate humans from other animals: 'The profound biological continuity between human and nonhuman animals masks an equally profound functional discontinuity between the human and nonhuman mind' (Penn, Holyoak & Povinelli 2008: 110). While many share this view, it remains unclear what identifiable features of human organisms as living systems constitute the mind, and mind is often equated with brain (Priest 1991). This brings us back to square one: we are different because our brains are different – bigger and better. However, if we consider the biological function of the brain, which is to control an organism's adaptive interactions with the environment, thereby sustaining its unity as a living system, it becomes clear that it is the nature of this environment and the manner in which an organism adaptively interacts with it, that must account for the bigger and better brain in humans: 'Living systems are cognitive systems, and living as a process is a process of cognition' (Maturana 1970: 4).

According to the 'social brain hypothesis', overall brain and the isocortex are selectively enlarged to confer social abilities in primates, allowing them to adapt in variable social and ecological environments across the life span and in evolution (Charvet & Finlay 2012). Still, the human brain differs in size and complexity from the brain of a chimpanzee or a gorilla believed to be our closest relatives. Moreover, the expression 'nonhuman mind' reflects our propensity to attribute human features to nonhuman animals: etymologically, *mind* is traced to Anglo-Saxon *munan* 'to think', and if we speak of non-human minds, we should also speak of non-human thought. And of course, the question in that case is how non-human thought, if we admit its existence, differs from human thought.

The obvious feature uniquely characteristic of our species as compared to all other species, including great apes, is language – interactional semiotic behaviour (Sebeok 1996; Premack 2007; Lakatos & Janka 2008; Jennings & Thompson 2012; Tattersall 2014, inter alia). It is a historical misfortune that, since Linnaeus (1758), the human species has been known under the name *Homo sapiens* rather than *Homo loquens*, as suggested by Herder (1772/2002). As was succinctly put by Müller (1861: 340), 'the one great barrier separating brute and man is Language. Man speaks, and no brute has ever uttered a word. Language is our Rubicon, and no brute will dare to cross it'.

The role of language in the development of human organisms as living systems has not only been underestimated in the established scientific paradigm, but simply misunderstood. It is a methodological fallacy to identify language with communication as exchange of information – with far-reaching epistemological consequences. Indiscrimination between communication as the process of establishing *common ground for perceptually guided interactions* between organisms of various levels of biological complexity (bees, birds, apes or what have you), and language as the uniquely human *orientational* (semiotic) *behavior based on taking into account what is not perceptually present* (Morris 1938), muddles up many researchers' thinking, often resulting in empirically unsound theoretical construals, as in the case of positing uninterrupted continuity between animal and human behavioural/mental capacities. While understanding language evolution remains one of the great mysteries of our species (Fitch 2010; Hauser et al. 2014), and there is no universal consensus on whether language evolved incrementally (Bickerton 2009) or appeared abruptly as a saltation (Chomsky 2012), there is no denying that linguistic behaviour – languaging as the overt manifestation of sapience – effectively sets humans apart from any other known species.

We can hope to come to a better understanding of our species when we begin to understand the difference between human and animal cognition from the point of view of biology (Maturana 1970). While cognition and understanding in general are summed up in the aphorism 'All doing is knowing, and all knowing is doing' (Maturana & Varela 1987: 26), it is the specific manner of operating in their cognitive domain (their doings) that distinguishes humans from other mammals: whatever humans do, they do it in language. As a species, humans are 'wise' because they can language – engage in coordinations of coordinations of cooperative interactions. Paradoxically, humans know little of what language is and what language does to them. Therefore, what they do in the course of interactions with the world, including others and self, is not informed by a practical epistemology based on understanding that, as living systems, they exist, or 'happen', in language, which becomes an epistemological trap (Kravchenko 2016a), preventing humans from seeing how they are part of a global ecology. To overcome this impasse, a change of perspective is needed.

Evolution, niche construction and language

Is the human brain bigger and better because of our genetically determined evolution, or could there be other factors at play in the development of our species? While a few decades ago evolution was seen as a rather conservative process in which nothing was created *de novo* and each new gene was believed to have arisen from an already existing gene (Ohno 1970), today evolutionary biologists acknowledge the important role of epigenetic phenomena in species evolution, abandoning the belief in genetic determinism (Maturana & Mpodozis 2000; Rapp & Wendell 2005; Lind & Spagopoulou 2018; Collens, Kelley & Katz 2019; Sarkies 2020, inter alia). Evolution is not 'just selfish genes mindlessly replicating themselves. It's a process in which the things animals do guide their own evolution' (Bickerton 2009: 11). Unfortunate metaphors, such as the 'blueprint metaphor' (that genes provide a blueprint for behaviour) or 'code biology' as the study of 'codes of life' (from the 'genetic code' all the way up to the 'codes' of language and culture), are extremely misleading (Deacon 2012; P. Bateson 2017; Kravchenko 2020a), and ecological genetics (Ford 1964; Real 1994) has become an important field of study in biology.

Organisms not only carry genes, they also interact with their environments, modifying 'at least some of the natural selection pressures present in their own' (Odling-Smee, Laland & Feldman 2003: 1). Therefore, ecology as a scientific study of the relationship of organisms with their environment (Haeckel 1866) is not just about behavioural patterns caused by various environmental factors, it is about interactions of an organism with the environment aimed at achieving the best fit between organism and environment – adaptation as 'survival of the fittest' (Darwin 1869).

Uexküll (1926) described such a fit as *Umwelt* – the surrounding (perceptual) world of an organism defined and determined by the organism's potential ability for interaction. To a human observer, however, an *Umwelt* is just part of what the observer distinguishes as the environment, an environmental niche occupied by an organism. In ecological psychology, the niche is defined as a set of affordances – possibilities for interaction offered to an organism by the environment (Gibson 1979). From a purely biological point of view, the niche is that part of the environment in which a living system exists as a unit of interactions; neither the living system nor its niche can be understood independently of each other (Maturana 1970: 4).

Epistemologically, the notion of niche as the ambience with which a living system can interact differs from the notion of environment:

> The niche is defined by the classes of interactions into which an organism can enter. The environment is defined by the classes of interactions into which the observer can enter and which he treats as a context for his interactions with the observed organism. The observer beholds organism and environment simultaneously and he considers as the niche of the organism that part of the environment which he observes to lie in its domain of interactions. Accordingly, as for the observer the niche appears as part of the environment, for the observed organism the niche constitutes its entire domain of interactions, and as such it cannot be part of the environment that lies exclusively in the cognitive domain of the observer. [...] [F]or every living system its organization implies a prediction of a niche, and the niche thus predicted as a domain of classes of interactions constitutes its entire cognitive reality. (Maturana 1970: 3)

It is important to note that the concepts *niche* and *environment* belong to the cognitive domain of the languaging observer: we exist as human beings in language using language for our explanations (Maturana 1988). When, however, biologists as observers begin to analyse humans and speak about the human ecological niche that must be taken into account in understanding human organisms as living systems, they tend to overlook the distinctions between niche and environment as distinctions made by the observer in language. This leads researchers astray in their attempts to understand what and how makes humans ecologically special, which is the case with niche construction theory (NCT) – a recently developed part of evolutionary biology (Laland, Odling-Smee & Feldman 2000; Magnani & Bordone 2010; Odling-Smee et al. 2013) – applied to human organisms (Kendal, Tehrani & Odling-Smee 2011; Fuentes 2017).

An ecological niche is not something external to, and independent of, an organism; by modifying its environment, an organism constructs its niche, transforming natural selection pressures. NCT emphasizes the ecological and evolutionary consequences of changes brought about by organisms in ecosystems, because, by creating habitats and resources used by other species, niche-constructing species affect the flow of energy and matter through ecosystems (Laland, Boogert & Evans 2014). But what *is* an ecological niche?

Trappes (2021: 7) defines an ecological niche as 'the environmental conditions, both biotic and abiotic, that permit the continued existence of an individual, population or species', obviously not seeing that such a definition is epistemologically flawed. We can speak of an ecological niche of an individual organism (second-order living system) or a population (third-order living system) because we can observe the classes of interactions into which these systems can enter. For example, depending on the pursued research goal, an ethologist can observe either the behaviour of an individual beaver in a pond or the behaviour of the entire population to which this beaver belongs. However, the ethologist cannot observe the behaviour of the species to which this population belongs because a species as a totality of populations of animals of a particular type that are able to breed with each other (such as beavers) is not a living system (a unit of interactions observed at a particular space-time). Because, as lineages formed by individuals, 'species occur outside of time' (Mpodozis 2022: 98), and because, as a distinction made in language, 'species' does not refer to something directly perceivable to an observer 'here and now', it is therefore, *an abstract concept*. The expression 'ecological niche of a species' does not make much sense if the words *ecology, niche,* and *species* are used strictly terminologically: the ecological niches of populations that constitute a species with a broad geographic distribution may considerably differ in detail, they are not uniform and invariant. After all, it is this variation in niche conditions that underlies the selection pressures as a major driving force of evolution – along with the changes brought about by organisms in ecosystems.

The evolutionary impact of such changes is not just a kind of add-on to genetic determinism:

> The manner in which a living system is compounded as a unit of interactions, whether by a single basic unit, or through the aggregation of numerous such units (themselves living systems) that together constitute a larger one (multicellular organisms), or still through the aggregation of their compound units that form self-referring systems of even higher order (insect societies, nations) is of no significance; *what evolves is always a unit of interactions defined by the way in which it maintains its identity. The evolution of the living systems is the evolution of the niches of the units of interactions defined by their self-referring circular organization,* hence, the evolution of the cognitive domains. (Maturana 1970: 4; emphasis added)

Niche construction and its legacy over time (ecological inheritance) are evolutionary processes. Populations of animals belonging to different species construct different niches; therefore, the evolution of living systems as units of interactions is affected by the degree to which the way in which they maintain their identity changes, bringing about changes in the niche (both quantitative and qualitative) over time. A living system adapts to such changes, inheriting the newly acquired modes of behaviour. In the case of humans, a major qualitative change in their evolution occurred with the rise of linguistic semiosis, or languaging, as a biological adaptation. As living systems, populations of humans (communities of talking animals) maintain their identity in the relational domain of languaging which becomes the definitive part of their niche. Linguistic semiosis – the ability to take into account in their interactions with the environment what is not perceptually present – transforms the cognitive powers of humans, allowing them to cross the boundaries of adaptation set for organisms by the immediately perceived affordances. Abstracting from the here-and-now of the niche as part of the environment in which a living system can interact with others and self (first-order consensual domain) and engaging in orientational semiotic activity as coordinations of coordinations of cooperative behavior (second-order consensual domain, or languaging), thereby becoming observers, was a 'big bang' in the evolution of humans, or, in Gregory Bateson's (2000) phrase, 'a difference that makes a difference'.

However, just like 'species', 'language' is an abstract notion, it refers to the uniquely human way in which collectives of talking organisms (communities, societies, nations) maintain their identity as living systems. To use a metaphor, all such living systems can dance, but they dance different dances on different floors in different time-spaces. In other words, they construct different niches, and it is these niches that become the objects of study to scientists as observers: as a notion, the niche 'lies exclusively in the cognitive domain of the observer'. There is no – and may not be – a 'human niche' as an observable class of interactions into which the totality of human living systems can enter – unless we use a God's eye view. What is distinguished in language as the species *Homo sapiens* is not a living system in its niche that can be observed. What is observed as the classes of interactions that a living system can enter is always the niche of either an individual human organism or a local population of humans 'dancing a dance' different from the 'dance' of the observer. When, however, the observer becomes the observed, the classes of interactions that the observer can enter and that specify the observer as a living system constitute not a niche but the environment; therefore, humans are *organism-environment systems* (Järvilehto 1998). The language of the observer (a particular kind of linguistic semiosis we call *a language,* such as English, Urdu or Swahili), as the way in which the identity of the population to which the observer belongs as a unit of interactions and in which the observer's organization as a living system is maintained, constitutes the observer's entire cognitive reality. Therefore, the cognitive realities of observers speaking different languages also differ.

Today, linguists are learning to speak differently about language, seeing continuity between life and language in languaging (Di Paolo, Cuffari & De Jaegher 2018; Cowley 2019) as our specific mode of living as observers (Raimondi 2014). At the same time, language is viewed as a biocultural niche (Sinha 2015), while evolutionary anthropologists emphasize the role of culture as 'a key element in the human niche' (Fuentes 2016: 16). This brings up the old questions about the relationship between nature and culture on the one hand, and between language and culture on the other.

There are many definitions of culture (Jahoda 2012), and the nature–culture dichotomy continues to be in the focus of attention in philosophy, psychology, anthropology, linguistics and many other fields of study. But what is culture from the point of view of biology in general, and evolutionary biology in particular? Without answering this question, we cannot hope to come closer to understanding the language–culture dichotomy and its epistemological implications.

Despite Occam's warning against multiplying entities (Schaffer 2015), the Cartesian legacy of epistemological dualism with its central dichotomy of subjective–objective, or mental/psychological–material/physical, continues to dominate our conception of the world, impeding our understanding of the phenomenon of humanness (Kravchenko 2022). Popper (1978/2011) even spoke of three worlds – the physical, the mental/psychological, and the world of the products of the human mind which, among other things usually identified with culture, included language. However, the 'mental/psychological world', or the mind, is just an epistemological construct devised for taxonomic purposes, not unlike the concept of biological species: it exists in our cognitive domain of distinctions made in language, and because of that we take it to be real. Yet, from the point of view of cognition understood as a biological function, there is no such thing as 'the mind' in the operation of the nervous system; 'the mind' is nothing but an explanatory notion (Maturana, Mpodozis & Letellier 1995: 25) used in our attempts to understand why and how humans differ from other mammals. Likewise, there is no such thing as 'the mental world' (as an extension of the notion of 'mind'), and Popper's 'third world' is simply the domain of shared human practices and artefacts that characterize their mode of living subsumed by the notion of 'culture'. Therefore, Popper's three worlds are reduced to two worlds, the physical (nature) and the human (culture) – an inherently contradictory dichotomy because, as physical bodies, human organisms are part of nature, which makes the dichotomy nature–culture highly problematic.

Remarkably, challenging Popper, Gibson (1979: 122) thought it 'a mistake to separate the cultural environment from the natural environment, as if there were a world of mental products distinct from the world of material products. There is only one world, however diverse, and all animals live in it, although we human animals have altered it to suit ourselves'. Taking up Gibson's idea of one world, Heras-Escribano and De Pinedo-García (2018) reject the nature–culture dichotomy in their analysis of landscapes as part of our natural environments, arguing that landscapes are a product of the interaction of humans and their environments. This line of argument could be continued to show that it is well-nigh impossible to provide an example of 'pure' nature in today's world, after the millennia of human history and the impact that human civilizations have had, literally, on everything we are used to thinking of as constitutive of nature. The established tradition to divorce nature and culture stems from the deeply entrenched belief in the existence of objective reality as the world of the physical that is there independent of what we, human subjects, think about this world and do in this world, continuously transforming it by bringing about changes in our praxis of the living – and we live in language as our relational domain of interactions. Viewed biologically, culture is the mode of living of a socially organized human population, and, as such, it is constitutive of the population as a living system. Therefore, because language is the way such a system maintains its identity, a language is *not* part of a culture; language *is* culture and there are as many cultures as there are languages (cf. Whorf 1958).

As a biological adaptation, language lies at the root of sapience. Because the evolution of the living systems is the evolution of their niches, and because languaging is constitutive of the niches of human populations as living systems (units of interactions), changes in the praxis of languaging lead to changes in the niches which can be evolutionarily beneficial for human populations but destructive for wider ecological systems, because we live in one world in which everything is connected with everything (Commoner 1971). We should realize that, being ecologically special, we bear responsibility for what we do as languaging beings. This calls for an ecological approach in the study of languaging and its role in the global ecology (Bang, Døør, Steffensen & Nash 2007; Do Couto 2014; Li, Steffensen, Huang 2020; Kravchenko 2020b; Steffensen & Cowley 2021).

The burden of being ecologically special

Humans are sapient because they can language – engage in species-specific interactional behaviour by taking into account what is not perceptually present. Over the millennia of evolution as a species, populations of talking animals have mastered this ability to abstract from the perceptually given aspects of the environment. This ability enabled them to cross the borderline of their ecological niche (their Umwelt) as living organisms and become organism–environment systems. The emergence of language as a second-order consensual domain in which components of the first-order consensual domain (iconic and indexical linguistic signs as orientational devices) began to be used without the consensual domain (the domain of perceived objects and phenomena to which human behaviour was oriented), acquiring the properties of symbols, marked a major evolutionary development: the human brain faced the challenge of guiding and controlling the biologically functional behaviour of individuals within a population/community as a living (third-order) system whose unity is sustained and supported by the relational domain of languaging that offers human-specific affordances for interactions (cf. Raczaszek-Leonardi & Cowley 2012). This novel aspect of the environment, generated by talking human organisms, became a natural selection pressure in its own, triggering an adaptive response from the organisms. Thus, populations of humans became living systems with a circular organization whose circularity was sustained by the manner of their operation in the environment – languaging. Humans did not invent language because they were 'wise'; they became 'wise' because of language, which is the alpha and omega of humanness.

However, the language myth (Harris 1981), the hallmark of orthodox linguistics which continues to rule the roost in the education systems in societies with developed literate cultures, makes humans turn a blind eye to the obvious: as organism–environment systems, we bring changes to this environment that affect the ecological niches of each and every living organism on the planet (Boivin et al. 2016), and we never give it a second thought. Used to viewing and describing the world in terms of the 'objective–subjective' and the 'natural–cultural' dichotomies, we do not realize that our way of life, characterized by an advanced stage of social and cultural development we proudly call 'civilization', puts a great burden on the world of the living. And this is a burden we are not willing to share: being ecologically special, we continue to be ecologically destructive.

As far as language studies go, and inasmuch as language is viewed and understood from a perspective different from the perspective defined by the code model of linguistic communication, namely from the perspective of a unified ecological language science (Steffensen 2011; Steffensen & Fill 2014; Kravchenko 2016b), the science of language is still in its infancy. Humans continue to play with language as if it were a fascinating toy or gadget 'out there', in the objective world that exists independent of what we think about it and, as a consequence of such thinking, do to it, forgetting that 'we are the world', that we are the ones who can 'make a brighter day'. To make a brighter day for every living creature in this world which we literally bring forth in language, we need to finally open our eyes to the simple fundamental truth: we are 'wise' because we can talk (and, later in our cultural-historical development, read and write). But do we, as organism–environment systems, talk the right talk and walk the right walk in this world? Regretfully, the answer is 'No'.

The entire cause-and-effect chain in the development of our species has been scandalously misunderstood, and our civilization today faces the dire consequences of this misunderstanding. It is not just the changing face of the earth we are witnessing, brought about by our restive minds. Because, as organism–environment systems, we come into this world as the enlanguaged world of humans in which we grow and develop as living systems, the relational domain of languaging is our cognitive domain in which we orient to affordances and realize values provided by language (Hodges 2014; Rączaszek-Leonardi & Nomikou 2015). Changes in the culturally–historically determined systems of values, which do not exist outside of language, affect the existential trajectories followed by societies and their individual members. While some of such changes, especially those caused by superficial changes in the physical dynamics of human organism–environment systems, may be insignificant, purposeful changes imposed on language by various language 'reformers', most of whom are linguists guided by the language myth with its code model of language as something external to communicating humans as living systems, may lead to dramatic changes in the entire system of values to which human individuals and societies orient, jeopardizing their very ability to sustain themselves as living systems. As may be clearly seen today, not only do humans become ecologically destructive to non-human forms of life on our planet; mindless of the place and role of language in the evolution of *Homo sapiens,* they themselves fall victims to their mode of living as they playfully destroy the brickwork of their 'house of being'.

Being a 'wise man' is a heavy burden. It is the burden of taking and carrying responsibility for everything that happens in the incessantly changing world dominated by humans. It is the duty of the strong to protect the weak. It is the moral obligation to do the right thing and keep the world of the living if not in harmony, then at least in balanced equilibrium. Because the world we live in is the world we make. And the world we make makes us what we are. If we understand this, we will find our path unwinding in this circle of life, a path to a brighter day and a better, ecologically minded civilization.

Note

1   I do not consider Chomskyan 'bio-linguistic' approach to language as an abstract computational system sitting in the mind/brain (Hauser, Chomsky & Fitch 2002) as having much to do with the science of biology.

References

Bang, J. C., Døør, J., Steffensen, S. V, & Nash, J. (2007). *Language, Ecology and Society: A Dialectical Approach*. London; New York: Continuum.

Bateson, G. (1972). *Steps to an Ecology of Mind: Collected Essays in Anthropology, Psychiatry, Evolution, and Epistemology*. Chicago, IL: University of Chicago Press.

Bateson, P. (2017). *Behaviour, Development and Evolution*. Cambridge: Open Book Publishers. Web. <http://books.openedition.org/obp/3880>.

Bickerton, D. (2009). *Adam's Tongue: How Humans Made Language, How Language Made Humans*. New York: Hill and Wang.

Bickerton, D. (2014). 'Some problems for biolinguistics'. *Biolinguistics*, 8: 73–96.

Boivin, N. L., Zeder, M. A., Fuller, D. Q., Crowther, A., Larson, G., Erlandson, J. M., Denham, T., & Petraglia, M. D. (2016). 'Ecological consequences of human niche construction: Examining long-term anthropogenic shaping of global species distributions'. *Proceedings of the National Academy of Sciences of the United States of America (PNAS)*, 113(23): 6388–96.

Call, J. (2006) 'Descartes' two errors: Reason and reflection in the great apes'. In S. Hurley, M. Nudds (Eds.), *Rational Animals?*, 219–34. Oxford: Oxford University Press.

Charvet, J. C., & Finlay, B. L. (2012). 'Embracing covariation in brain evolution: Large brains, extended development, and flexible primate social systems'. *Progress in Brain Research*, 195: 71–87.

Chomsky, N. (2012). *The Science of Language: Interviews with James McGilvray*. Cambridge: Cambridge University Press.

Clowry, G. J. (2014). 'Seeking clues in brain development to explain the extraordinary evolution of language in humans'. *Language Sciences*, 46: 220–31.

Clutton-Brock, T., & Harvey, P. H. (1980). 'Primates, brains and ecology'. *Journal of Zoology*, 190(3): 309–23.

Collens, A., Kelley, E., & Katz, L. A. (2019). 'The concept of the hologenome, an epigenetic phenomenon, challenges aspects of the modern evolutionary synthesis'. *Journal of Experimental Zoology*, Part B, 332(8): 349–55.

Commoner, B. (1971). *The Closing Circle: Nature, Man, and Technology*. New York: Alfred A. Knopf.

Cowley, S. J. (2014). 'Bio-ecology and language: A necessary unity'. *Language Sciences*, 41(Part A): 60–70.

Cowley, S. J. (2019). 'The return of *languaging*: Toward a new ecolinguistics'. *Chinese Semiotic Studies*, 15(4): 483–512.

Darwin, C. (1869). *On the Origin of Species by Means of Natural Selection, or the Preservation of Favoured Races in the Struggle for Life* (5th ed.). London: John Murray.

Deacon, T. W. (1997). *The Symbolic Species: The Co-evolution of Language and the Human Brain*. New York: W. W. Norton & Co.

Deacon, T. W. (2012). *Incomplete Nature: How Mind Emerged from Matter*. New York: W. W. Norton.

Di Paolo, E. A., Cuffari, E. C., & De Jaegher, H. (2018). *Linguistic Bodies: The Continuity between Life and Language*. Cambridge, MA: The MIT Press.

Do Couto, H. H. (2014). 'Ecological approaches in linguistics: A historical overview'. *Language Sciences*, 41: 122–8.

Evans, V. (2015). *The Crucible of Language: How Language and Mind Create Meaning*. Cambridge: Cambridge University Press.

Fitch, W. T. (2010). *The Evolution of Language*. Cambridge: Cambridge University Press.

Ford, E. B. (1964). *Ecological Genetics*. London: Methuen.

Fuentes, A. (2016). 'The extended evolutionary synthesis, ethnography, and the human niche: Toward an integrated anthropology'. *Current Anthropology*, 57, Suppl. 13: 13–26.

Fuentes, A. (2017). 'Human niche, human behaviour, human nature'. *Interface Focus*, 7: 20160136.

Gibson, J. (1979). *The Ecological Approach to Visual Perception*. Boston, MA: Houghton-Mifflin.

Gibson, K. R. (2002). 'Evolution of human intelligence: The roles of brain size and mental construction'. *Brain, Behavior and Evolution*, 59: 10–20.

Givón, T. (2002). *Bio-Linguistics. The Santa Barbara Lectures*. Amsterdam, Philadelphia: John Benjamins.

Haeckel, E. (1866). *Generelle Morphologie der Organismen*. Berlin: G. Reimer.

Harris, R. (1981). *The Language Myth*. London: Duckworth.

Harris, R. (2005). *The Semantics of Science*. London, New York: Continuum International Publishing Group Ltd.

Hauser, M. D., Chomsky, N., & Fitch, W. T. (2002). 'The faculty of language: What is it, who has it, and how did it evolve?' *Science*, 298: 1569–79.

Hauser, M. D., Yang, C., Berwick, R. C., Tattersall, I., Ryan, M. J., Watumull, J., Chomsky, N. & Lewontin, R. C. (2014). 'The mystery of language evolution'. *Frontiers in Psychology*, 5(401): 1–12.

Heras-Escribano, M., & De, Pinedo-García M. (2018). 'Affordances and landscapes: Overcoming the nature–culture dichotomy through Niche Construction Theory'. *Frontiers in Psychology*, 8: 2294.

Herder, J. (1772/2002). 'Treatise on the Origin of Language'. In M. Forster (Ed.), *Herder: Philosophical Writings (Cambridge Texts in the History of Philosophy*, 65–164). Cambridge: Cambridge University Press.

Hodges, B. H. (2014). 'Righting language: A view from ecological psychology'. *Language Sciences*, 41: 93–103.

Hofman, M. A. (2003). 'Of brains and minds. A neurobiological treatise on the nature of intelligence'. *Evolution and Cognition*, 9: 178–88.

Hofman, M. A. (2014). 'Evolution of the human brain: When bigger is better'. *Frontiers in Neuroanatomy*, 8 article 15: 1–12.

Hummer, J. (1985). 'Human and animal intelligence: A question of degree and responsibility'. *Between the Species*, 1(2): 28–36.

Humphrey, N. K. (1976). 'The social function of intellect'. In P. P. G. Bateson and R. A. Hinde (Eds.), *Growing Points in Ethology*, 303–17. New York: Cambridge University Press.

Jahoda, G. (2012). 'Critical reflections on some recent definitions of "culture"'. *Culture & Psychology*, 18(3): 289–303.

Järvilehto, T. (1998). 'The theory of the organism-environment system: I. Description of the theory'. *Integrative Physiological and Behavioral Science*, 33: 317–30.

Jennings, R. E., & Thompson, J. J. (2012). 'The biological centrality of talk'. In A. V. Kravchenko (Ed.), *Cognitive Dynamics in Linguistic Interactions*, 33–63. Newcastle upon Tyne: Cambridge Scholars Publishing.

Kendal, J., Tehrani, J. J., & Odling-Smee, J. (2011). 'Human niche construction in interdisciplinary focus'. *Philosophical Transaction of the Royal Society B*, 366: 785–92.

Kravchenko, A. V. (2016a). 'Constructivism and the epistemological trap of language'. *Constructivist Foundations*, 12(1): 110–12.

Kravchenko, A. V. (2016b). 'Language as human ecology: A new agenda for linguistic education'. *New Ideas in Psychology*, 42: 14–20.

Kravchenko, A. V. (2020a). 'A critique of Barbieri's code biology'. *Constructivist Foundations*, 15(2): 122–34.

Kravchenko, A. V. (2020b). 'Why ecolinguistics?' *Ecolinguística: Revista brasileira de ecologia e linguagem (ECO-REBEL)*, 6(2): 18–31.

Kravchenko, A. V. (2021). 'Approaching linguistic semiosis biologically'. *Rivista Italiana di Filosofia del Linguaggio (RIFL)*, 15(2): 139–158.

Kravchenko, A. V. (2022). 'Language and the nature of humanness (opening a discussion)'. *Slovo.ru: Baltic Accent*, 3: 7–24 (in Russian).

Kravchenko, A. V., & Payunena, M. V. (2017). 'Education: A value lost?' In A. Dudziak & J. Orzechowska (Eds.), *Język i tekst w ujęciu strukturalnym i funkcjonalnym*, 239–46. Olsztyn: Centrum Badań Europy Wschodniej Uniwer-sytetu Warmińsko-Mazurskiego w Olsztynie.

Lakatos, L., & Janka, Z. (2008). 'Evolution of human brain and intelligence'. *Clinical Neuroscience*, 61(7–8): 220–9.

Laland, K., Odling-Smee, J., & Feldman, M. W. (2000). 'Niche construction, biological evolution and cultural change'. *Behavioral and Brain Sciences*, 23(1): 131–75.

Laland, K. N., Boogert, N., & Evans, C. (2014). 'Niche construction, innovation and complexity'. *Environmental Innovation and Societal Transitions*, 11: 71–86.

Lamb, S. (1999). *Pathways of the Brain: The Neurocognitive Basis of Language*. Amsterdam, Philadelphia: John Benjamins.

Lavoisier, A. (1789). *Traité elémentaire de chimie*. Third paragraph. Paris: Chez Cuchet.

Li, J., Steffensen, S. V., & Huang, G. (2020). 'Rethinking ecolinguistics from a distributed language perspective'. *Language Sciences*, 80: 101277.

Lind, M. I., & Spagopoulou, F. (2018). 'Evolutionary consequences of epigenetic inheritance'. *Heredity*, 121: 205–9.

Linnaeus, C. (1758). *Systema naturæ* (10th ed.). Stockholm: Laurentius Salvius.

Magnani, L., & Bardone, E. (2010). 'Chances, affordances, and cognitive niche construction: The plasticity of environmental situatedness'. *International Journal of Advanced Intelligence Paradigms*, 2(2/3): 235–53.

Maturana, H. R. (1970). *Biology of cognition*. BCL Report 9.0. Urbana, IL: University of Illinois.

Maturana, H. R. (1978). 'Biology of language: The epistemology of reality'. In G. Miller & E. Lenneberg (Eds.), *Psychology and Biology of Language and Thought: Essays in Honor of Eric Lenneberg*, 27–63. New York: Academic Press.

Maturana, H. R. (1985). 'Comment by Humberto R. Maturana: The mind is not in the head'. *Journal of Social and Biological Structures*, 8(4): 308–11.

Maturana, H. R. (1988). 'Ontology of observing: The biological foundations of self-consciousness and of the physical domain of existence'. *The Irish Journal of Psychology*, 9(1): 25–82.

Maturana, H. R. & Mpodozis, J. (2000). 'The origin of species by means of natural drift'. *Revista Chilena de Historia Natural*, 73(2): 261–310.

Maturana, H. R., & Varela, F. J. (1987). *The Tree of Knowledge: The Biological Roots of Human Understanding*. Boston, MA: Shambhala.

Maturana, H. R., Mpodozis, J., & Letelier, J. C. (1995). 'Brain, language, and the origin of human mental functions'. *Biological Research*, 28: 15–26.

Milton, K. (1981). 'Distribution patterns of tropical plant foods as an evolutionary stimulus to primate mental development'. *American Anthropologist*, 83(3): 534–48.

Morris, C. W. (1938). 'Foundations of the theory of signs'. In O. Neurath, R. Carnap, C. W. Morris (Eds.), *International Encyclopedia of Unified Science*. Vol. 1, Part 2, 1–59. Chicago: The University of Chicago Press.

Mpodozis, J. (2022). 'Natural drift: A minimal theory with maximal consequences'. *Constructivist Foundations*, 18(1): 94–101.

Müller, F. M. (1861). *Lectures on the Science of Language. First Series*. London: Longman and Roberts.

Ohno, S. (1970). *Evolution by Gene Duplication*. Berlin: Springer.

Odling-Smee, F., Laland, K., & Feldman, M. (2003). *Niche Construction: The Neglected Process in Evolution (MPB-37)*. Princeton; Oxford: Princeton University Press.

Odling-Smee, J., Erwin, D. H., Palkovacs, E. P., Feldman, M. W., & Laland, K. N. (2013). 'Niche construction theory: A practical guide for ecologists'. *The Quarterly Review of Biology*, 88(1): 3–28.

Penn, D. C., Holyoak, K. J., & Povinelli, D. J. (2008). 'Darwin's mistake: Explaining the discontinuity between human and nonhuman minds'. *The Behavioral and Brain Sciences*, 31: 109–30; discussion 130–78.

Pepperberg, I. M. (2002). *The Alex Studies: Cognitive and Communicative Abilities of Grey Parrots*. Cambridge, MA: Harvard University Press.

Popper, K. (2011). 'Three worlds. The Tanner lecture on human values, delivered at The University of Michigan, April 7. (1978)'. In *The Tanner Lectures on Human Values I*, 141–67. Cambridge: Cambridge University Press.

Premack, D. (2007). 'Human and animal cognition: Continuity and discontinuity'. *Proceedings of the National Academy of Sciences of the United State of America*, 104(35): 13861–7.

Priest, S. (1991). *Theories of the Mind: A Compelling Investigation into the Ideas of Leading Philosophers on the Nature of the Mind and Its Relation to the Body*. Harmondsworth: The Penguin Books.

Rachels, J. (1990). *Created from Animals: The Moral Implication of Darwinism*. Oxford: Oxford University Press.

Raimondi, V. (2014). 'Social interaction, languaging and the operational conditions for the emergence of observing'. *Frontiers in Psychology*, 5, Article 899. doi: 10.3389/fpsyg.2014.00899.

Raimondi, V. (2019). 'The bio-logic of languaging and its epistemological background'. *Language Sciences*, 71: 19–26.

Rączaszek-Leonardi, J., & Cowley, S. J. (2012). 'The evolution of language as controlled collectivity'. *Interaction Studies*, 13(1): 1–16.

Rączaszek-Leonardi, J., & Nomikou, I. (2015). 'Beyond mechanistic interaction: Value-based constraints on meaning in language'. *Frontiers in Psychology*, 6: 1579.

Rapp, R. A., & Wendel, J. F. (2005). 'Epigenetics and plant evolution'. *New Phytologist*, 168: 81–91.

Real, L. A. (Ed.) (1994). *Ecological Genetics*. Princeton, NJ: Princeton University Press.

Roth, G., & Dicke, U. (2005). 'Evolution of the brain and intelligence'. *Trends in Cognitive Science*, 9(5): 250–7.

Sagsan, M., & Medeni, T. (2012). 'Understanding "Knowledge Management (KM) Paradigms" from social media perspective: An empirical study on discussion group for KM at professional networking site'. In M. M. Cruz-Cunha, P. Gonçalves, N. Lopes, E. M. Miranda, G. D. Putnik (Eds.), *Handbook of Research on Business Social Networking: Organizational, Managerial, and Technological Dimensions.* Vol. 1-2, 738-55. Hershey, PA: IGI Global.

Sarkies, P. (2020). 'Molecular mechanisms of epigenetic inheritance: Possible evolutionary implications'. *Seminars in Cell & Developmental Biology*, 97: 106-15.

Savage-Rumbaugh, S., & Lewin, R. (1994). *Kanzi: The Ape at the Brink of the Human Mind.* New York: Wiley.

Schaffer, J. (2015). 'What not to multiply without necessity'. *Australasian Journal of Philosophy*, 93(4): 644-64.

Schaik, C. P. van, Isler, K., & Burkart, J. M. (2012). 'Explaining brain size variation: From social to cultural brain'. *Trends in Cognitive Science*, 16: 277-84.

Schoenemann, P. T. (2009). 'Evolution of brain and language'. *Language Learning*, 59(Suppl. 1): 162-86.

Sebeok, T. A. (1996). 'Signs, bridges, origins'. In J. Trabant (Ed.), *Origins of Language*, 89-115. Budapest: Collegium Budapest Workshop Series.

Sherwood, C. C., Subiaul, F., & Zawidzki, T. W. (2008). 'A natural history of the human mind: Tracing evolutionary changes in brain and cognition'. *Journal of Anatomy*, 212: 426-54.

Sinha, C. (2015). 'Language and other artifacts: Socio-cultural dynamics of niche construction'. *Frontiers in Psychology*, 6, Article 1601. https://doi.org/10.3389/fpsyg.2015.01601.

Steffensen, S. V. (2011). 'Beyond mind: An extended ecology of languaging'. In S. J. Cowley (Ed.), *Distributed Language*, 185-210. Amsterdam, Philadelphia: John Benjamins.

Steffensen, S. V., & Cowley, S. J. (2021). 'Thinking on behalf of the world: Radical embodied ecolinguistics'. In W. Xu & J. R. Taylor (Eds.), *The Routledge Handbook of Cognitive Linguistics*, 723-36. New York and London: Routledge.

Steffensen, S. V., & Fill, A. (2014). 'Ecolinguistics: The state of the art and future horizons'. *Language Sciences*, 41: 6-25.

Tattersall, I. (2014). 'An evolutionary context for the emergence of language'. *Language Sciences*, 46: 199-206.

Trappes, R. (2021). 'Defining the niche for niche construction: Evolutionary and ecological niches'. *Biology and Philosophy*, 36: 31.

Uexküll, J. von (1926). *Theoretical Biology*. New York: Harcourt, Brace & Co.

Whorf, B. L. (1958). *Language, Thought, and Reality: Selected Writings of Benjamin Lee Whorf.* New York: The Technology Press of MIT.

Willemet, R. (2013). 'Reconsidering the evolution of brain, cognition, and behavior in birds and mammals'. *Frontiers in Psychology*, 4. doi:10.3389/fpsyg.2013.00396.

6

Varieties of Expression and Enlanguaged Cognition in the Context of a Radicalized Ecolinguistics

Rasmus Gahrn-Andersen

Introduction

In their review of the state-of-the-art of contemporary ecolinguistics (e.g. for a more recent overview, see Fill & Penz 2018), Steffensen and Fill (2014) point out how this particular field of research is characterized by a twofold locus:

> On the one hand, ecolinguistics is a scientific enterprise that aspires to grasp the complexities of the-thing-we-call-language and, on the other, it attempts to reach beyond the scientific community by raising consciousness about the interdependence between discursive practices and ecological devastation. (p. 21)

The latter locus resonates with the fact that the field of ecolinguistics, since the early 1990s, has been increasingly concerned with how language interrelates with issues pertaining to ecology and, more specifically, environmental problems such as animal welfare and climate change (cf. Fill 1996: 13). Thus considered, ecolinguistics research grounds on the basic constructivist assumption pushed by Halliday (1990) that language shapes, if not all, then at least significant parts of our reality and, equally important, can be seen as a 'perpetuator' of ideologies (cf. 1990). As stated by Fill (1996), it is thus assumed that ideologies such as sexism and classism are ''contained' in the grammar of our languages' (p. 13). Steffensen and Fill (2014) elaborate on this point by stressing how ecolinguistics should not take ecological problems at face value but instead engage with the daunting task of reformulating such problems with the purpose of proposing novel solutions to the major challenges of our time. As an example of such a reformulation, Steffensen and Fill mention how ecolinguistics has tended to pass on problematic folk dichotomies (such as the nature–culture distinction) rather than sought to provide adequate reformulations. In view of the former locus, it is worth noting how ecolinguistics is fundamentally driven towards theoretical ingenuity. For as Fill (1996) concludingly remarks, ecolinguistics is more than the systematic investigation of individual texts in accordance with established branches in linguistics. It seeks, besides from novel methodological and empirical investigations, 'some new theorizing' (p. 14) on the nature of language. Based on insights from radical linguistics and, more specifically, the Distributed Language Perspective (Cowley 2009), Steffensen and Fill make a case for situating ecolinguistics between, on the one hand, strictly biological sensemaking – in the sense of recognizing that language is a unique phenomenon pertaining to humans – and, on the other hand, the formalized ontologies of traditional linguistics which reduce language to a disembodied and abstract phenomenon including main tenets of twentieth-century linguistics such as Saussure (1916) and Chomsky (1965) – for a critique, see Kravchenko (2016) and Cowley (2019). Effectively, Steffensen and Fill's distinction sets the direction for future paths of investigation within theoretical ecolinguistics. Such paths might be diverse and heterogeneous considering that the distinction opens up a *Spielraum* of considerable dimensions which come with no particular intrinsic theoretical load besides from avoiding falling into the two extremes of the spectrum.

This brings me to the purpose of the current chapter which is to investigate a rarely discussed but nevertheless central topic to ecolinguistics: the role of linguistic meaning. As my starting point, I take inspiration from a particular observation made by semiologist and philosopher Felix Guattari (1995), who posed a direct challenge to linguistic formalization by arguing that meanings should not be understood through content–form dyads. More concretely Guattari (1995) stressed the importance of resituating semiology 'within the scope of an expanded, machinic conception which would free us from a simple linguistic opposition between Expression/Content, and allow us to integrate into enunciative assemblages an indefinite number of substances of Expression, such as biological codings or organizational forms belonging to the socius' (pp. 23–34). I take this quote to be central to Guattari's (1995) view on language as expressed in his late work, *Chaosmosis: An Ethico-aesthetic Paradigm*. With this quote and, furthermore, the general exposition of this work, Guattari motivates the need for moving beyond the object of study of classical linguistics, arguing that we should consider placing emphasis on the 'a-signifying semiological dimension' related to enunciative assemblages (see Figure 6.1 for an overview). The necessity of such a move is motivated on at least two basic insights: First, that language-use – and, more concretely what is analytically at least amendable to form–content distinctions – should not be considered as solely definable for the outcome in human communication exchanges. Second, that a complex interplay exists between different kinds of expressions which effectively renders strict form–content distinctions useless. Indeed, as shown in the quote, Guattari stresses how other kinds of expressions (ranging from biological codings to human social organizing) are fundamentally 'a-signifying'. In evoking this particular neologism, Guattari introduces a somewhat tricky term given that it might cause one to believe that non-linguistic modes of expression simply do not involve any signification – and, hence, 'meanings' – at all. Yet, what Guattari simply has in mind is that such modes are a-signifying in the sense that their meaning-making function is not amendable to the Saussurean form–content distinction and, more specifically, that meanings exist over against the signs which are assumed to express or carry them.

In the context of theoretical ecolinguistics research, Guattari's mentioning of the varieties of expressions can be taken to pinpoint an important, hitherto unexplored venue. It begs the question of how to move beyond semantical analyses by acknowledging the diversity of expressions that influence the meaning-making activities in languaging activity? Surely, the implications of such a move cannot be exhaustively analysed by means of a single paper. Thus, I situate my contribution as a continuation of the so-called radicalized ecolinguistics which

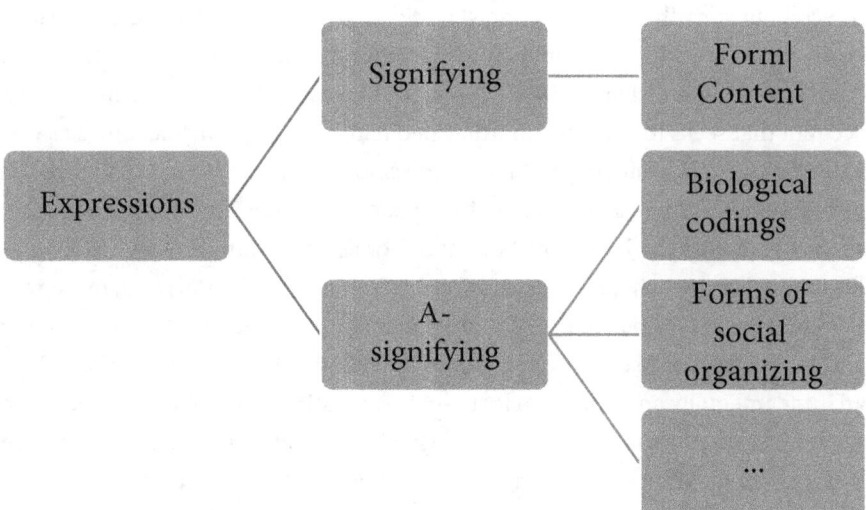

Figure 6.1 Varieties of expression.

'traces languaging to a symbiosis of sensorimotor activity and encultured behaviour. Rather than start with a lexicogrammar (or correct "ways of speaking"), such models play to objectifications of language (in a scientific and/or prescriptive sense)' (Cowley 2022: 15). A radicalized ecolinguistics (see also, Steffensen & Cowley 2021) shares certain basic assumptions with the Distributed Language Perspective. Not only has the latter informed Steffensen and Fill's articulation of the *Spielraum* for future research in theoretical ecolinguistics (cf. above), the basic distributed assumption that language is 'dynamics first, symbols afterwards' (cf. Cowley 2009) is effectively what Cowley (2022) mentions as one of the defining traits of a radicalized ecolinguistics (cf. the quote above). Before engaging with issues revolving around such radicalization in relation to the topic of significance, however, I first consider an example of a less radical position in ecolinguistics which has already acknowledged that linguistic meanings are irreducible to a narrow linguistic ontology.

Bang and Døør's dialectical framework

As argued by proponents of Distributed Language research, it would be a mistake to assume that ecolinguistics research yet has to acknowledge that the meaningful outcome of linguistic interaction is irreducible to interlocutors' cognitive processing of pre-established and formalized word-meanings (cf. Thibault 2011). Accordingly, in what follows, I explore one example of a theoretical contribution in ecolinguistics that comes somewhat close to embracing Guattari's negative claim against traditional linguistics. Specifically, the dialectical ecolinguistic theory of Bang and Døør (1993, 2000) comprises a very good example of an account that seeks to show the multifaceted nature of linguistic meanings as well as their context-dependency (which, needless to say, is an important counterpoint to Saussurean formalism). Despite these positive traits, it can be argued that we should go a step further than Bang and Døør's contribution when seeking to find room for the varieties of expression as identified by Guattari and, moreover, that this step entails pushing a radical agenda. This is especially due to how Bang and Døør safeguard semantics and, consequentially, the assumption that words are fundamentally amendable to form–content distinctions.[1] Not only does such a view treat linguistic tokens as ontologically separate from cognition, it also rests on the assumption that linguistic sense-making unfolds as mind-internal operations or at least relies on internal correlates in order for communication to take place. In what follows, I present a critical scrutiny of Bang and Døør's theory. The purpose in doing so is twofold: First, I wish to highlight some aspects and assumptions pertaining to their theory that I take to be problematic for the development of a positive account that allows for an integration of Guattari's insights. Second, I aim to show that, despite certain issues, Bang and Døør's framework nevertheless can be used to inform our attempt at integrating the varieties of meanings in the context of a more radical approach to language and cognition.

Initially, it is worth considering how Bang and Døør (1993, 2000) challenge mainstream linguistics for its widespread tendency of seeking to naturalize and objectivize language research. Thus, they argue, it is a mistake for linguists to imitate natural scientists for the simple reason that there is no such thing as language-use free of human values. On similar lines, Finke (2020) has more recently criticized science by arguing in favour of a 'serious science' which 'is open to the problems of the present [and] can claim to be trusted for the future' (p. 5) that acknowledges that rationalism is nothing but nostalgia (p. 9). In the case of Bang and Døør, the countering of scientism in linguistics shows itself from how they abandon the core formalist assumption that language as a phenomenon can be uncovered as a thing in itself with predefined rules and meanings. Instead, Bang and Døør argue, we should embrace the Wittgensteinian point that the nature of 'language' depends on its various modes of instantiations or, simply, the different language games that we play. Wittgenstein (2009) is famous for his pragmatic argument concerning the fact that the meaning of language is not determined in advance but rather remains dependent on its manifestations and, hence, how it is actually put to use. Accordingly, Bang and Døør observe how linguistic meanings are never fully predetermined or pre-given but also influenced by various contextual factors. Thus, as they formulate it, 'every word, every text gets some part of its meaning, and its semantic force, from the situation [...] There is no context-free or situation-free meaning' (p. 9). In this connection, we can identify one of their core claims, namely that 'language and ecolinguistics are parts of a culture, a social formation, and a praxis; therefore, language and linguistics are constituted by the core contradictions of our social praxis' (p. 2). Moreover, we find two central points which they use as means for qualifying their dialectical theoretical framework:

The first point is that language and linguistics are constituted by – as well as constitutive of – human practical activity or, in Bang and Døør's terminology: *praxis* (cf. 2009). This substantiates their observation concerning the relativity of linguistic meanings to human social doings while it also emphasizes that linguistics is just as much a cultural product as plain language-use. To put it differently, linguistics is just an enlanguaged practice amongst the myriad of other practices: we engage in meaning and it makes no sense to treat linguistics as an objective science alongside, for instance, physics and chemistry.[2]

The second point is that a dialectical relation exists between, on the one hand, the *situation* which instantiates and materializes linguistic activity in the form of *texts* and, on the other hand, the *environment* which surrounds the former.

I take both of these points to illustrate that Bang and Døør's dialectical approach generally acknowledges the variety of expressions. It does so by treating language-use as part of (practical) activity more generally and, hence, as being intrinsically constituted by a multitude of factors. Bang and Døør recognize, at least in principle, that language-use is irreducible to linguistic conventions but equally interplays with biological and societal factors all of which are expressed through our linguistic coordination. With these two points in mind, one is therefore left with the impression that Bang and Døør's dialectical theory comprises a sufficient ecolinguistic basis for not just integrating Guattari's insights but also pushing a radical agenda in ecolinguistics.

Yet, if we scrutinize how different modes of expression are actually taken into account by Bang and Døør, we find that their theory is fundamentally subdued to expressions understood as signifyings and, moreover, that such signifyings are conceptualized in basic accordance with the traditional form–content distinction of traditional semantics. What I take the above-mentioned quote by Guattari to indicate is that a-signifying elements should not necessarily be considered as being articulated as part of human language-use but might also be considered as being constitutive of its levels of signification. This is an important point because it means that the heterogeneity of meanings is irreducible to semantics in the traditional sense. In the remaining part of this section, I attempt to show how Bang and Døør's theory overlooks precisely this constitutive dimension by prioritizing the articulated dimension of language-use.

In introducing a set of three different logics (i.e. a *bio-logic*, a *socio-logic* and an *ideo-logic*) Bang and Døør illustrate that there is more to human language-use than what is strictly ascribed to it by a traditional linguistic ontology. Indeed, language-use is irreducible to 'language' understood as system of formalized rules, meanings and resources. Instead, it forms part of our existence and unfolds through – in the sense of manifests – these different logics (cf. 2000: p. 8). As such, the fact that we can single out such logics and show how they interplay with wordings and other language-specific utterances in actual communication underlines how other ontologies than the strictly formalized ontology of classical linguistics interplay with human meaning-making processes and, hence, language. Thus, Bang and Døør (2000) write:

> We propose that we start regarding our language-use as **life-significant,** i.e. that our talk has both a *socio-logical significance* and a *bio-logical significance*. When language has a socio-logical significance it influences and co-conditions our social life. When language has a bio-logical significance it influences and co-conditions our biological life. There is, however, even more at stake. When we talk, our talking has an ideo-logical significance, too. Our language-use colours and co-conditions our thought processes, even though they are not present in a linguistic medium, but in pictures, images, feelings, emotions, sensations, or perceptions. (p. 3)

With this focus on the life-significant aspects of language-use they come to acknowledge that linguistic significance (or: formalized denotative meanings) is not solely definable of communication. Thus, the obvious strength of Bang and Døør's theory is that it recognizes that language-use affords meanings other than those pertaining to language-use in a narrow, Saussurean sense.

Although Bang and Døør thus seem to be moving away from traditional linguistics given their acknowledging of the workings of these different logics, it can nevertheless be argued that they safeguard at least two problematic assumptions characteristic of Saussurean linguistics. Critically, the presence of these effectively entails that Bang and Døør's contribution is at odds with the radical agenda in ecolinguistics. While the first assumption testifies to how their contribution is unsuitable for a proper integration of the varieties of expressions as identified by Guattari, the second assumption shows how Bang and Døør's theory fails to satisfy a vital element pertaining to what the radical agenda is, namely a commitment to anti-representationalism. As I will argue in the following, the two assumptions are interconnected.

On the one hand, Bang and Døør recognize that what Guattari thematizes as 'a-signifying elements' have constitutional relevance to our languaging activity and should therefore be taken into account by the linguist whenever they are deemed to be relevant. On the other hand, they fail to go all the way as they merely consider these logics as factors that accompany language-use and, hence, not as something that is necessarily constitutive of the former. This is most readily evident in relation to their point concerning the manifestations of the three different *logics*. For as they write in the quote above, language manifests the significance related to the logics regardless of whether the logic pertains to the biological, the social or the ideological environment (cf. Bang &

Døør 1993: 8). Thus conceived, we come to see that Bang and Døør's approach remains conventional given that it takes as its level of analysis that of signification (understood in the narrow linguistic sense) and, more specifically, unfolds through the analysis of word meanings. Thus, as they put it:

> [A]ny utterance is only a part of a dialogue and is more or less restricted as a *potential of meanings* by the syntacticosemantical organisation of the utterance, by the situational context constituted by the present persons and by the other utterances produced in direct or indirect relation to the utterance in question. (Bang & Døør 2000: 16; my emphasis)

'Meaning' – understood as situational outcomes based on linguistic interaction – interrelates with the 'mind' (cf. 2000: 15). Thus, ideo-logical factors for instance, should not be attributed to a 'linguistic medium' but rather to agent-intrinsic factors such as 'pictures, images, feelings, emotions, sensations, or perceptions' (2000: 3). The fact that especially mind internalism is assumed to play a key role in language-use and communication is underlined by Bang and Døør as they state that when preliminary engaging with a text, the agent creates 'an idea, an image, of a situation and context of and for the following texts' (2000: 14). Thus, the actual text or conversation as well as the context it embodies is assumed to have an internal correlate in the form of *an idea*. Bang and Døør explicitly stress the necessity of creating an 'idea of the context of the dialogue and of the discourse' in order to engage meaningfully in a conversation. So, although 'bio-soc dominance' ontologically influences the communication (cf. p. 14), the meaning-making activities and, hence, the significance pertaining to language-use shouldn't be taken to exist independently of certain biological and socio-material factors which themselves are not amendable to traditional linguistic description per se.[3] On the contrary, as I will argue in the following, such factors play a crucial part in language-use thus underlining the fact that the investigation of linguistic phenomena requires an interdisciplinary focus.

Enlanguaged cognition: A radical take

It makes little sense to treat language and cognition in adult humans as separable phenomena (see, for instance, Maturana [1988] for an account on their inseparability). Indeed, much human cognition is enlanguaged. Moreover, as Finke (2020) somewhat provocatively articulates, 'it is the cognitive function of language not the communicative which is fundamental' (p. 10). Certainly, we can think of particular kinds of cognition which need not involve language. This, for instance, is the case in the flexible adaptive behaviour of non-linguistic animals and bacteria. Nevertheless, the reverse doesn't hold given that cognition is essentially characteristic of the doings of any living agent. Indeed, as Autopoietic Enactivists (see Thompson 2004) have claimed, a deep continuity exists between cognition and the living or, simply, life and mind. Whether such continuity, which has been thematized by amongst others Godfrey-Smith (1996), also extends to include language lies beyond the scope of the current chapter to investigate. Nevertheless, I'm going to pick up one of the major implications of the said continuity for linguistics research: that language-use involves cognizing. Consequently, 'language' should not be treated as a stand-alone phenomenon but rather as being intertwined with human thinking, here understood in the broadest possible sense of our enacted, socio-material doings. On the view defended here, cognition does not solely reduce to instances of overtly reflective behaviour which are commonly said to involve *representation-hunger* and as occurring *offline* but, equally so, play out in purely embodied instances (see Clark & Toribio 1994). Cognition also happens strictly *online* and, hence, is inseparable from our pre-reflective actions as an embodied agent stands over against the environment in strictly dynamical – and, thus, relational – manner.[4] Amongst proponents of anti-representationalist cognitive science, online cognition is treated as the prevalent mode in which our thinking unfolds. There has been a recent upsurge in anti-representationalist attempts at showing that even cognitive phenomena which are traditionally treated as involving essential offline components (e.g. memory and imagination) can in fact be explained in dynamical, online terms (see Degenaar & Myin 2014; Kiverstein & Rietveld 2018).

One implication of such a dynamical view for the theorization of language is that it would be misleading to assume that 'stand-alone' words comprise epistemically isolated entities that have an intrinsic and exhaustible meaning-potential in their own right. The somewhat radical implication of such an insight for contemporary linguistics including ecolinguistics is that there is no meaning without the presence of meaning-makers, thus rendering it useless to assume that linguistic tokens are somehow imbued with essential traits. Yet, the criticism goes even more to the core given the defining trait of online cognition, namely as put in the terms of Hutto and Myin (2013), that there are no 'consumers' to pick up content precisely because content is involved neither on the brain-side nor on the world-side in strictly online cognition. In this connection, Kee (2020) has recently argued that words are tool-like in the sense that we engage with them with the purpose of using them for specific purposes, etc. Thus, the use of words whether written or spoken enmeshes with our cognition as we enact them in a dynamical relation to our environment. Another strong indicator of this inseparability is that language-use does not reduce to the spoken or the written but extends to how human basic perception – or what proponents of *Radical Enactivism* term as 'basic cognition' (see Hutto & Myin 2013) – relies on concept-relative skills and knowhow (see Gahrn-Andersen 2021; Gahrn-Andersen 2022). And considering how perception feeds into cognitive faculties such as memory and imagination, it is indeed difficult to see how any cognitive behaviour pertaining to linguistically competent human beings can be completely devoid of conceptual influences.[5] Effectively, the view I'm pushing challenges mentalist models that take language as a medium for transmitting thoughts and, further, that assume that utterance activity relies on the presence of an internal correlate in the form of represented word-meanings that exist inside the head of the language-user. Here I'm acknowledging Merleau-Ponty who pointed out that our speech doesn't rely on the existence of pre-extant images but rather, in a progressive manner, fulfils – or in Merleau-Ponty's (2010) terms: *accomplishes* – our thinking as we're going on (p. 207).

Also, language-use is irreducible to a formalist linguistic ontology given that our enlanguaged doings exhibit a degree of significance which goes beyond the mere usage of words and, further, the pre-existing meanings and references as assumed by traditional linguists. This brings us back to Guattari whose mentioning of the varieties of expression should be read as an acknowledgement of the fact that other kinds of 'significance' impact on the way in which linguistic utterances are perceived. Moreover, his point concerning the necessity that we free ourselves from the classical form–content distinction underscores that it is not simply enough to take the said distinction as being an essential part of language and then, subsequently, add-up by considering how non-linguistic contextual factors influence the reception of such meanings as in the case of Bang and Døør. By contrast, given how a form–content distinction in principle can always be (super)imposed retrospectively as a way of mapping out recursive and, hence, significant aspects in communication, it is important to stress how this distinction is more of an epistemic tool of the researcher than an objective mapping of essential correspondence relations that are intrinsic to our 'language' (for a similar point, see Harris 1997, 2000).

Meanings are, as Bang and Døør also recognize, often inseparable from social practices. Whether happening in relation to established, highly conventionalized practices or not, language-use will always have a practice-significant dimension.

The reason for this is that it is part of our existence (qua life-significant) meaning that we engage in such activity in order to achieve something else. This is also central to Wittgenstein's introduction of the concept of 'language games'; namely that the different ways in which language-users 'combine' words remain dependent on certain conventions (i.e. rules) and are closely intertwined with the social activity that language-use enables. Successful communication relies on the skilful expression of words (and the mastering of grammar, syntax, prosody and other factors that have been delineated by linguists). However, this does not mean that there are a finite number of language games to be played and that can be mapped once and for all. On the contrary, what Wittgenstein (2009) effectively shows is that 'language' is a flexible medium in the sense that it allows for a potentially infinite variety of modes of expressions that are used for engaging in activity that either tacitly or overtly exhibit linguistic phenomena (e.g. wordings, concepts). Moreover, we can always imagine a particular new language game as being played in such and such a way. What Bang and Døør fittingly highlight as the 'life-significance' of language-use does not just relate to the fact that we rely on linguistic resource when we communicate with others about the state of the ecology, what we had for dinner last night or when our train is supposed to arrive, but also that the so-called bio- and socio-logical significance comprise constitutive elements to how we humans exist in language. To put it differently, both our biology and our sociality co-condition the manner in which we become enmeshed in language. In other words, language cannot be reduced to a representational medium. For contrary to Bang and Døør's claim, such enmeshing does not entail that biological and social factors are content-relatedly expressed in our communication. With this point in mind, I will now seek to show how the varieties of expressions singled out by Guattari, can also be shown to have a constitutional relevance to our language-use.

On the constitutional relevance of the logics

In a recent Special Issue edited by Stephen J. Cowley, which thematizes the connection between biosemiotics and radical linguistics, Robert Prinz and I argue in favour of life-mind-language continuity (see Gahrn-Andersen & Prinz 2021). Specifically, we seek to uncover the generative basis of Maturana's (1988) notion of *languaging* and, thus, what Maturana in a slightly more technically way terms as 'second order consensual coordination'. In so doing, we want to avoid ascribing a constitutive role to informational content in human cognition and language use. Drawing on the case of evoneering and, more specifically, how advanced technical devices are implanted into or attached to the bodies of human agents, we argue that embodied hierarchies of molecular coding play a key enabling role to not just human languaging but also plain actions that are imbued with socio-practical significance. The latter kind of activity involves a vast range of doings from queueing to grasping, running, etc. – all of which need not revolve around linguistic utterances but nevertheless are part of human practice-based behaviour. Cowley (2022) broadens this view when suggesting that the brain relies on natural evoneering as it seeks 'to master the techniques of material culture' (p. 2). As he rightly submits, this occurs in an unintended manner – where intentionality is understood in the classical sense of Franz Brentano and, hence, as involving mental representations – meaning that no offline cognition (or accompanying representations) is required for the performance of the action in question.

Turning to our enlanguaged behaviour, we can hypothesize at least two different conditions that differ with respect to how they are connected with Bang and Døør's socio- and bio-logics, namely when (1) behaviour relies on the performer of a given action having relevant skill sets construed through a past of interactions based on linguistic resources and (2) when an action is ascribed practical significance as it is framed by members of one or more practices to which the performer of the action also belongs. In this sense, it can be argued that activities, things, people, etc. have the potential for becoming enlanguaged for an agent as they are denotatively demarcated – or simply, 'pointed out' (cf. Merleau-Ponty 2010; Gahrn-Andersen 2021) – by others as it happens in ostensive language games which play a foundational part in language teaching (cf. Wittgenstein 2009). We find instances of (1) in basically all doings that are somehow dependent on the agent's habituated linguistic skills and knowhow including acts of *languaging* in the Maturanian sense. Such activities involve the meshing of what Bang and Døør term as socio-logics and bio-logics because it not only emerges out of first-order consensual coordination (i.e. biological sense-making) but also depends on a specific history of doings and things in accordance with others. Thus, it is constrained by certain norms and routines which are traceable to social communities. In being somewhat narrower, (2) are instances where members of a community with language-relative skill sets *frame* the actions of someone else to this particular someone who lacks similar skills and, hence, engages in first-order coordination (as described by Maturana 1988). This is the case, for instance, in infant communication where caregivers engage in acts of languaging as they ostensively identify certain (embodied) acts of the child, things in the environment, etc. with the purpose of teaching the child their significance, not just denotatively but also in relation to the practice which situates the interaction. While the caregiver's languaging activities rely on the aforementioned meshing of bio- and socio-logics, the infant's action including orientation towards an object is grounded in bio-logics; at least in the outset. But once the child is *chafed* sufficiently (cf. Gahrn-Andersen & Cowley 2017), she or he will self-adjust to the sensed perturbations to the extent that aspects of his or her action potential changes from being strictly first-order coordinative to becoming second-order coordination or: languaging. Of course, in general, the practice is fluent meaning that in infancy (1) and (2) are more or less in constant interplay and in frequent overlaps as the child gradually becomes acquainted with how his or her languaging relates to practical purposes, people and the surrounding world more generally.

As to how the denotative, the practical and acquired skills interplay, it makes sense to consider Halliday's (2016) depiction of Nigel (a pseudonym for his own son, Neil). Nigel engages in acts of languaging within an idiosyncratic practice constructed by him and his father. The idiosyncratic nature of their interactions is manifested through Nigel's use of ditto phrases and wordings. For instance, he would say 'chuffa stúck' when his little toy train is stuck and he requires assistance to get it out (cf. Halliday 2016: 6). Indeed, the uninitiated observer would initially struggle with coming to terms with the significance of this utterance. Or that is, at least, until they find out that Nigel enacts a practice that involves onomatopoeia. But Nigel's languaging mirrors common practices as the utterances connects certain wordings with certain actions and, in fact, even elliptical speech since the request to pick up the train is not verbally explicated by Nigel. Clearly, Nigel does not still exist fully in language nor does he have sufficient linguistic skills for making himself understood outside the tightly coupled interaction with his caregiver. Nevertheless, Nigel is on his way in the sense that his conceptual attaching of for instance 'chuffa' onto his little toy trains come with a degree of generality and trans-practicality. So once Nigel starts understanding *sameness* at eighteen months, he becomes capable of identifying things belonging to particular classes across contexts (cf. Halliday 2016: 42). Moreover, as Halliday explains, the linguistic skill sets of Nigel are under constant refinement as the caregiver's reiteration of aspects of his languaging chafes Nigel to adjust to 'normal' English and, hence, adopt certain 'discourses':

> The adult's response as we have said is in normal English, with all the grammatical words and morphemes added in place; gradually, the child will incorporate these into his discourse too. But it will still be the ordinary everyday discourse of the home and the neighbourhood: the unselfconscious, unplanned and unwritten-down language of daily life. (Halliday 2016: 6)

Indeed, what comes to integrate the bio-logics with the socio-logics (including their merging in acts of idiosyncratic languaging such as 'chuffa') is how expressional significance is irreducible to localized, strictly situated encounters. Rather than unfolding through tight agent-device couplings, it comes to constitute as well as draw on what I in lack of better terms characterize as an overreaching *praxis-logic*. The reason that I chose to evoke this neologism is that, in being enlanguaged, it involves both the bio- and socio-logical. In other words, neither of the two alone would suffice. Specifically, a praxis-logic is synonymous with the ways in which practical behaviour is organized in the realm of a given practice and, hence, what pertains to its members practical understanding of what belongs to the practice in question (e.g. in terms of the things, doings, sayings that are characteristically constitutive of the said practice). Moreover, in reifying practices, they involve global, and not just local, significance. Here:

> 'Global' should here be understood in the sense of our socio-material engagements being irreducible to localised interactions bound to a particular territory or spatio-temporal realm. On the contrary, thanks to the denotative dimension of enlanguaged cognition, we can make sense of artefacts, objects etcetera across situations (i.e., on a global scale) as we draw diachronically on our conceptual knowhow. (Gahrn-Andersen & Prinz 2021: 116)

Indeed, the sameness that is a distinctive quality pertaining to eighteen-month-old Nigel's languaging is a testimony of the fact that he is beginning, albeit slowly, to engage in a praxis-logic in the sense that he is gradually becoming aware of the fact that his languaging connects with things and events beyond the immediacy of a situation. For instance, Halliday gives the following account of a 23-month-old Nigel:

> Nigel knew about zoos; he had been to one and had been particularly impressed with the lions. On this occasion, his mother and I were planning to take him to the aquarium. Nigel heard us discussing it, but he did not know what an aquarium was. This was how he reasoned it out: (1; 11)
> *We not going to see a rào (= lion). Vòpa (= fishes). There will be some wàter.*
> (Halliday 2016: 43)

Besides from Nigel's striking skills in reasoning it is also worth noting how he has gained the ability of relating to known things and phenomena (i.e. lions, fishes and water) as well as the practice-specific activity of seeing (in the sense of observing animals in captivity) with a high degree of generality. Thus, seeing as a general activity clearly is not restricted to seeing lions in a zoo but also fishes in a hitherto unknown practice (= an aquarium) which nevertheless have common traits with a zoo (which Nigel is already familiar with) in the sense that it is about seeing animals which comprises a trans-practice phenomenon. Thus, he exhibits how bio- and social-logically driven acts of languaging are flexibly adaptively enacted so that they exhibit a praxis-logic in the sense that they connect with complexes of certain material structures, animals, doings, norms and habit whose generality and trans-situationality exceeds the locus of Nigel's localized interactions.

Concluding remarks

In embracing Guattari's point concerning the varieties of expressions, the chapter explores the role of significance in the context of a radical perspective on enlanguaged cognition and ecolinguistics. I have argued in favour of enlanguaged cognition in the attempt at showing that a praxis-logic can be said to integrate various logics (specifically socio- and bio-logics), grant different practice-constitutive elements (e.g. things, people, doings, norms) their significance and, further, allow for the ongoing of human practices. Acts of languaging (and ostensive engagements) play key roles in this connection as they not only integrate different logics but also interrelate amongst themselves. Languaging is key because it connects skills with the practice-specific phenomena.

On the pre-reflective, non-represented level of human languaging – understood as complex agent-environment and agent-agent dynamics – there is indeed no signified meanings in the form–content dyads. Yet, it is always possible to descriptively reduce aspects of our languaging activity to such dyads. This is because conceptual distinctions such as this are first brought into play through linguistic practice as the linguist (specifically understood as an Maturanian observer) observes recurrent real-world dynamics (languaging) and 'chooses' to map them by means of (equally recurrent) conceptual distinctions within a dominant praxis-logic. The contingency of the form–content dyad is underlined by how other possible descriptive categories could easily be evoked instead including the Peircean triadic sign. Surely, the view is then subsequently introduced through ostensive language games through childhood as caregivers are teaching the child the seeming basis of languaging, namely denotative relations between a 'word' and things in the environment.

Notes

1. As Fill (2001) observes, Bang and Døør have not only pushed theoretical ecolinguistics but, equally so, made headway into applied ecolinguistics through their detailed analyses of various kinds of texts.
2. Similar observations are found in Kravchenko (2016) as he makes the critical Maturanian-inspired point that the 'epistemic cut' between the observed and the observer should be eliminated (cf. p. 108). As noted by Zhou (2022), Kravchenko's view is signalling the fact that some ecolinguistic contributions are becoming increasingly concerned with epistemology (p. 9). Indeed, as shown by this important point pertaining to Bang and Døør's theory, concerns related to epistemology in ecolinguistics can be traced back to the 1990s. More recently, Finke (2020) claims how changes to our culture change our knowledge and, thus, suggests that any scientific inquiry remains fundamentally enculturated and, hence, dependent on the evocation of certain values and norms (cf. p. 9).
3. Bang and Døør hint at this when stating that 'The first dimension is the bio-logics. A present text, or an utterance, has a physical or biological conditioned existence – and without the biological dimension the text or utterance could not exist. • The second dimension is the ideo-logics. The utterance, or text, has mental aspects, some mental conditions or implications without which it would not be identifiable as an utterance/text. The utterance is a form of social activity and therefore we introduce the term socio-logics. Without a social praxis there would be no natural language nor linguistic sign nor text. A natural language is a cultural medium which stylizes and formalizes forms of social interactions' (Bang & Døør 2000: 9–10). Yet, although thus recognizing the constitutive role of the different logics, they nevertheless fail to show how these logics are amendable to expressions others than those involving form–content.
4. As Thibault mentions, the radical, naturalizing of language which characterizes both Distributed Language research and radical ecolinguistics (cf. Steffensen & Fill 2014) is strongly inspired by theoretical developments in cognitive science which 'has taken the form of a shift from classical or first-wave (internal symbol manipulation) and second-wave (connectionist) cognitive science to third-wave theories and models of embodied, embedded distributed cognition and the place of languaging behavior in these' (Thibault 2011: 211).
5. It should be noted that I'm not advocating in favour of an all-encompassing conceptualism. I don't think that the richness of perceptual experiences, for instance, can be reduced to the 'meanings' of concepts.

References

Bang, J. C., & Døør, J. (1993). Eco-linguistics: A framework. http://www.jcbang.dk/main/ecolinguistics/Ecoling_AFramework1993.pdf. Accessed 22 February 2022.

Bang, J. C., & Døør, J. (2000). 'Ecology, ethics & communication: An essay in eco-linguistics'. In A. V. Lindø & J. Bundgaard (Eds.), *Dialectical Ecolinguistics: Three Essays for the Symposium 30 Years of Language and Ecology in Graz December 2000*. Odense: Syddansk Universitet.

Chomsky, N. (1965). *Aspects of the Theory of Syntax*. Cambridge, MA: MIT Press.

Clark, A., & Toribio, J. (1994). 'Doing without representing'. *Synthese*, 101: 401–31.

Cowley, S. J. (2009). 'Distributed language and dynamics'. *Pragmatics and Cognition*, 17(3): 495–508.

Cowley, S. J. (2019). 'The return of languaging: Toward a new ecolinguistics'. *Chinese Semiotic Studies*, 15(4): 483–512.

Cowley, S. J. (2022). 'Ecolinguistics reunited: Rewilding the territory'. *Journal of World Languages*. https://doi.org/10.1515/jwl-2021-0025.

Degenaar, J., & Myin, E. (2014). 'Representation-hunger reconsidered'. *Synthese*, 191: 3639–48.

Fill, A. (1996). 'Ecolinguistics – State of the art 1996'. In J. C. Band, J. Døør, R. J. Alexander, A. Fill & F. C. Verhagen (Eds.), *Language and Ecology: Eco-Linguistics – Problems, Theories and Methods – Essays for the AILA '96 Symposium*, 11–16. Odense: Odense University.

Fill, A. (2001). 'Ecolinguistics: State of the art 1998'. In A. Fill & P. Mühlhäusler (Eds.), *The Ecolinguistics Reader: Language, Ecology and Environment*, 43–53. London: Continuum.

Fill, A., & Penz. H. (2018). 'Ecolinguistics in the 21st century'. In Alwin Fill & Hermine Penz (Eds.), *The Routledge Handbook of Ecolinguistics*, 437–43. London: Routledge.

Finke, P. L. W. (2020). 'Go for the Gaiacene! Knowledge, culture and corona'. *Ecolinguística: Revista brasileira de ecologia e linguagem (ECO-REBEL)*, 6(4): 4–12.

Gahrn-Andersen, R. (2021). 'Conceptual attaching in perception and practice-based behavior'. *Lingua*, 249: 102960.

Gahrn-Andersen, R. (2022). 'Concrete concepts in basic cognition'. *Philosophia*, 50(3): 1093–116.

Gahrn-Andersen, R., & Cowley, S.J. (2017). 'Phenomenology & sociality: How extended normative perturbations give rise to social agency'. *Intellectica*, 67(1): 379–98.

Gahrn-Andersen, R., & Prinz, R. (2021). 'How cyborgs transcend Maturana's concept of languaging: A (bio)engineering perspective on information processing and embodied cognition'. *Italian Journal of Philosophy of Language* (RIFL), 15(2): 104–20.

Godfrey-Smith, P. (1996). 'Spencer and Dewey on life and mind'. In M. Boden (Ed.), *The Philosophy of Artificial Life*, 314–31. Oxford: Oxford University Press.

Guattari, F. (1995). *Chaosmosis: An Ethico-aesthetic Paradigm*. Bloomington and Indianapolis: Indiana University Press.

Halliday, M. A. K. (1990). 'New ways of meaning: The challenge to applied linguistics'. *Journal of Applied Linguistics*, 6: 7–36.

Halliday, M. A. K. (2016). *Aspects of Language and Learning*. Heidelberg: Springer.

Harris, R. (1997). 'From an integrational point of view'. In G. Wolf, & N. Love (Eds.), *Linguistics Inside Out: Roy Harris and His Critics*, 229–310. Amsterdam: John Benjamins.

Harris, R. (2000). *Rethinking Writing*. London: Athlone Press.

Hutto, D. D., & Myin, E. (2013). *Radicalizing Enactivism: Basic Minds without Content*. Cambridge, MA: MIT Press.

Kee, H. (2020). 'Horizons of the word: Words and tools in perception and action'. *Phenomenology and the Cognitive Sciences*, 19(5): 905–32.

Kiverstein, J., & Rietveld, E. (2018). 'Reconceiving representation-hungry cognition: An ecological-enactive proposal'. *Adaptive Behavior*, 26(4): 147–63.

Kravchenko, A. V. (2016). 'Two views on language ecology and ecolinguistics'. *Language Sciences*, 54: 102–13.

Maturana, H. (1988). 'Reality: The search for objectivity or the quest for a compelling argument'. *The Irish Journal of Psychology*, 9(1): 25–82.

Merleau-Ponty, M. (2010). *Phenomenology of Perception*. London: Routledge.

Saussure, F. (1916). *Cours de linguistique générale*. Paris: Payot.

Steffensen, S., & Cowley, S. J. (2021). 'Thinking on behalf of the world: Radical embodied ecolinguistics'. In W. Xu & J. R. Taylor (Eds.), *The Routledge Handbook of Cognitive Linguistics*, 723–36. London: Routledge.

Steffensen, S. V., & Fill, A. (2014) 'Ecolinguistics: The state of the art and future horizons'. *Language Sciences*, 41: 6–25.

Thibault, P. J. (2011). 'First-order languaging dynamics and second-order language: The distributed language view'. *Ecological Psychology*, 23(3): 210–45, DOI: 10.1080/10407413.2011.591274.

Thompson, E. (2004). 'Life and mind: From autopoiesis to neurophenomenology. A tribute to Francisco Varela'. *Phenomenology and the Cognitive Sciences*, 3: 381–98. DOI: https://doi.org/10.1023/B:PHEN.0000048936.73339.dd

Wittgenstein, L. (2009). *Philosophical Investigations* (4th edition). Oxford: Blackwell Publishing.

Zhou, W. (2022). 'Ecolinguistics: A half-century overview'. *Journal of World Languages*.

Part Two

From Discourse to Worldly Action

7

Ecolinguistics for Ethical Leadership

Arran Stibbe

Introduction

For all the destruction it has caused, the coronavirus pandemic has also shone a spotlight on the nature of industrialized civilization, provoked reflection on its flaws and kindled a determination to rebuild a different kind of civilization in its wake. This can be seen in the simple alliterative slogan 'Build Back Better' promoted by the US White House, but also in more searching comments in the media and social media. Dave Hollis (2020) invites us into reflection: 'In the rush to return to normal, use this time to consider which parts of normal are worth rushing back to.' Sonya Renee Taylor (2020) describes some aspects of 'normal' that we certainly would not want to return to:

> We will not go back to normal. Normal never was. Our pre-corona existence was not normal other than we normalized greed, inequity, exhaustion, depletion, extraction, disconnection, confusion, rage, hoarding, hate and lack ... We are being given the opportunity to stitch a new garment. One that fits all of humanity and nature.

The stitching metaphor is a powerful call to reconstruct a socially just society and protect the ecosystems that life depends on. The journalist Peter Baker (2020) also uses a textile metaphor in conjunction with a light metaphor to inspire renewal: 'disasters and emergencies do not just throw light on the world as it is. They also rip open the fabric of normality. Through the hole that opens up, we glimpse possibilities of other worlds.' Arundhati Roy (2020) uses a parallel metaphor where the hole in the fabric becomes a portal: 'historically, pandemics have forced humans to break with the past and imagine their world anew. This one is no different. It is a portal, a gateway between one world and the next.'

Breaking away from the horrors of what was 'normal', imagining the world anew, and stitching a garment that fits all of humanity and nature will require *ethical leadership* to build a new, more ethical and sustainable society. It will require ethical leadership not just from CEOs, politicians and people who have official leadership roles in organizations, but from everyone who has the opportunity and ability to influence how other people see the world.

The practice of leadership is conducted primarily through words. As Drew Westen (2011) points out, 'The stories our leaders tell us matter, probably almost as much as the stories our parents tell us as children, because they orient us to what is, what could be, and what should be.' Similarity, Geoff Mead (2014: 3) writes: 'Successful leadership depends on the stories we tell and the stories we live and how well they speak to the need of our time.' This makes ethical leadership of great concern to ecolinguistics, since one of the key roles of ecolinguistics is to reveal the stories we live by, challenge them and contribute to the search for new stories to live by. This chapter explores what ecolinguistics can contribute to both the theory of ethical leadership and practical leadership training, and what theories of ethical leadership can contribute to ecolinguistics.

Ecolinguistics

In the past, the term 'ecolinguistics' was applied to a diverse range of areas of study, but has become increasingly aligned with other ecological humanities subjects in its focus on engaged inquiry that takes into consideration not only humans but other species and the ecosystems that life depends on. Sibo Chen (2016: 109) performed a critical analysis of seventy-six journal articles on ecolinguistics and came to the conclusion:

> Ecolinguistics seeks to explore linguistic phenomena found in inter-language, inter-human, and human-nature relationships from the perspective of ecological philosophy. In contrast to other subfields of linguistics, ecolinguistics adopts 'ecosophy' as its principle normative framework.

Other areas of linguistics such as critical discourse analysis explore issues including racism, sexism and homophobia from a normative framework, which is usually orientated towards opposing oppression and creating a fairer and more equitable society. There is, however, little point in building an equal society if its consumption patterns destroy the ecosystems that life depends on because it would be unsustainable and could not continue into the future. An ecosophy, by definition, is a normative framework that takes into consideration not only humans but other species and the physical environment. What makes a form of linguistics ecolinguistics is not a particular methodology or approach but a more general care that extends beyond an individual human, beyond a group of humans, to encompass all humans as well as future generations, other species and the wider ecosystems that life depends on, and an orientation towards practical action to make a difference. Ecolinguistic studies have examined issues such as the representation of animals in industrial farming; the obsession with profit and economic growth; discourses of consumerism; the language of environmentalism; indigenous and traditional discourses of nature; nature writing; the relationship between language diversity and biodiversity, and a wide range of other areas, using a wide range of linguistic techniques, but all grounded in an explicit or implicit ecosophy.

It is not just the end-goal that distinguishes ecolinguistics from other forms of linguistic enquiry. An ecological perspective influences *what* ecolinguists see as language and *where* they see language as located. While prevailing structuralist and poststructuralist views of language see it as a fixed system existing within the minds of native speakers, ecolinguists have increasingly been seeing language as existing within the interactions of humans with other humans, other species and the physical environment, i.e. within ecology (Cowley 2018: 47). To illustrate this by analogy: messaging between trees along mitochondrial networks can be occasioned by the external environment (e.g. an attack by pests) and can lead to physical changes (surrounding trees raising their defences), which has consequences for the future survival of the trees. The messaging itself is part of the life-sustaining interaction of organisms with other organisms and the physical environment so is part of ecology. In the same way, messaging among humans is influenced by the mental, social, biological and physical environment, and can influence behaviour, which in turn has consequences for the ecosystems that life depends on.

The term 'languaging' is used in ecolinguistics for this ecologically embedded linguistic interaction (Steffensen 2009; Cowley 2014, 2018; Steffensen & Fill 2014; Steffensen & Cowley 2021). Steffensen (2011: 203) writes that 'when languaging, human beings create a meshwork of bio-socio-ecological relations'. Protassova (2012: 214) describes how 'all linguistic activity is languaging. As the manner of operating in a consensual domain, it serves to coordinate human behaviour in everyday life. It represents the integrated action of thinking, making sense, verbal structuring, and adapting to the world of experiences'. The term 'languaging' is a deliberate use of a verb for something which is usually referred to as a noun, 'language', in order to draw attention to how it exists only within interaction, rather than existing separately in the minds of speakers or as a reified 'thing' such as 'English' or 'Chinese'.

Clearly, the coordination of human behaviour is central to leadership and the concept of languaging helps capture the processes of leadership as it happens in the world. Since languaging influences and is part of the ecological systems that life depends on, languaging is of central concern not just for leadership, but ethical leadership.

Ecosophy

What unites ecolinguistics and ethical leadership is the concept of 'ecosophy'. The term originated with Félix Guattari (see Guattari 2014) and Arne Næss (see Naess 1995). While Guattari's conception of ecosophy as a link between minds, social structures and the environment is highly relevant to ecolinguistics and languaging, it tends to be Næss's (1995: 8) more practical definition that is used by ecolinguists:

> By an ecosophy I mean a philosophy of ecological harmony ... openly normative, it contains both norms, rules, postulates, value priority announcements and hypotheses concerning the state of affairs ... The details of an ecosophy will show many variations due to significant differences concerning not only 'facts' of pollution, resources, population, etc., but also value priorities.

Whether consciously or unconsciously, an ecosophy is what guides the practice of ecolinguists. While ecolinguists are more or less explicit about their ecosophy in their writing, all are using a philosophical framework that considers humans, other species and the physical environment when they are making judgements about linguistic issues. The concept of ecosophy is equally applicable to ethical leaders, who use their ecosophy to critically analyse the stories that shape their institution and society and use language in ways that align with their ecosophy in the search for new stories to live by.

The following is an example of an explicit ecosophy, a shortened version of Stibbe (2021a: 14), which is also the ecosophy that is informing this chapter:

Ecosophy in one word: *Living!*

Explanation

- **Valuing living:** The exclamation mark in *Living!* is normative, indicating 'to be valued / celebrated / respected / affirmed', and it applies to all species that are living.

- **Now and the future:** *Living!* includes the ability to live with high well-being in the present, the near future and for future generations.
- **Environmental limits:** *Living!* into the future requires massive overall reduction of consumption and transformation of practices in all sectors to keep within environmental limits.
- **Social justice:** All must have the means to live with high well-being even as total consumption is reduced. This necessitates redistribution of resources from over-consumers to under-consumers.
- **Deep adaptation:** Environmental changes that make the Earth less hospitable for life are already locked in, and ways to allow *Living!* as far as possible in the declining conditions of the world must be found.

An ecosophy is a complex ethical framework in the mind of an analyst or leader that changes over time as they are exposed to ideas and experience, and so can only be partially captured in a snapshot like this.

Ecosophy relies on reflection. Cohen and Qualters (2007: 110) call for 'leadership that values reflective ethical inquiry as an ongoing practice for empowering ethical awareness, investigation and responding'. Despite the inability to fix an ecosophy in time, making an ecosophy explicit demonstrates the criteria that ecolinguists and ethical leaders are using when making ethical judgements about communication practices. There cannot, of course, be a 'neutral' position beyond an ecosophy when dealing with issues of the injustice and the ability of the earth to support life. As Desmond Tutu once said:

> If you are neutral in situations of injustice, you have chosen the side of the oppressor. If an elephant has its foot on the tail of a mouse and you say that you are neutral, the mouse will not appreciate your neutrality. (Tutu in Brown 1984: 19)

Treating racist discourse or discourse which promotes harm to the natural world neutrally, by pointing out interesting linguistic features without any kind of explicit or implied judgement would be a highly political act in itself: complicity in current unequal and environmentally destructive social arrangements. For both ecolinguists and ethical leaders, aligning their action with their ecosophy is a way to display integrity. According to Liu (2017: 265), 'Integrity refers to the extent to which leaders act consistently in line with their core values and is strongly associated with leadership authenticity'.

Of course, ethical leaders often work not individually, but as part of a wider team. There is a balance between the leader imposing their own ecosophy and demanding others work towards it, with conversation to discover shared values that everyone is motivated to work towards together. The problem is that in industrial societies the prevailing values often disregard the interest of other species and the ecosystems that support life, so there is a danger that a shared ecosophy will be weakened down to the lowest common denominator. Cels (2017: 762) represents an approach which is both top-down in imposing an ecosophy and dialogic:

> Ethical leaders ... articulate the values and norms that others should be concerned about and orchestrate a conversation about these norms and values with and between the people whose efforts are vital to achieving moral and practical objectives.

A potential way forward is for leaders to work with the team to advance a subset of their own personal ecosophy that is shared by the whole team, while gently encouraging the team to move in the direction of a stronger joint ecosophy. An example would be if the leader has an ecosophy of 'no exploitation of animals for products' while the team has a weaker ecosophy, then they could start working together on an ecosophy of 'reducing the exploitation of animals for products' that would be compatible for all. This could eventually be strengthened as the team's ecosophy evolves. In general, any team will be made up of individuals who have their own ecosophy, and leaders (whether appointed or impromptu leaders) can work with elements that are shared across the team while also trying to influence the team to take on a stronger ecosophy (i.e. one with more care for other people, other species and the ecosystems that life depends on). The result is a community of practice with inclusive, engaged participation, but where ethical values are not compromised by the lowest common denominator.

The search for new stories to live by

This chapter uses an approach to ecolinguistics first described in Stibbe (2015) and developed further in Stibbe (2017, 2018, 2019, 2020, 2021a, 2021b). The approach can be summarized as conducting linguistic analysis of texts that are prevalent in a culture to reveal the 'stories we live by', judging those stories using an ecosophy, resisting stories that oppose that ecosophy, and searching for 'new stories to live by' that resonate and promote the ecosophy. The term 'stories' here refers to cognitive structures in the minds of individuals which influence how they think, talk and act. The 'stories we live by' are stories that are spread widely across a particular culture in a process that van Dijk (2009: 19) calls 'social cognition'.

To give an example: If an analyst had an ecosophy which saw animals as beings with intrinsic value, then they would analyse prevailing cultural texts to reveal the ways that they represent animals and judge them as destructive if they represent animals as resources who are worthless in their own right (Stibbe 2012). Of most interest are not individual texts but larger patterns that run across numerous texts, e.g. the discourse of the animal product industries (Glenn 2004; Arcari 2017). Where these larger patterns are common within the analyst's culture they can consider them 'stories we live by', and the task is to move away from destructive stories and search for 'new stories to live by'. In this case, the analyst may search cultures around the world for inspirational forms of language which convey messages that align with their ecosophy, i.e. messages that confirm the intrinsic value of animals.

Ethical leadership

The previous sections described an ecolinguist as an engaged inquirer who actively seeks to change the society and culture they are part of, based on linguistic theory and an ethical framework that includes consideration of other people, other species and the physical environment. This activity has certain parallels to ethical leadership: the ethical base for action, the critique of current social arrangements, and the intention to influence and change the worldview and actions of others. Two questions arise. First, can the practice of ecolinguistics be considered as a form of ethical leadership in its own right? If so, can a form of ecolinguistics be usefully applied not only by academic linguists but by leaders of all kinds, from those leading their company and community to those leading their society? The answers to these questions depend, of course, on how 'ethical leadership' is defined and characterized. This section examines some concepts of ethical leadership from the business literature that could potentially be rethought along ecolinguistic lines to serve wider interests than the predominant goals of organizational business.

The most frequently cited theory of ethical leadership is Brown and colleagues (2005: 120) which characterizes ethical leadership as follows:

> Ethical leaders are models of ethical conduct who become the targets of identification and emulation for followers. For leaders to be perceived as ethical leaders and to influence ethics-related outcomes, they must be perceived as attractive, credible, and legitimate. They do this by engaging in behaviour that

is seen as normatively appropriate (e.g., openness and honesty) and motivated by altruism (e.g., treating employees fairly and considerately). Ethical leaders must also gain followers' attention to the ethics message by engaging in explicit ethics-related communication and by using reinforcement to support the ethics message.

The emphasis on communication that reinforces ethical messages aligns with ecolinguistics since a central task of ecolinguistics consists of finding forms of language which promote a particular ethical framework (ecosophy). Brown and colleagues call for 'explicit' ethics-related communication but conveying ethical values does not need to be done explicitly in terms of stating what is right, wrong, moral or immoral. Ecolinguistics shows how texts convey ethical values more subtly, between the lines, often being more effective for being implicit (Stibbe 2021a).

A problematic aspect of Brown and colleagues' characterization of ethical leadership is the passive nature of the ethical framework, which rests only on what is 'seen as normatively appropriate' by society. In industrial societies, there are many things that may be seen as 'normatively appropriate' that are causing suffering and harm to current and future generations such as factory farming, exploitation of workers in developing countries, or the single-minded pursuit of profit and economic growth. The ecosophy of an ecolinguist or ethical leader will go far further than the prevailing norms of an unequal and unsustainable industrial society. This passivity has been questioned by Kaptein (2019: 1136), who argues that ethical leadership does not just follow ethics but also leads it:

> Contrary to Brown et al.'s (2005) suggestion, an ethical leader is not only a moral person and a moral manager who demonstrates normatively appropriate behaviour and follows the current ethical norms. An ethical leader is also a moral entrepreneur who creates new ethical norms [...] [and] contributes to the development of both society and the trust of stakeholders.

The term 'moral entrepreneur' was originally coined by Howard Becker to refer negatively to self-righteous moral crusaders as well as more positively to those who have a genuine altruistic and humanitarian ethical framework and take action to change the prevailing ethics of the society they live within in line with that framework. Becker (1995: 169) gives the example that '[a]bolitionists were not simply trying to prevent slave owners from doing the wrong thing, they were trying to help slaves to achieve a better life'. A more modern example is the international campaign to ban landmines, which Faulkner (2007) describes as successful due to moral entrepreneurs. In their attempt to challenge prevailing cultural stories about what is good, bad, moral, immoral, ethical and unethical on the basis of a deeply held ecosophy, ecolinguists and ethical leaders could be considered moral entrepreneurs in this sense.

While Brown and colleagues' vision was of influencing direct followers to change their behaviour, the issues that ecolinguistics faces are global issues of vast cultural and spatial extent and require widespread social change. As Visser and Courtice (2011: 28) point out, 'sustainability leadership … is geared towards bringing about profound change, whether in our political and economic systems, our business models and practices, or in the broad social contract with stakeholders and society'. Visser and Courtice use the term 'sustainability leadership' rather than 'ethical leadership', although what they mean is very much the same thing: 'A sustainability leader is someone who inspires and supports action towards a better world' (Visser & Courtice 2011: 27).

The term 'sustainability leadership' has the disadvantage of being associated with the dominant sustainable development discourse, as used by the United Nations, which has been accused of being anthropocentric and failing to challenge prevailing ideologies of economic growth (Hickel 2017). The term 'ethical leader' is more general, which has the positive aspect of potentially including anyone who has an influence on others. It is vital, of course, that consideration of other species and the ecosystems that life depends on is wrapped up into the definition of 'ethical'. An ethical system which considered only the human would, after all, be incomplete since any desired state for humanity depends entirely on the ability of the planet to support life into the future.

Visser and Courtice's (2011: 29) model of sustainability leadership consists of three aspects. First, the context of leadership which includes the ecological, political, economic and organizational context. Secondly, the traits of an individual leader, which include caring, morally driven, holistic thinker and altruistic. Thirdly, leadership actions, which include informed decisions, performance accountability and stakeholder transparency. It therefore combines trait-based leadership (Zaccaro 2007) with situational theories of leadership (Blanchard et al. 1993). From an ecolinguistic perspective, the extension of context beyond the immediate institutional situation to take account of the social and ecological context is important. However, what is missing is a sense of the leader intervening in the social structures around them to create change. Visser and Courtice's model is static and does not address the moment-by-moment discursive struggle to define and re-define reality that leaders necessarily play a role in through their language. As Heizmann and Liu (2018: 41) point out:

Much of this strand of the sustainability leadership literature resonates with competency-based approaches to leadership development and is focused on distilling surface-level and generalised behavioural patterns that effective sustainability leaders ought to develop. In doing so, sustainability leadership is not only divorced from the context of the diverse meaning-making frameworks in which it is embedded [...] but it is also too often constructed through the logic of an anthropocentric worldview.

That's not to say that competency-based approaches are entirely irrelevant to ecolinguistics since it would be possible to define competencies in critical language awareness of the stories that industrial civilization is based on, ethical reflection, and the ability to use language in innovate ways that can contribute to new stories to live by. However, a more dynamic approach is necessary to capture the world-building aspects of languaging.

One of the most useful dynamic characterizations of leadership is that of Smircich and Morgan (1982: 258):

> Leadership is realised in the process whereby one or more individuals succeeds in attempting to frame and define the reality of others [...], They emerge as leaders because of their role in framing experience in a way that provides a viable basis for action, e.g., by mobilising meaning, articulating and defining what has previously remained implicit or unsaid, by inventing images and meanings that provide a focus for new attention, and by consolidating, confronting, or changing prevailing wisdom.

The process described by Smircich and Morgan parallels ecolinguistics by linking languaging (in their words *framing, defining, articulating* and *mobilising meaning*), with revealing the stories we live by (which they describe as *prevailing wisdom* that has *previously remained implicit*), *confronting* and *changing* those stories, and acting in ways which provide new stories to live by (*a focus for new attention*). Drath and Palus (1994: 4) present a similar view of leadership as primarily based in meaning and influencing underlying stories about the world (which they call 'world versions'):

> Meaning can be thought of as a cognitive and emotional framework (an internal structure of ideas and feelings) that allows a person to know (in the sense of understand) some world version (a representation of the way things are and the way they ought to be) and that places the person in relation to this world version. Given this way of thinking about meaning, meaning-making then consists of the creation, nurturance, and evolution (or revolution) of these cognitive and emotional frameworks. When the making of such frameworks happens in a community of practice ... then we can say that leadership is happening.

Within these models, leadership is an active process, something which emerges within interaction as individuals inspire others to rethink the world around them. This approach to leadership parallels the more dynamic approach to language in ecolinguistics.

The move from 'language' to 'languaging' could be mirrored in a move from 'a leader' to 'leadering'. The term 'leadering' emphasizes that the phenomenon of being a leader exists in real time in real interaction rather than being a fixed property of a person – 'leadership is happening' as Drath and Palus put it above, rather than 'someone is a leader'. While 'leadering' is a useful term for the discussion here, the term 'way-making' may be more suitable to capture both the active process of leadering and the way it opens up new paths to the future through discovering new stories to live by. As Heizmann and Liu (2018: 41) point out, 'an emerging body of critical leadership studies is highlighting the need to conceive of leadership in more relational, practice-based and dialogic terms'. The dialogic is, of course, central to an ecolinguistic approach. However, while both Drath and Palua and Smircich and Morgan's models are dynamic and rooted in languaging, they lack an ethical dimension.

One theory of leadership that is particularly up-front about ethics is *Transformative Leadership*. This theory is usually articulated for educational settings but could be applied more broadly. Carolyn Shields describes how the 'notions of promise, liberation, hope, empowerment, activism, risk, social justice, courage, or revolution' are at the heart of transformative leadership (Shields 2010: 559). For Shields (2010: 562), transformative leadership consists of 'a combination of both critique and promise; attempts to effect both deep and equitable changes; deconstruction and reconstruction of the knowledge frameworks that generate inequity; acknowledgment of power and privilege'. The emphasis on 'the socially constructed nature of society' (Shields 2010: 571) and the approach of deconstructing knowledge frameworks and reconstructing new ones, parallels ecolinguistics and its aim to reveal the stories we live by and search for new stories to live by. Like most critical theory, however, the ethical focus is primarily on power inequality between human groups, rather than a wider consideration of how power influences the ecosystems that life depends on. It is possible to take the deconstructive and reconstructive focus of Transformational Leadership, expand it beyond the educational realm and beyond the human-only-world, to create the kind of engaged and active leadership that could address the social structures at the heart of an unsustainable society.

So far, this chapter has been building up a picture of ethical leaders as critically engaged with the texts, discourse and stories that their selves, organizations and societies are built on, questioning them according to their own personal ecosophy and conveying new stories to live by. There is one problem with this though, in that it represents the leader as acting individually rather than within an institutional context. It sees the ethical leader as a solo hero. Heizmann and Liu (2018: 41) point out that an overemphasis on individual agency can 'obscure the ways in which individuals are constituted as subjects through organisational and institutional discourses, which legitimise certain truth claims and organisational practices of sustainability leadership'. These broader discourses can constrain leaders to serve the interests of a narrow set of stakeholders rather than the broader community of life. Heizmann and Liu (2018: 54) therefore describe how '[o]n an individual level, leadership-as-practice development involves building learners' critical, self-reflexive capacities to challenge underlying beliefs that shape, and often constrain, their situated contexts (e.g., the primacy of business rationalities, individualist notions of leadership)'. In terms of languaging, this involves awareness of the institutional constraints to inspirational forms of language that can build new stories to live by. Giddens' (1991) model of *structuration* is useful here, as all leaders will have some agency to use language creatively in ways that accord with their ecosophy, while having institutional constraints which can punish them for stepping out of line or force them out of the organization completely if they go too far. The ideal compromise is perhaps Deborah Meyerson's (2001) model of the 'tempered radical' – a leader who uses their agency to push the boundaries of acceptable discourse but not so far that they find themselves forced out of their position and lose the power to contribute to change entirely. By extending boundaries and visibly getting away with it, leaders can move those boundaries permanently, opening up new paths for others in the process.

Communicative modes

The discussion so far in this chapter has focused on languaging as a way of shifting the stories we live by, but there are other communicative modes beyond language which play an important role in constructing social reality. Liu (2017: 263) writes:

> [W]hile ethical leadership in mainstream theorising is assumed to be a cognitive exercise, leaders' bodies in fact play a significant role in the social construction of ethical leadership. Their bodies (both their exposure and concealment) become particularly potent when leaders are depicted via the interplay between visual and verbal modes in the media.

If ethical leadership is a performance, then the bodies of the performer also play a role: gendered bodies, old or young bodies, muscular bodies, bodies clothed in particular ways, bodies close or distant, bodies displaying jewellery, and bodies performing particular gestures and postures. Gardner writes that '[t]he ultimate impact of the leader depends most significantly on the particular story that he or she relates or embodies, and the reception to that story on the part of audiences' (in Mead 2014: 2). Liu (2017: 273) makes the interesting point:

> As disembodied patriarchs, close-up and low-angle photographs of the CEOs cropped at the head and shoulders inspired a sense of awe and power. Their bodies were cloaked in dark business suits that blended seamlessly into dark backgrounds and accentuated their image as disembodied 'heads'.

Liu also describes how representations of female leaders, non-white leaders, or both, frequently emphasize their full bodies rather than just their heads. The non-display of the body is, therefore, meaningful in itself, and can reinforce binaries of leadership as rationalist control rather than an embodied belonging in the world.

The more general point here is that it would be artificial to separate embodied communication from words, or words from the diagrams, charts, images and photographs which accompany them in print or PowerPoint presentations. Ecolinguistics must necessarily go beyond language to achieve its goals, and ethical leadership will need embodied awareness and awareness of visual and other semiotic modes in addition to language.

An ecolinguistic approach to ethical leadership

Essentialist theories of ethical leadership see an 'ethical leader' as a particular kind of person – someone distinct from others through traits such as 'integrity and trustworthiness [...] high power inhibition, high moral reasoning levels, internal locus of control, low Machiavellianism, agreeableness, conscientiousness, and social responsibility' (Liu 2017: 256). This neo-Aristotelian focus on virtues (Meyer et al. 2019) has the danger of limiting ethical leaders to a small group of exceptional individuals and creating unrealistic expectations (Cullen 2020: 1). There was shock and surprise, for instance, when Aung San Suu Kyi started acting in ways which did not align with the 'ethical leader' identity that had been imposed on her (Beech 2017). And if all there was to ethical leadership was an essentialist identity then linguistics would have little relevance.

Much more relevant for ecolinguistics are postmodern theories which see identity as 'fluid, fragmentary, contingent, and, crucially, constituted in discourse' (Benwell & Stokoe 2006: 17). Discursive theories see identity as existing only in the outer levels of performance within a discursively constrained context rather than the inner levels of being a particular kind of person. As Cullen (2020: 1) describes, 'leadership is "done" by imperfect human beings who try to avoid violating their own ethical standards while at the same time navigating the realities of social and organizational life'. The advantage of seeing leadership that is something that is 'done' or 'performed' is that it can be done by anyone, in any situation, not just an elite group of virtuous people or a set of people who have been allotted to particular leadership roles by society. As Mead (2014: 41) puts it, 'leadership is a universal facet of human interaction in which we all participate from time to time'. He calls for 'Narrative Leadership', which he defines as 'the conscious use of stories and storytelling to make meaning with and for other people' (p. 94).

By 'story', Mead primarily means narrative, but it could equally be 'story' in the more general ecolinguistic sense of a cognitive structure which influences how individuals or cultural groups think, talk and act. And 'storytelling' could equally be the use of linguistic features that convey these cognitive structures. Ecolinguistics can provide a wealth of understanding of how linguistic features convey underlying stories which leaders can use to shape their own communicative patters and convey stories that align with their ecosophy.

This chapter is converging on a characterization ethical leadership built from a combination of ecolinguistic theory and ethical leadership theory. Ethical leadership can be considered a performance, through language and other symbolic modes, where an individual attempts to resist the destructive stories that a group of people live by and reshape the reality of the group through providing new beneficial stories to live by. It is a real-time process of 'leadering' (performing the identity of a leader) through 'languaging' (interaction through words and other modes), where what is considered 'beneficial' or 'destructive' is relative to the individual's ecosophy.

An example

Alexander (2009: 113) gives an example of this form of leadership in his analysis of a lecture given by the Indian scholar and environmental activist Vandana Shiva. He notes how 'Shiva critically delineates how the myths associated with neo-liberal projects and "solutions" are being formulated' and resists these myths (or stories) through showing the harm that they cause. In the next step, Shiva provides 'counter-concepts, alternative metaphors and a different view of the world' (p. 114), or, in ecolinguistics terms, new stories to live by. An example that Alexander gives is as follows: 'Shiva re-invigorates [...] devalued notions like smallness. "Small farmers" is a positively loaded, affirmative term as used by Shiva. Shiva rewrites and re-iterates a counter-current to structural metaphorical thought, namely: SMALL IS GOOD (and by implication LARGE IS BAD)' (Alexander 2009: 124). In this way, Shiva is using language activity in ways that convey a new story about the world, one where, unlike dominant stories, smallness is valued.

Shiva's explicit calling into question of the stories that underlie industrial civilization is evident in a more recent interview with the BBC. In the interview, Shiva (2021) states:

> Colonialism and industrialism have destroyed the Earth and indigenous cultures through four false assumptions. First, that we are separate from nature and not a part of nature. Second, that nature is dead matter, mere raw material for industrial exploitation. Third, that indigenous cultures are inferior and primitive, and need to be 'civilised' through civilising missions of permanent colonization. Fourth, that nature and cultures need improvement through manipulation and external inputs.

Here she uses the term 'assumption' in a similar way to the 'story' of ecolinguistics, and at other times she uses the term 'myth'. Shiva makes the new stories to live by (which are, in fact, ancient ones) explicit in the following statement:

> I evolved the concept of Earth Democracy on the basis of my philosophy and practice that we are part of the Earth, and human freedom and human wellbeing depends on other species. We are not superior to other species, we are inter-beings. Anthropocentrism is a violent construct. Earth Democracy allows us to shift from economies and cultures that kill and democracies that are dead to living economies, living democracies, living cultures of the Earth, sharing her abundance, respecting her limits. (Shiva 2021)

In this statement Shiva explicitly describes her ecosophy, and the new stories that she considers beneficial, including stories of environmental limits, sharing, democracy and culture rooted in the earth. In addition to this, throughout her interview, Shiva uses language features which convey these stories, for example:

> Yesterday, women from my region in the Himalayas gathered at Navdanya for a millet festival. The Green Revolution [that revolutionised India's farm

production in the 1960s–70s] named them 'backward' and 'primitive' grains. But they [yield] 10 times more nutrition using 10 times less water. Members of Navdanya were calling me during lockdown to say that the Gardens of Hope we started provided food for their families and communities in spite of lockdown. Food and culture are the currency of life. And while we are overwhelmed by disease and death, a living food culture can show the light to the path of life. For me, food sovereignty is sovereignty over your life, livelihood and health. We are interconnected, therefore food sovereignty is an ecological process of co-creation with other lifeforms. (Shiva 2021)

In this extract, Shiva denounces the way that the technocratic Green Revolution frames traditional agriculture as 'backward' and 'primitive'. She resists the framing by pointing out how efficient traditional agriculture is. Shiva then applies an alternative framing of 'life' to traditional food culture, in the metaphors *food is the currency of life* and *a path to life*, and in the phrase *a living food culture*. This gives enormous positivity to traditional food practices by representing them as literally vital. Shiva also performs an *ecocultural identity* (Stibbe 2020) through the inclusive pronoun 'we' in 'we are interconnected', which includes both humans and 'other lifeforms', and by placing both humans and other lifeforms as the agent of a process of 'co-creation'. In this way, Shiva challenges dominant stories and uses linguistic features in ways that convey stories of sharing and interconnection that resonate with her ecosophy.

This example, then, is a moment of leading through languaging, where Shiva uses language in ways which could potentially shift the audience's views of reality. The audience in this case is distributed spatially and temporally – they receive the words when they listen to interview. Whether or not it is an *effective* performance of ethical leadership depends on the impact it has on readers. And whether it can be considered a *beneficial* performance of ethical leadership depends on whether the stories that are being conveyed align with the ecosophy of the analyst. According to the ecosophy described above (*Living!*), this is a form of beneficial ethical leadership because it values all humans and all species and works towards their continued living into the future through sustainable food production.

Conclusion

The apparatus of ecolinguistics, including the ongoing development of an ecosophy to judge stories against, active critical analysis of the texts which shape society to reveal the stories we live by, and promotion of new stories to live by, are tools that can be used to perform ethical leadership. This could be in one-to-many situations such as the example discussed above of Shiva, or in more intimate communication one-to-one or within a group of people who are working together. Ethical leadership could be performed by someone who has an official leadership role, or by the most junior member of a team who calls out damaging stories and the linguistic features which convey them and inspires others to rethink reality along the lines of new stories to live by. Everyone, whatever level they are in society, is constrained in their expression by the structures of that society, so a key aspect of ethical leadership is understanding those constraints and pushing boundaries (gently) to contribute to a discursive shift that weakens the constraints and opens up paths to new forms of expression.

Ecolinguists themselves may not perceive themselves as performing ethical leadership through their professional practice. However, ecolinguistics research and outreach activities have been shown to have an impact on how others perceive the world around them and act in their personal and professional lives (Roccia 2020; Roccia & Iubini-Hampton 2021). Ecolinguists can have an impact on their students, on the teachers they lead professional development sessions for, on the executives of corporations that they run workshops for, on NGOs they work with in creating campaigns, on the local communities that they cooperate with, and publishers, counsellors, tourist guides, poets, creative writers and others who come across their work indirectly (Roccia 2020; Stibbe 2021c). If ecolinguists see themselves as performing ethical leadership through their work and draw from theories of ethical leadership, languaging and leading to inform their practice, then the discipline of ecolinguistics could become even more engaged and make an even greater difference to the world.

For ecolinguistics to play a role in the development of ethical leadership it is necessary to conduct future research which investigates leadership performance of all kinds to (a) gain a deeper understanding of the detailed linguistic techniques that individuals use to shape the reality of others in line with their ecosophy; (b) gain a deeper understanding of how the ecosophy of an individual interacts with the ecosophies of others within a group who are working together towards a common goal, and (c) to understand different kinds of discursive constraints within institutions and ways of overcoming those constraints to create lasting change in the kind of discourse that is acceptable. Also of vital importance is research into the effectiveness of leadership communication. It is a necessary condition of ethical leadership that words are used in ways that convey stories that align with the individual's ecosophy. However, that is not sufficient, since those stories must also be persuasive to the audience. Audience response research, therefore, is also necessary.

The understandings gained through this kind of further research could be infused in education of all kinds from primary to PhD level, in workplace professional development, and in the education of ecolinguists themselves. The pressing and urgent reason for doing this is that industrial civilization is unsustainable and its future cannot be left in the hands of a few individuals who society has designated as 'leaders'. Instead, we need individuals at all levels to question the stories that shape their self, workplace, community and society, according to an ecosophy which considers not only humans but also other species and the physical environment. We need those individuals to contribute to the search for new stories to live by that can build an ecological civilization that safeguards the ecosystems that all life depends on. In other words, in the wake of Covid as we reinvent society we need everyone to perform ethical leadership in all the situations that they find themselves in, and ecolinguistics can provide tools to contribute to that.

References

Alexander, R. (2009). *Framing Discourse on the Environment: A Critical Discourse Approach*. New York: Routledge.

Arcari, P. (2017). 'Normalised, human-centric discourses of meat and animals in climate change, sustainability and food security literature'. *Agriculture and Human Values*, 34(1): 69–86.

Baker, P. C. (2020). '"We can't go back to normal": How will coronavirus change the world?' *The Guardian*, 31 March.

Becker, H. (1995). 'Moral entrepreneurs: The creation and enforcement of deviant categories'. In N.J. Herman (Ed.), *Deviance: A Symbolic Interactionist Approach*, 169–178. Boston: Rowman & Littlefield.

Beech, H. (2017). 'What happened to Myanmar's human-rights icon?' [online]. *The New Yorker*. Available from: https://www.newyorker.com/magazine/2017/10/02/what-happened-to-myanmars-human-rights-icon. Accessed 8 January 2022.

Benwell, B., & Stokoe, E. (2006). *Discourse and Identity*. Edinburgh: Edinburgh University Press.

Blanchard, K. H., Zigarmi, D., & Nelson, R.B. (1993). 'Situational leadership after 25 years: A retrospective'. *Journal of Leadership Studies*, 1(1): 21–36.

Brown, M. E., Treviño, L.K., & Harrison, D.A. (2005). 'Ethical leadership: A social learning perspective for construct development and testing'. *Organizational Behavior and Human Decision Processes*, 97(2): 117–34.

Brown, R. M. (1984). *Unexpected News: Reading the Bible with Third World Eyes*. Philadelphia: Westminster John Knox Press.

Cels, S. (2017). 'Saying sorry: Ethical leadership and the act of public apology'. *The Leadership Quarterly*, 28(6): 759–79.

Chen, S. (2016). 'Language and ecology: A content analysis of ecolinguistics as an emerging research field'. *Ampersand*, 3: 108–16.

Cohen, P., & Qualters, D. M. (2007). 'Ethical leadership: The AIR model empowers moral agency'. *Journal of Human Values*, 13(2): 107–17.

Cowley, S. J. (2014). 'Bio-ecology and language: A necessary unity'. *Language Sciences*, 41: 60–70.

Cowley, S. J. (2018). 'Life and language: Is meaning biosemiotic?' *Language Sciences*, 67: 46–58.

Cullen, J. G. (2020). 'Moral recovery and ethical leadership'. *Journal of Business Ethics*, 175: 458–97.

Drath, W., & Palus, C. (1994). *Making Common Sense: Leadership as Meaning-making in a Community of Practice*. Greensboro, NC: Center for Creative Leadership.

Faulkner, F. (2007). *Moral Entrepreneurs and the Campaign to Ban Landmines*. Amsterdam: Rodopi.

Giddens, A. (1991). *Modernity and Self-identity: Self and Society in the Late Modern Age*. Redwood: Stanford University Press.

Glenn, C. B. (2004). 'Constructing consumables and consent: A critical analysis of factory farm industry discourse'. *Journal of Communication Inquiry*, 28(1): 63–81.

Guattari, F. (2014). *The Three Ecologies*. London: Bloomsbury Academic.

Heizmann, H., & Liu, H. (2018). 'Becoming green, becoming leaders: Identity narratives in sustainability leadership development'. *Management Learning*, 49(1): 40–58.

Hickel, J. (2017). Five reasons to think twice about the UN's Sustainable Development Goals [online]. Available from: http://blogs.lse.ac.uk/southasia/2015/09/23/five-reasons-to-think-twice-about-the-uns-sustainable-development-goals/.

Hollis, D. (2020). The rush to return to normal [online]. *Instagram post*. Available from: https://www.instagram.com/p/B-J_3PPnFW5/?hl=en. Accessed 8 Jan 2022.

Kaptein, M. (2019). 'The moral entrepreneur: A new component of ethical leadership'. *Journal of Business Ethics*, 156(4): 1135–50.

Liu, H. (2017). 'The masculinisation of ethical leadership dis/embodiment'. *Journal of Business Ethics*, 144(2): 263–78.

Mead, G. (2014). *Telling the Story: The Heart and Soul of Successful Leadership*. Oxford: John Wiley & Sons.

Meyer, M., Sison, A. J. G., & Ferrero, I. (2019). 'How positive and neo-Aristotelian leadership can contribute to ethical leadership'. *Canadian Journal of Administrative Sciences / Revue Canadienne des Sciences de l'Administration*, 36(3): 390–403.

Meyerson, D. (2001). *Tempered Radicals: How People Use Difference to Inspire Change at Work*. Boston: Harvard Business School Press.

Naess, A. (1995). 'The shallow and the long range, deep ecology movement'. In A. Drengson & Y. Inoue (Eds.), *The Deep Ecology Movement: An Introductory Anthology*, 3–10. Berkeley: North Atlantic Books.

Protassova, E. (2012). 'Bilingual Finnish-Russian children describing pictures in their two languages'. In A. Kravchenko (Ed.), *Cognitive Dynamics in Linguistic Interactions*, 214–240. Newcastle upon Tyne: Cambridge Scholars Publishing.

Renee Taylor, S. (2020). 'We will not go back to normal'. [online]. *Instagram post*. Available from: https://www.instagram.com/p/B-fc3ejAlvd/. Accessed 8 Jan 2022.

Roccia, M. (2020). 'Changing lives and professional practice: A report on the impact of ecolinguistics'. *Language & Ecology*: 1–49.

Roccia, M., & Iubini-Hampton, J. (2021). 'The stories we live by and the stories we won't stand by: Measuring the impact of a free online course in ecolinguistics'. *Journal of World Languages*, 7(1): 58–79.

Roy, A. (2020). 'The pandemic is a portal'. *The Financial Times*, 3 April.

Shields, C. M. (2010). 'Transformative leadership: Working for equity in diverse contexts'. *Educational Administration Quarterly*, 46(4): 558–89.

Shiva, V. (2021). Vandana Shiva on why the food we eat matters [online]. Available from: https://www.bbc.com/travel/article/20210127-vandana-shiva-on-why-the-food-we-eat-matters. Accessed 8 Jan 2022.

Smircich, L., & Morgan, G. (1982). 'Leadership: The management of meaning'. *The Journal of Applied Behavioral Science*, 18(3): 257–73.

Steffensen, S. V. (2009). 'Language, languaging, and the Extended Mind Hypothesis'. *Pragmatics & Cognition*, 17(3): 677–97.

Steffensen, S. V. (2011). 'Beyond mind: An extended ecology of languaging'. In S.J. Cowley (Ed.), *Distributed Language*, 185–210. Amsterdam; Philadelphia: John Benjamins Pub. Co.

Steffensen, S. V., & Cowley, S. J. (2021). 'Thinking on behalf of the world: Radical embodied ecolinguistics'. In *The Routledge Handbook of Cognitive Linguistics*. London: Routledge.

Steffensen, S. V., & Fill, A. (2014). 'Ecolinguistics: The state of the art and future horizons'. *Language Sciences*, 41: 6–25.

Stibbe, A. (2012). *Animals Erased: Discourse, Ecology, and Reconnection with the Natural World*. Middletown, CT: Wesleyan University Press.

Stibbe, A. (2015). *Ecolinguistics: Language, Ecology and the Stories We Live by*. 1st ed. London: Routledge.

Stibbe, A. (2017). 'Critical discourse analysis and ecology: The search for new stories to live by'. In J. Richardson & J. Flowerdew (Eds.), *The Routledge Handbook of Critical Discourse Analysis*, 497–509. London: Routledge.

Stibbe, A. (2018). 'Positive discourse analysis: Re-thinking human ecological relationships'. In A. Fill, & H. Penz (Eds.), *The Routledge Handbook of Ecolinguistics*, 165–178. London: Routledge.

Stibbe, A. (2019). 'Education for sustainability and the search for new stories to live by'. In J. Armon, S. Scoffham & C. Armon (Eds.), *Prioritizing Sustainability Education: A Comprehensive Approach*, 233–43. London; New York: Routledge.

Stibbe, A. (2020). 'Towards a grammar of ecological identity'. In T. Milstein & Castro-Sotomayor (Eds.), *Routledge Handbook of Ecocultural Identity*, 416–430. Abingdon, Oxon; New York: Routledge.

Stibbe, A. (2021a). *Ecolinguistics: Language, Ecology and the Stories We Live By*, 2nd Edition. London: Routledge.

Stibbe, A. (2021b). 'Ecolinguistics as a transdisciplinary movement and a way of life'. In A. Burkette & T. Warhol (Eds.), *Crossing Borders, Making Connections: Interdisciplinarity in Linguistics*, 71–88. Boston: De Gruyter Mouton.

Stibbe, A. (2021c). *Ecolinguistics and Its Impact on People's Life and Work Practices*. Research Excellence Framework 2021 Impact Case Study.

van Dijk, T. (2009). *Society and Discourse: How Social Contexts Influence Text and Talk*. Cambridge: Cambridge University Press.

Visser, W., & Courtice, P. (2011). Sustainability leadership: Linking theory and practice. *SSRN Electronic Journal*.

Westen, D. (2011). 'What Happened to Obama?' *New York Times*, 6 August.

Zaccaro, S. J. (2007). 'Trait-based perspectives of leadership'. *American Psychologist*, 62(1): 6–16.

8

Landscape Sentience

Elizabeth Oriel, Deepta Sateesh and Amal Dissanayaka

Introduction

Stepping outside the lines of exclusive human language exceptionalism that contributes to extinction and extractive earth-based practices, how do we listen to the land? With Steffensen and Cowley's (2021) re-drawing of new inclusive linguistic lines, such that language and the living world are interdependent, this chapter poses multispecies case studies on listening to land, to place, along with ways that colonial vocabularies have shaped elephant ecology from modalities that do not listen to the land nor non-human inhabitants.

It is a fairly recent (in the last few hundred years) relational pattern that humans do not perceive themselves as belonging to the land but, instead, viewing the land as belonging to humans; this shift corresponds with a loss of conversation across land and people in industrialized cultures such that land is not regarded as a communicator. For systems theorists like Gregory Bateson, Humberto Maturana and Francisco Varela, ecosystems are understood as informational, as communicative, and as cognitive. 'Our cognitive process (the cognitive process of the observer) differs from the cognitive processes of other organisms only in the kinds of interactions into which we can enter, such as linguistic interactions, and not in the nature of the cognitive process itself' (Maturana & Varela 2012: 49). Bateson (2000) suggests how cognition and evolution are mirrored and interdependent, and here we extend this notion to land. Land too comprises a sphere of relationships, defined by their participation and interactions, that are physical, cognitive and communicative. The vocabularies of land, which are mere metaphors for many in modernist culture, hold diverse realities and practices for farmers, hunters, and ecosystem people (Guha & Gadgil 1995).

For inhabitants of Lesotho, a being's life, or *bophelo,* is conceived entangled with their multispecies community and is inextricably linked to the concept of well-being. The word *bophelo* means the individual, homestead, village, nation, religious realms and the earth, all at once. For *bophelo* to exist, it must reside in all spatio-temporal realities (Germond & Cochrane 2010). This word, that expresses an ontology of well-being as intricately connected across all scales, contrasts with the dominant worldview that draws distinct boundaries separating landscapes, humans, plants, elephants, water bodies, etc. This notion and lexicon of continuity across land and beings echoes Indigenous and some traditional/emergent approaches to earth/environment as living, sentient and as a communicator.

We explore here multiplicities in language, moving from and towards land, and the ways that words and their sensory perceptions shape engagement with landscape, in ways that degrade or support multispecies thriving. This kind of socio-ecological phenomena is part of co-generation that Ingold describes as correspondence, as the 'dynamic of lives going along with one another' (Ingold 2020: 9). Bringing this meshwork into the field of linguistics, Steffensen and Cowley (2021) present a form of distributed language in radical ecolinguistics that offers an embodied approach to the study of how human language contributes to bioecologies. Resilient lifeways within emplaced cultures generally orient around practices of close attentiveness and communication within a field of sentient beings and relations. Human–wildlife conflict is a symptom of lines of separation, loss of listening to the land and disregard for the intertwined world as *bophelo*. And those dwelling *with* land, farmers are positioned closest and best to hear the land speaking; these groups usually have marginal voices and consultative power in land designs.

In South Asia, the rapid global changes which left behind slow listening and observation has roots in colonial rule, which left landscapes as simplified and subjugated spaces. A challenging systemic repercussion of loss of landscape heterogeneity and sentience for farmers and wildlife has increased human–wildlife conflict. The conversations that many dwellers engaged with in shifting cultivation, seeking permission for fire, reciting poems to elephants, speaking a terrain-generated vocabulary rooted in specific material operations which were multi-directional. With the loss of *ancient dialogues and the emergence of universal monologues in colonial and extractive logics*, how can lands' voices be accessed to aid in thinking about land designs and practices, especially when sharing terrain with co-dwellers such as elephants?

The shapes and contours of land and weather are assemblages, complex meeting places that shape numerous relationships that, in turn, shape them, continually. Landscapes as speaking actors are often silenced by global histories and localized influences and histories that have broken terrestrial relationalities and accountabilities. Lands that host human–elephant conflicts are often degraded systems and spaces, with exhausted and over-chemically sprayed soils, with plant communities altered by overgrazing, fires, invasive species and lack of traditional cultivation patterns that maintained biodiversity.

Human–elephant conflict is a territorial issue, as elephants lose access to traditional terrain due to agriculture and development, with subsistence cultivation transforming into a sedentary economic enterprise across colonial and postcolonial times. Territories are altered, and farmers and elephants are in conflict over access to terrain and vegetation. Territory is a central feature of this conflict, and yet territories are rarely consulted in modernist approaches to land. A central question of this chapter is how land has been heard and articulated over time, and how land-based relationships are being cultivated or lost.

This ecolinguistics volume offers an opportunity to include lands' qualities, forms of communication that are most often ignored in planning policies and in managing human-wildlife relations. The natural world has languages which root into the larger relational patterns of the living world, such as movement, permeability, flux, and symbiosis. As Steffensen and Cowley write, 'language must be seen in terms of symbiosis, not symbols' (2021: 726); languaging co-generates across bioecological contexts.

We present research from Southern India and south-eastern Sri Lanka on how territory speaks and differentiates, through movements of water permeating and shaping landscapes, how territory is categorized and measured, with settlement often as a means of subjugations. We also present findings from interviews about land base relations and listening to land with farmers in the UK and US, two Indigenous tradition holders, and others. While the first two case studies reveal land as an actor in the polarized relations of humans and elephants, the interviews offer other perspectives from direct experience of land as sentient and voiced. Each case study was conducted through ethnography during the period 2018–21, learning with diverse actors, places, experiences and relationships. These contexts reveal qualities of places and experiences and how these communicate in human languages, interspecies dialogues, practices and poetry that involve/d care, and the colonial and postcolonial breaching of these deep relations. Including lands' voices in conservation and policy spheres and in diverse scholarship is an essential ingredient, we contend, in human–elephant thriving cohabitation. Ecolinguistics can offer guidance.

Vayal-nad, describing a monsoonal ground

Our first case is the *Vayal-nad* which is an undulating landscape, characteristic of mounds and swales, situated within an escarpment that stretches along the western land-sea region of India (see Figure 8.1). There are a multitude of material grounds (Ingold 2011) that are ecologically sensitive including the *sholas* (high slopes of forest-grassland complexes) (MoEF-GoI 2009), streams, subterranean material movements and water holding systems. This case study narrative is situated in a porous, damp, enlivened *ecotone* (Neimanis 2012); a world inhabited by diverse dwellers in multiple grounds. The proposition to consider is of *vayal-nad*, which translates as a 'place of low grounds', or swamps. This is a fluid place rich in vegetal, animal and material diversity that is home to monsoon rains that drench this terrain for over six months in a year. When it is not raining, the atmosphere is warm and sultry, and the atmosphere is moist in presences of mist, fog and dew.

Vayal-nad is home to communities (human and other-than-human) who follow rhythms of rain and movement of materials. These communities include tribal peoples and multitude terrestrial, subterranean, avian and arboreal beings (IUCN 2012; Raman 2018). Tribal peoples encounter other-than-human beings in their everyday lives, while fetching water, firewood, honey, fruits and berries, and while growing, harvesting and wandering through the terrain on foot. Correspondingly, these other-than-human beings saunter through paddy fields, bamboo thickets, vegetable patches, orchards, coconut and coffee plantations, and *vayals* to feed and access water.

Today, the region continues to be rich in cultural heritage and natural processes, a place held in temporal liminalities in which multitudes of tribal peoples dwell within densely vegetated undulations. In this landscape, inhabitants practice ancient methods of tending to plants, caring for the other-than-human, and nurturing the earth (Raman 2018). Human inhabitants, like other-than-human beings, were mobile, engaging in shifting cultivation practices called *punam* (Thurston & Rangachari 1909: 124–30). They moved through a complex world of relational practices making home in watery grounds, simultaneously attending to the environment. This kind of inhabitation is responsive; it is a lived experience.

Figure 8.1 *Vayal*, Human–Elephant 'conflict' area, village and forest edge, Muthanga area, Wayanad, 2018 (Image courtesy: Deepta Sateesh).

Vayal-nad was governed by local tribes (Logan 1887). After a number of revolts (Ravi n.d.) between the late 1700s and early 1800s, it was taken by the British Empire. By 1830, the region was surveyed and annexed into the Madras Presidency, placing the region in the hands of the British administration. This is *settlement*, a term for revenue-generating land and its management (Powell 1892). Settlement of the region, through mapping of the surface, its land uses, soil make-up, ownership and yield, divided land from water (on the surface), creating new economic frames for either protection or production of land. This separated its inhabitants as human (cultural) and non-human (natural). Through this act of spatialization, *vayal-nad* became *Wayanad*, with the map being used to administer the region.

Colonizing by 'corridors', defining habitat

Against the above pre-disciplinary narrative of *vayal-nad* is 'Wayanad', a *habitat* known by colonial surveying and recording the surface of the terrain depicted in maps. This territory of Wayanad is dominated by agriculture, while the western and northern fringes are forests, rocky outcrops and have a rich agro – and eco-biological diversity. Many of these are legally termed as 'Reserve

Forests', owned and managed by the Forest Department (Brandis 1883); they include large tracts of plantations primarily of teak, and smaller privately held *areca* nut, coconut, coffee and jackfruit plantations. Reserve Forests were surveyed and demarcated in a Forest Settlement map, and guarded from humans by officials (IFA 1878). Amidst these land uses and entwined into the 'forests' is a recent legal category of land use, the 'elephant corridor', within which elephants are seemingly designated to roam. This description is a result of understanding places from a distance – as viewed from above, and other-than-human beings viewed from afar – devoid of immersive engagement (Edney 1997).

Correspondences versus conflicts – drawing lines

Vayals are today seen as places of human–elephant conflict – a misreading or reduction of the *vayal* as a productive 'land' has caused the view that anything that hampers efficient production of crops is 'destructive' (Gadgil et al. 2011: 241). Trajectories of elephant wanderings continually cross designed boundaries between forest and village, revenue land and protected areas. In places the lines have been marked as physical constructions – walls, electric fences, deep trenches – to prevent elephants from moving along and deepening ancient lines of correspondences, of diverse ambulatory pathways, moving through diverse landscapes.

There is a more fundamental issue than the intervention of physical boundaries – the conflict is not so much that elephants wander into the fields and plantations, but that the 'habitat' of the elephant has been delegated to 'corridor' (Gadgil et al. 2011) and elephants are held to this territory permanently, their relations with landscape assumed to be associated only with 'corridors' (relations erased and place territorialized, these fixed meanings implicit in vocabulary). The 'corridor' is a notion imagined by humans who are distant from context, seeing the region from above, thus drawn to separate them from the everyday life of human inhabitants through universal regulatory mechanisms and laws, either categorizing them as destructive to the forest, or held to responsibilities of being stewards protecting the forest (FRA 2006). This is the world of conservation practice. On the 'other side' of the line are market-oriented productive fields. When production decrease is attributed to elephants 'raiding' these areas, it is a conflict. This is a man-made conflict created by the drawing of permanent lines to control and manage, where they may actually be temporally negotiated ones, through different sorts of time including diurnal, lunar, seasonal and annual rhythms.

Hardening habitat – fixing language through laws

The drawing of the corridor as a line in a map, like the line 'contains the river' (da Cunha 2018), attempts to contain the elephant and its movement. Elephant movement is used to define the limits of this corridor, without considering that both humans and elephants inhabit this low-lying dynamic terrain, negotiating each other's spatial appropriations across time. Traditionally, there may have been ways and means of co-existing, when there was a different understanding, perhaps not of seeing the 'other' but relating through kinship (Harvey 2019), as correspondence, care and co-operation, rather than competition. However, the 'corridor' designation delegates specific areas marked in a map as elephant habitat, and erases their ordinary temporal wanderings (beyond these areas) treating them as 'destructive' (Fairhead & Leach 2011). This short-term analysis serves economics, while ignoring the deep relations amongst sentient inhabitants, atmosphere and earth that continue to develop over long durées of following multitude rhythms, this understanding embedded in myths, oral stories and situated practices.

Fixed forms of representations hold space and time in the moment of surveying, a moment of dryness when there is no rain; the information depicted in this imagery is deemed true, and used to manage the landscape and its inhabitants. Interestingly, it is not possible to contain elephants within the designated forested areas through physical boundaries. Maps are visual representations of a moment in the past (Edney 1997), particularly of survey of land use and its productivity, constructing the notion of surface by settlement, and movement of water (geology) through 'cracks' or gaps in the layers of materials/soils. By embedding our imaginations in the processes of seeping and soaking, considering the terrain as alive, with waters oozing from the earth and suspended in the atmosphere, traditional *punam* cultivation practices can be better understood to operate through a seasonally negotiated gradients of wetness.

Through this watery imagination, the *vayals* may be described as dynamic shifting grounds (rather than conflict zones); this allows us to move away from problem–solution mode that tends to focus on policy and law as corrective measures, instituted by fixed forms of representation such as maps. This is quite different from customary law, based on ethical engagements of continual practices that perpetuate respectful relationships (Tobin 2013).

Vayal as an inclusive, responsive and participative ground

Elephants have been known to be gardeners (Campos-Arceiz & Blake 2011) – as they move through the terrain of the Nilgiris, they feed on bamboo, get intoxicated on ripe jackfruit, selectively feed on mango and banana plants (Baskaran & Desai 2013). What appears to be a messy affair, based on records of what they leave behind, is a threshold between death and birth, of seeds strewn in dung, of depressions made by their feet for rainwaters to soak and overflow. This way of seeing positions elephants and their everyday movements and practices, as initiators of new growth enriching earth rather than being 'destructive' (Fairhead & Leach 2011). Human inhabitants of these shared places understand their temporal rhythms of moving through the undulating wet earth-atmosphere ecotone, and consider them in their everyday practices, through redundancies of planting, and negotiating through nightwatches in *machans*, that is, elevated sheltered platform.

Figure 8.2 *Vayal*, ground of multiple practices and inhabitants, Muthanga area, Wayanad 2018 (Image courtesy: Deepta Sateesh).

Reimagining vocabularies as practices

Through the above reappropriation, the word *vayal-nad* holds a certain understanding in the human dweller's vocabulary and perhaps needs to be considered a verb. Morton calls this 'ambient poetics' that is significant in ecomemesis.[1] For him, this is an attempt to 'break out of the normative aesthetic frame, go beyond art' (Morton 2007: 31). Today, *vayal* is generally a local term for paddy fields; however, if one spends time in the forests and wetlands of this region, as do the inhabitants, all low-lying areas are referred to as *vayals*. This indicates a relational understanding rather than a 'land use' designation – that these swales are where water gathers, being wet most of the time. In order to grasp this significant yet simple practical understanding of wateriness, we draw from wet ontologies (Steinberg & Peters 2015) that privilege wateriness, a gradient of material conditions between least wet and most wet, here, held between the Ghats and the Deccan Plateau. These low-lying grounds are seamlessly joined with other grounds of different kinds of wetnesses, such as *kavu* (sacred grove/ medicinal garden/ shrine), *kadu* (wild dense vegetal growth/ forest/ grove/ thicket/ woods/ orchard), *thottam* (farm/ plantation/ orchard/ garden/ food forests) and so on. Each is an anchor for trajectories of movements of diverse dwellers, materials and processes (see Figure 8.2).

Within this wet framing, one can say that the vocabulary of terrain (in the situated tongues) includes other-than-human worlds. *Vayal* is not just paddy fields, nor the recent conversions into banana plantations; it is a place of gatherings of different kinds – for water to seep, soak and collect, where non-human inhabitants bathe and drink, forage on plants that situate themselves and grow near wet soils; wet soils that soak water and nutrients seep into, and humans who dwell along with these practices, attending to the changes through engaging with wetness – cultivating during the monsoon and winter (wettest seasons), while leaving fallow during the less wet times. This is an enlivened ground of corresponding in a world that is open to change, dwelling in an *open whole* (Kohn 2013). The *vayal* may be experienced as a place of temporal appropriations and engagement for both humans and elephants, amongst other sentient beings. Here, during the monsoon, paddy is planted, and post-monsoon, elephants wander into the fields as they favour milk sap from young paddy, while feeding on bamboo.

Ancient cultivation practices continue in some places inhabited by forest dwellers who have not been 'settled' by the Forest Rights Act, and although they dwell in less temporal ways, they continue to practice cultivation that shifts with the seasons, making place through experience (rather than making space as delineated in drawings). Elephants defy the corridor, moving through this wet ground of the Ghats and beyond, foraging on a multitude of foods, young paddy, bamboo, wetland grasses, wayfaring through waters, dense vegetation, and traversing hill slopes, continually moving, pausing only for nutrition and rest. The corridor does not consider the conditions of wetness in earth and atmosphere, nor of movements and rhythms of and through *vayal, kavu, kadu, thottam*, that defy the 'corridor'. While 'corridor' assumes a singular definition, the situated local vocabulary seems to be embedded in a linguistic register of temporal relations, processes that are enmeshed with and inclusive of material understandings.

Sri Lankan land-based rhetoric and practices that are eclipsed by vertical power structures

We now shift focus from the Indian *vayal-nads* to Sri Lanka. In the following, we trace land as a voice in ancient cultivations (*chena*) through the colonial period, and the transition for many small-scale farmers in the 1980s from subsistence towards economic cultivation. Among countries with free-ranging Asian elephants, Sri Lanka has the highest density of elephants and the third highest density of humans (Prakash et al. 2020). One elephant dies each day from the conflict making localities fraught with multispecies attempts at defending territories. Despite these tensions, farmers often say, 'this is elephant land', acknowledging their rights to territory and a land-based ethics of equalized access. We trace aspects of subsistence cultivation that emerge through languages that are verbal and somatic; historical practices are repositories of relational perspectives and practices to learn with/from in imagining a multispecies peaceful coexistence.

Chena cultivation

Chena is a Sinhalese term for subsistence practices of slash-and-burn cultivation that shifts and moves across time and space, mimicking animals' and plants' lifeways that work with seasonal and climatic rhythms. Crops were grown only in rainy seasons, and fields were shifted which regenerated soils. Traditional *chena* is rarely practised now as agrochemicals, and irrigation are the norm, and a loss of community-based methods leave many farmers working alone.

Chena was a socio-ecological tradition and dialogue across land and farmer, informed over millennia of observation and practice, and was shaped by topography, hydrology and species' inter-relationships. The lands' voices were interactive, and were actively listened to and spoken with.

The relationship between *chena* and wild animals was a mutually nurturing one. Farmers' management techniques promoted growth on their farms while negotiating with other species. Accordingly, the architecture of the *chena* land played a prominent role in human–elephant relations. Generally, *chena* cultivation was in a round shape and crops most likely to be accessed by wild animals were in the middle. Animal repellent crops such as chili and gingelly were on the edges. The main watch hut was sited in the middle while sub-watch huts were in the surroundings. Furthermore, *chena* is a collective practice of cultivation by groups of farmers (Irangani 2020). Crop protection methods were mostly targeted against elephant attacks. Most of the time, elephants enter abandoned *chena* land after the harvest which provides a good source of food. It was a kind of mutual understanding between the human and elephant.

Sinhalese folklore provides many clues to the persisting human–elephant relations in ancient Sri Lanka. The following folk poetry was recited by farmers in ancient Sri Lanka when they guarded their crops.

> Lassana himawathē māwē pesennē
> Duk dena ali ethun pannā harinnē
> Rekmena deviyan wele bath budinnē
> Duppathkama nisai mama pel rakinnē

> Beautiful paddy fields are ripening
> and it's the result of the hard work of the farmer.
> Farmers have to protect the cultivation from elephants and
> tusks usually during the whole night. Also, God's protection
> gives them food security.
> They believe they have to do this because of poverty.

Farmers did not kill wild animals. Conversely, the traditional farmer played the role of wild animal guardian. The farmer who practised fire-fallow cultivation warned the animals inhabiting the land before setting the blaze through singing a prayer. Beginning with three hoots the farmer calls upon the divine spirits protecting the land including the ancestors and all living beings inhabiting the land such as reptiles, worms, birds, and all living in sheaths, holes, pits, every living being from the tiniest ant to the biggest elephant, asking them to leave the land while seeking permission to set fire. While the lead farmer performs this prayer, other farmers walk around the land warding off any animals left there (Kahandagamage 1999).

Accordingly, the *chena* farmer played the role of forest guardian as well. The burning of *chena* fields was also a gradual process. First, the dried palms of the forest boundary were dumped into the inner *chena* area. Its perimeter was covered with fresh raw wet branches cut on the same day to limit the possibility of spreading the fire. The burning is not performed by any farmer but by the leader of the farming group or by the village *Anumethirala*.[2] It is not performed on windy days or even at midday under general weather conditions. These guardianship roles were communicative, speaking with and being informed by the forest, plants, animals and weather.

Irrigated cultivation and the Grand Civilization

The story of hydrology in Sri Lanka was a matter of reverence for rivers and waterways. People took an active role through tank creation in moistening the land for themselves, plants and other animals. This stewarding of water systems has been a form of dialogue across land, wetness and water and human inhabitants. The village tank-based irrigated cultivation is the most prominent and widespread agriculture activity in ancient Sri Lanka. This system is identified as *ellanga gammana* or Cascaded Tank-Village system which has been declared as one of the Globally Important Agricultural Heritage Systems (GIAHS) (Food and Agriculture Organization 2018). Permanent allocation of lands and forest for wildlife fuelled the harmony between humans and elephants (Rathnayake et al 2018). The system encompasses tanks along a gradient that catch sediment, and have other functions, while upland forest and other trees and grasses protect the water and provide for wildlife. Basically, the upper half of the tank facilitates wildlife activities while most of the human activities are concentrated around the bottom half.

Tanks embody not only hydrological legacies going back thousands of years but also agricultural heritage in Sri Lanka. Most of the tanks are concentrated in the dry zone (Keane 1905). They were man-made and the ancient tank was only one part of a village, consisting of agricultural land, settlements and forest areas. Panabokke et al. (2002) identified 15,373 small tanks in Sri Lanka and 50 per cent of them are abandoned. Most of these tanks are evidence of advanced technology and development in the ancient water-works. This balanced agrarian economy underwent a radical change with colonization.

Colonial landscaping of agriculture and the turning point of HER of Sri Lanka

The longevity of *chena* practices with forest and wildlife continuity suggests the sustainability of these traditional approaches. The colonial period that began with Dutch, Portuguese, and then British rule of the entire island altered land-based conversations and this loss of dialogue explains the rise of human–elephant conflict. By 1843, 230,000 acres in the upcountry were taken over by colonial rulers for coffee cultivation (Snodgrass 1966). Most of the areas used for commercial estates used to be forested areas. In 1840 the Crown Land Ordinance enabled acquisition of lands that belonged to the common masses letting ecosystems collapse, which ultimately led to the emergence of the human–wildlife conflict (Silva 1981). Many traditional residences were lost in the expanding cultivation, and liveable land declined dramatically, resulting in a high population density in the highlands.

Coffee, cocoa and tea were cultivated in the commercial plantations, but the desired amount of harvest was not attained due to wild animal damages. The capture and killing of wild animals including wild elephants was legalized to control the situation. The elephant kraal of Panamura was an enclosure where wild elephants were held. All government policies were directed at promoting commercial plantations while neglecting rural agriculture. As a result, the rural sector crumbled while epidemics such as malaria and smallpox claimed thousands of lives. Others migrated to other areas to save lives (Talagune 1998). Consequently, many villages were abandoned and destroyed, and soon they became wilderness.

With the passage of the Fauna and Flora Protection Ordinance No. 2 of 1937, forest limits were defined. As a result, most of the villages were confined to forested areas along with their illustrious agricultural past (www.nfms.lk). With the collapse of the dry zone rural sector the country's food security plunged into a serious crisis, and by the Second World War the British rulers were in deep trouble. Re-development of the rural sector began in the first quarter of the twentieth century with development of agricultural settlements and water sources in rural areas.

The reciprocity and listening of subsistence practices that persisted in the face of elephant incursions were reduced in economic and industrial modes of cultivation to one voice speaking over the others, and subsuming the others. Wetness and water in the tanks (and as in India from section above) were a primary feature of small-scale self-sufficiency for humans that also benefitted

Figure 8.3 Elephant browsing, Uda Walawe National Park, Sri Lanka, 2018. (Image courtesy: Elizabeth Oriel.)

elephants and formed a land-based dialogue across water and practices to help that water disperse; many were abandoned in colonial times. The structural (landscape) changes that took place in the agriculture sector of Sri Lanka displaced not only wild animals in their traditional habitats but also rural communities in their traditional lands. Further, this process changed the traditional face of human–elephant relations. Traditional practices reveal respect in the warnings before burning the vegetation, close attention to atmosphere and place, and the kind of call and response of situated relations that involve listening to landscapes (see Figure 8.3).

Listening to languages of the land: Some perspectives

In this section, embodied relations with land come to the fore, as examples of modes of listening to landscapes. These offer multiple perspectives and tools that answer to the implications of findings from the previous multispecies landscape analyses, with practical ways to relate and listen. Diverse relations and communications with land were gathered from conversations[3] with ten land dwellers in the United States and the United Kingdom. These oral histories were collected in 2021 through the snowball effect (a sampling method for qualitative research) with prompts to speak about personal experiences and each's cultural eco-heritage. Across disciplines, place and placelessness (or current states of atopia) are centred within critiques of modernism and globalization, processes that dismantle the thousands-year-old ties across nature–culture that sustained life.

Land as one, land as many, land as both runs across the narratives, with three mentioning land as a unified whole. For Indigenous chaplain Tahnahga Yako (Minnesota, USA), the 'land is a being, producing life, renewal and rebirth'. She describes connecting to the heartbeat of the Earth when she drums in ceremony which connects her heart to the Earth's heartbeat; this is a central feature of ceremony, she says. Similarly, the land is both one entity and a community of living entities for UK-based regenerative farmer, Rebecca Hosking (Devon, UK). She refers to land as a 'she' which older farmers used to do in Devon; she imagines it may come from British nautical culture, thinking of land as a vessel. 'A sense of life', 'a presence' is how one describes her sense of who land is. She describes the sense of life entering her, and an exchange happening between her and the land.

Several described an ineffable quality to land and to land's vocabularies, speaking to the limits of human language, and recalling Campagna's (2018) assertion of a magic and the ineffable as an alternative reality to Technis. Several respondents say they leave their mental thoughts and their primary verbal language aside when they listen to land. One says there is a place on the river where she meets with her deceased parents; the ability to meet them is particular to that riverine locale. Invisible realities are highlighted in these experiences which are generally devalued in dominant culture.

One inhabitant emphasized differences in land and staying attentive to the needs and interests of each place. 'The land is diverse across small and larger localities, a microhabitat underneath a tree, an expanse of grass in several acres or across a broad plateau – each possesses unique qualities and characteristics based on all the relationships of topography, vegetation, climate, soil, microbes, and much more.'

Languages of land

The diverse languages of the land are experienced sensorially and in energetic ways. These vocabularies are found in changing colours, scents, sounds, touch and in all the ways the land teaches one limits, in water availability, in access to heat from wood. The land provides limits to the self, which emerges through periods of abundance and scarcity, normative cycles of drought and wetness, heat and cold, wind and calm.

Fragrance is one language of the land that was mentioned in two conversations. Gary Nabhan (Arizona, USA) said each place has a lexicon of fragrance:

> I live in the Sonoran Desert, one of the largest and most diverse deserts in the world. And for 40 years, I've been tracking the lexicon of volatile oil fragrances from the plants and the soil. That is what gives people the impression when there's a thunderstorm that the desert smells like rain. There's a sense of how the land communicates, immediately before the rain, you get a wave of floral fragrances that have evolved, so that plants can communicate to other plants and to animals about the humidity, ozone, and wind changes. There's an incredible release of volatile oil, aromatic fragrances that communicate to toads to come up out of the soil where they've been dormant for months, and communicates a sense of elation and wellbeing to humans. The desert has additional reasons [besides attracting pollinators] for producing these aromatic oils to protect against solar radiation, temperature, stress and other environmental stressors that are hazards. Those very same volatile oils reduce stress in humans when exposed to them. They don't just function on wildlife and on other plants, they also function on humans.

Fragrance is also a form of the land's primary language for college president Ann Filemyr (New Mexico, USA), as is the wind. The land speaks through wind, a form of breath, just as humans do. Both Filemyr and Yako find the origin of human languages with sounds of water and wind moving, sounds from the Earth, and different languages reflect unique localities.

Yako describes communication with land as having two-way directionality. 'It takes me years to understand this connection, what is going on with the land.' Communications are complex, taking place with ancestors, the soil and plants. When she collects plant medicines, she says, 'I tell them why I'm there, I put down two offerings for them, I give them my lineage. I say, "this is why I'm here, this is who I'm harvesting for," and I ask them to tell me when I have enough.'

The land 'communicates on all levels of my sensory awareness/perception. In one state the land is feeding you, and in another state, you're feeding the land', says artist Ondé Chymes (New Mexico, USA). 'We feed the land by honoring it. Living on the land in the high desert with a well, you are aware the source of water is the sky. You understand the relationship between rainfall and the water you use in your home and garden. City people turn on the faucet and have no idea where their water comes from.' Living with a well is a way of listening.

Hosking says the land speaks to her on her farm in patterns and rhythms of disturbance and then rest (reminiscent of shifting cultivation). Hosking utilizes pulse grazing on her sheep farm; animals are moved often, leaving fields to rest, mimicking natural processes when predators would push herbivores to new ground. She explains:

> If there is too much mud, that is the land saying 'You're hurting me,' by overgrazing. Another way the land communicates is in the color of the foliage on the pastures. It is a short pasture and then it grows into flowers. But once it goes to seed, it's browning, and that's a signal for us to send the animals in ... 'Now is my time to share my seed' [she speaks here for plants].

One theme is how humans give back to the land. Yako offers food in certain places to the land and to ancestors, as do other respondents. She also offers prayers. Not wanting to impose one's emotional state or thoughts onto land came up with two people; negotiating land relations from the context of dominant culture requires care and caution.

How do those who perceive land as sentient, as a communicator track the impact of extractions, intensifications through development that leave soils, waterways, and landscapes depleted and devoid of life? Land that is over-grazed, clear-cut, cut into for mining – these sites can be viewed as spaces of trauma. Land as both matter and psyche exhibits both sorts of trauma. Hosking says:

> Each field and each parcel of land has personality. They have spirits, and it looks like an overall entity when you're dealing with it. But actually, when you break it down, it is the vast community that is creating the spirit of that character. I describe land that has been completely overworked as 'Stepford fields', because they have no personality left, and they have no character, they're really submissive and they do just what they're told. Whereas the fields I work here have still got a spark about them. And they will spit you out if you don't behave properly. If you overgraze the fields, they will make your animals sick. They take it away from you if you misbehave with them.

Nabhan describes the process of healing wounded lands through bringing stories from the past and re-interpreting them, re-shaping them for the new generation. Silence, he says, is also a language, and when he is in silence, then he hears the languages of animals.

Listening to the land

Listening to the land requires slowness, stillness and a removal from densely human-built spaces. Some described the stillness and quiet as difficult to find in modern lifestyles. Several described listening as a somatic experience, sensorial, while one says for her it is not related to her mind or body, but is vibrational, energetic. Filemyr says the removal from the domestic sphere is key to listening to land:

> Stepping away from human settlement is such an ancient practice. Native cultures have preserved that practice, whether it's called 'vision quest' or the Lakota call it 'going up on the hill.' That practice was everywhere. We have the testimony in the Bible and in the lives of the saints. This was understood, that there are things to learn that you cannot get except by going direct to the wild.

Observation, attention and presence are central to listening to land.

Nabhan attests to the centrality of working the land in listening and being in relationship to place. All other organisms participate in shaping the land, he says, and humans are not excluded. He says, 'the dumber than nails assumption is that caretaking is a privilege, not an obligation … To really understand the land, you have to be in the dirt, dirt under your fingernails, participating with the land, restoring it, protecting it, or co-managing it with animals and other organisms.'

Discussion

Listening to the land is a nonlinear complex affair, correlated with situated transformations and collectivities across multiple nature–cultures. Listening to the land through particular vocabularies, of sound, tactility and activated senses requires multispecies sentience, rooted in distributed cognition, and as Steffensen (2018) writes, symbiotic relations. This exploration of the *languaging* of human–elephant–land practices and knowledge, develops and grounds Steffensen and Cowley's (2021) radical embodied ecolinguistics in fractious terrain in South Asia. We add to these colonial and modernist land patterns, US- and UK-based interviewees' experiences with terrestrial vocabularies, as they attest to the intelligence in land's biotic communications, and to the subjective and ineffable relations with land that require humans to join into ecologies instead of ecologies fitting into human priorities. These contribute to Val Plumwood's (2008) call for an ethics of place. Vertical power structures (colonial and global) have imposed fixed abstract relations between inhabitants and their environment, distancing them from each other. Here, we asked questions of colonial and modernist environmental knowledge, extractions, simplifications that universalize, and erase pasts and contexts, ignoring inherent characteristics of topography, weather, plant communities, hydrologies and stories. As radical embodied ecolinguistics (2021) asserts, conversing in situated vocabularies requires an ethical orientation, to distributed sentience and self-determination, which has been lost in many regions. It requires experiential approaches beyond visual representations of alphabets, lines on maps and imposed settlements. And yet, those who listen and respond to situated vocabularies are usually excluded from land-use planning and decision-making processes (Döring & Ratter 2018). The situated understandings emphasize tacit knowledges acquired through multiple engagements in and with the world, through everyday ancient material practices of cultivation, temporally appropriating commons with other sentient beings, and transmission through everyday practices, poetry, songs, fables and lived experiences. The possibilities for diverse understandings and expressions of place-based relations are seen in these more-than-human vocabularies, by re-appropriating words and practices, and going beyond the fixed definitions towards new descriptions.

Notes

1. Ecomemisis is an author's evocation of their own environment (Morton 2007).
2. The *Anumethirala* is a villager who works as a messenger of the god that communicates between the people and the god.
3. A number of interviewees gave permission for their names to be used and others did not.

References

Baskaran, Nagarajan, & Desai, Ajay A. (2013). 'Frugivory and Seed Dispersal by the Asian Elephant Elephas Maximus in the Tropical Forests of Nilgiri Biosphere Reserve, Southern India.' Edited by Meena Venkataraman. *Journal of Threatened Taxa*, 5(14): 4893–97.

Basso, Keith (1996). *Wisdom Sits in Places: Landscape and Language among the Western Apache*. Albuquerque: University of New Mexico Press.

Bateson, Gregory (2000). *Steps to an Ecology of Mind: Collected Essay in Anthropology, Psychiatry, Evolution, and Epistemology*. Chicago: University of Chicago.

Brandis, Dietrich (1883). *Forest Administration*. Madras: Government Press.

Campagna, Federico (2018). *Technic and Magic: The Reconstruction of Reality*. London: Bloomsbury Publishing.

Campos-Arceiz, Ahimsa, & Blake, Steve (2011). 'Megagardeners of The Forest – the Role of Elephants in Seed Dispersal'. *Acta Oecologica*, 37(6): 542–53.

Da Cunha, Dilip (2018). 'River Literacy and the Challenge of a Rain Terrain'. In Venkat D. Rao (Ed.), *Critical Humanities from India: Contexts, Issues, Futures*, 177–204. London and New York: Routledge.

De Certeau, Michel (1984). *The Practice of Everyday Life*. Berkeley: University of California Press.

Döring, Martin, & Ratter, Beate (2018). 'Senses of Place in the North Frisian Wadden Sea: Local Consciousness and Knowledge for Place-Based Heritage Development'. In Egberts Linde, & Schroor Meindert (Eds.), *Waddenland Outstanding: History, Landscape and Cultural Heritage of the Wadden Sea Region*, 293–304. Amsterdam: Amsterdam University Press.

Edney, Matthew (1997). *Mapping an Empire – The Geographical Construction of British India, 1765–1843*. Chicago: The University of Chicago Press.

Fairhead, James, & Leach, Melissa (2011). *Misreading the African Landscape – Society and Ecology in a Forest-Savanna Mosaic*. 2nd ed. Cambridge: Cambridge University Press.

Food and Agriculture Organization (2018). *Sri Lanka among Globally Important Agricultural Heritage Systems*. FAO in Sri Lanka, Food and Agriculture Organization of United Nations.

FRA (2006). *The Scheduled Tribes and Other Traditional Forest Dwellers (Recognition of Forest Rights) Act*.

Gadgil, Madhav, Krishnan, B. J., Ganeshaiah, K. N., Vijayan, V. S., Borges, Renee, Sukumar, R., & Noronha, Ligia (2011). 'Report of the Western Ghats Ecology Expert Panel'.

Germond, Paul, Cochrane, James R. (2010). 'Healthworlds: Conceptualizing Landscapes of Health and Healing'. *Sociology*, 44: 307–24.

Guha, Ramachandra, & Gadgil, Madhav (1995). *Ecology and Equity: The Use and Abuse of Nature in Contemporary India*. London: Routledge.

Harvey, Graham (2019). 'Animism and Ecology: Participating in the World Community'. *The Ecological Citizen*, 3: 79–84.

Indian Forest Act (1878). Act No. VII in *A Collection of the Acts Passed by the Governor General of India in Council in the Year 1878*. Calcutta: Office of the Superintendent of Government Printing.

Ingold, Tim (2011). *Being Alive: Essays on Movement, Knowledge and Description*. London: Routledge.

International Union for Conservation of Nature (IUCN) (2012). 'World Heritage Nomination – IUCN Technical Evaluation Western Ghats (India) – ID No. 1342 Rev'.

Irangani, M. K. L. (2020). 'Sustainable Principles of Indigenous *Chena* Cultivation and Management in Sri Lanka: Lessons for Contemporary Agricultural Problems'. *International Journal of Scientific and Research Publications*, 10(11): 46–54.

Kahandagamage, Piyasena (1999). *Information of Chena* (Hene Withthi: Sinhala Medium Book). Colombo 10: S. Godage Publishers.

Keane, Captain Sir John (1905). *Report on Irrigation in Ceylon*. Colombo: Government Press.
Kirksey, S. Eben, & Helmreich, Stefan (2010). 'The Emergence of Multispecies Ethnography'. *Cultural Anthropology*, 25(4): 545–76.
Kohn, Eduardo (2013). *How Forests Think – Towards an Anthropology beyond the Human*. Berkeley: University of California Press.
Latour, B. (2017). *Facing Gaia: Eight Lectures on the New Climatic Regime*. Cambridge: Polity Press.
Logan, William (1887). *Malabar Manual*. Madras: Government Press.
Maturana, Humberto, & Varela, Francisco (2012). *Autopoiesis and Cognition: The Realization of the Living*. London: D. Reidel Publishing Company.
Ministry of Law and Justice (2002). *The Biological Diversity Act (BDA), 2002*. India: National Biodiversity Authority of India.
MoEF-GoI (Ministry of Environment and Forests, Government of India) (2009). 'Serial Nomination of the Western Ghats of India: Its Natural Heritage – For Inscription on the World Natural Heritage List'. India.
Morton, Timothy (2007). *Ecology without Nature*. Cambridge: Harvard University Press.
Neimanis, Astrida (2012). 'Hydrofeminism: Or, on Becoming a Body of Water'. In Henriette Gunkel, Chrysanthi Nigianni & Fanny Söderbäck (Eds.), *Undutiful Daughters: Mobilizing Future Concepts, Bodies and Subjectivities in Feminist Thought and Practice*, 96–115. New York: Palgrave Macmillan.
Panabokke, C. R., Sakthivadivel, R., & Asoka Dias Weerasinghe (2002). *Evolution, Present Status and Issues Concerning Small Tank Systems in Sri Lanka*. Sri Lanka: International Water Management Institute.
Phillimore, Reginald H. (1945). *Historical Records of the Survey of India, Volume III, Eighteenth Century*. Dehradun: The Surveyor General of India.
Plumwood, Val (2008). 'Shadow Places and the Politics of Dwelling'. *Australian Humanities Review*, 44(2): 139–50.
Powell, Baden Henry (1892). *The Land-Systems of British India, Being a Manual of the Land-Tenures and of the Systems of Land-Revenue Administration Prevalent in the Several Provinces – Volume III – Book IV: The Raiyatwari and Allied Systems*. Delhi: Low Price Publications.
Prakash, T. G., Supan, Lahiru., Wijeratne, A. W., & Prithiviraj, Fernando (2020). 'Human-Elephant Conflict in Sri Lanka: Patterns and Extent'. *Gajah*, 51: 16–25.
Raman, Cheruvayal (2018, May 20). Personal Interview.
Rathnayake, R. M. N. B., Hapugoda, Mahesh, Ariyarathna, Manoj, & Weerakoon, Rumesh (2018). 'Using Agricultural Information System to Enhance the Sustainability and Forcastability. In the Ellanga Traditional Cascade Tank-Village System In Sri Lanka'. *Asia Proceedings of Social Sciences*, 3(1): 35–9.
Ratnatunga., P. U. (1979). *Sri Lanka Wewas and Reservoirs Album*. Colombo, Sri Lanka: Sri Lanka Freedom from Hunger Campaign.

Ravi, J. (n.d.). 'What Were the Salient Features of Peasant Revolt in South India'. Accessed from https://www.preservearticles.com/education/what-were-the-salient-features-of-peasant-revolt-in-south-india/13891.

Silva, A. T. Mahinda (1981). *'The Evolution of Land Policies in Sri Lanka; an Overview'*. Training material 23/III, Training Programme on Settlement Planning and Management, Ministry of Land and Land Development and Food and Agriculture Organization.

Snodgrass, Donald R. (1966). *Ceylon: An Export Economy in Transition*. Homewood, IL, Irwin: Publication of the Economic Growth Center, Yale University.

Steffensen, Sune Vork (2018). 'The Microecological Grounding of Language: How Linguistic Symbolicity Extends and Transforms the Human Ecology'. In Alwin Fill & Hermine Penz (Eds.), *The Routledge Handbook of Ecolinguistics*, 393–405. London: Routledge.

Steffensen, Sune. Vork., & Cowley, Stephen. J. (2021). 'Thinking on Behalf of the World: Radical Embodied Ecolinguistics'. In X. Wen & J. Taylor (Eds.), *The Routledge Handbook of Cognitive Linguistics*, 723–36. London: Routledge.

Steinberg, Philip, & Peters, Kimberley (2015). 'Wet Ontologies, Fluid Spaces: Giving Depth to Volume through Oceanic Thinking'. *Environment and Planning D: Society and Space*, 33(2): 247–64.

Talagune, A. B. (1998). *Rural Development of Sri Lanka – History and Evolution, Rural Development and Development, Wijerama Lionel*. (Ed). Colombo: Rural Development Training and Training Institute.

Tobin, Brendan (2013). 'The Role of Customary Law in Access and Benefit-Sharing and Traditional Knowledge Governance: Perspectives from Andean and Pacific Island Countries'. United Nations University (UNU)/World Intellectual Property Organization (WIPO). Retrieved from: https://www.wipo.int/export/sites/www/tk/en/resources/pdf/customary_law_abs_tk.pdf. Accessed 15 January 2022.

Thurston, Edgar, & Rangachari, K. (1909). *Castes and Tribes of Southern India. Volume IV – K and M*. Madras: Government Press.

9

Considering Cows in Australian Dairy Discourse

Alison Rotha Moore

Troubling oneself

After a writing retreat with a friend a few years ago, where we helped look after a small herd of rescued cows including a twenty-year-old cow who needed hand feeding, my friend wrote to say, 'I troubled myself to look up the milk supply chain when I got back (until the age of 47, I had never actually wondered about it …).'

This got me pondering on the rhetorical work that must have been going into keeping cows' milk positioned as a good human food and how that work has been changing. Equally, I wondered how my friend and I (female mammals like cows, and also professional linguists working on language and ideology) could for so long have been insensible to the ethical and environmental harms this near ubiquitous food entails (Poore & Nemecek 2018; Hampton et al. 2021), especially in a context of increasing public concern in Australia and elsewhere about animal welfare and the climate emergency[1] (Coleman 2019). In 2022 the average Australian consumed approximately 93 litres of milk, along with 15 kilos of cheese, over 3 kilos of butter and nearly 10 kilos of yoghurt (Dairy Australia 2022). Ninety-seven per cent of households bought milk regularly (Dairy Australia 2023).

So I began looking at this puzzle from an ecolinguistic angle, tracing changes in discursive representations of milk and milk products in the Australian dairy industry over the twentieth and early twenty-first centuries identified in relevant texts from national, state and industry archives and private/ephemeral collections online, and current campaigns and supplementary material online. Industry discourse is selected here as a key domain of first-order 'languaging'

(Thibault 2011) of the kind that 'extends ... human-organism-environment systems' through which extension our 'situated here-and-now activities', such as eating, are 'transformed and empowered by our access to sociocultural resources, which has had drastic consequences for all ecological systems on Earth' (Li et al. 2020: 5). But, as Li and colleagues also point out, language, on its slower timescales, 'stabilizes social coordination and enables human cognition to function more efficiently'. Herein lies the possibility, even if small, of change.

In this chapter I argue that if we are going to move towards an ecologically favourable civilization, we need to change how we speak, think and act regarding dairy. In short, we need to change dairy praxis.[2] This will involve a critical and creative reconfiguring of food industry discourses, among others.

To some extent we can see change in progress already. It is by no means the case that meanings and practices around dairy are fixed and monoglossic. There have been notable shifts and tensions in how milk and dairy have been positioned. These shifts sometimes appear designed to address public questioning about the desirability of cows' milk, but at other times appear designed to deflect or prevent such questioning (cf. Dupuis 2002 in the US context; Moore 2015, 2019; Moore & Evans forthcoming).

Two early examples of this relation between historical pressures on the dairy industry and contemporaneous dairy advertisements in Australia show how dairy discourse can be understood as languaging, 'activity in which wordings play a part', which happens 'above all, *for* someone' and which 'informs acting and perceiving' (Cowley 2022: 418). (1) A poster published in 1911 advertises 'Milk in sealed bottles'. This languaging invokes a concern for contamination and adulteration of milk which lasted, in Australia, until the 1930s, due to persistent fears about pasteurization's effectiveness in Australia's hot climate (Colclough 2008). In 1911, promoting dairy involved combatting views that milk was an inherently unhealthy food (Royal Commission 1913; Thorley 2014; see Dupuis for US accounts). (2) Approximately fifty years later, a poster 'Only butter with fish' reflects different a set of concerns and desires linked the growing popularity of margarine in Australia in the 1960s, which in turn was tied to rising costs of living and to expanded European migration (Abbott 2015).

The advertisement for butter uses what systemic functional descriptions of interlocutor 'engagement' call a 'disclaim, counter' move, where a locution 'invoke[s] a contrary position which is then said not to hold' (Martin & White 2005: 120; cf. White 2020). The position invoked in the butter advertisement is something like '[y]ou might think that margarine and butter are interchangeable', which is then countered. Note that the (interpersonal) modal adjunct 'only' is doing important work here. By contrast, the earlier 'sealed bottles' advertisement relies largely on invoking an ideational logic, offering a solution to known safety issues. Each advertisement seems designed at least in part to address a negative assessment of dairy that was circulating at the time, without those negative views being explicitly presented.

In my main example below, in order to illustrate my argument that dairy discourses need to change if we are to have ecocivilization in the future, I discuss a 2013–20 video campaign by Dairy Australia. I explore how (human) languaging in and around this industry shapes the conditions of existence for human and non-human participants.

My overarching aim is to critically evaluate alignments between the goals of ecocivilization on the one hand, and the values and priorities that seem to be promoted by current dairy industry languaging on the other hand, with a view to identifying specific areas of discourse most in need of need of challenging.

The critical concepts around which this evaluation is framed largely emerge from the industry discourse that I analyse. Whorf (1956) is useful here, for his argument that habitual ways of using language have a profound effect on individual cognition and social belief systems, since language and culture 'had grown up together' (156). A further lens is ecofeminism, taken as 'an intellectual and experiential understanding of the mutually reinforcing interconnections among diverse forms of oppression' across lines such as gender, sexuality, species (Gaard 2013: 596) and, following Adams and Donovan (2007), it is important to attend both to individual experiences (for humans and others) and to the structures and systems that shape them, although there is no space to make all these interconnections central to this chapter. In this chapter I strive to using both scholarly and industry sources in a critical way.

The chapter proceeds by summarizing known tensions between the project of ecocivilization and current dairy praxis, drawing on industry-led and critical accounts. It then briefly reviews key research on dairy discourse. My own close analysis of an Australian dairy advertisement follows. I finish with implications for where dairy praxis most needs to be challenged, and how ecolinguistics might make a contribution to such a challenge.

Dairy and (eco)civilization

Given the current ecological crisis, it is pressing to ask, 'What would an ecocivilized food system look like, and how would it position the dairy cow?'

Before moving on it is necessary to outline the 'drastic consequences' that dairy has been associated with. The consumption of milk and dairy in westernized countries seems to be declining, but it is still large and is growing in the Global South. For example, in Australia 1.34 million cows (Dairy Australia 2023) currently live lives tightly organized around maximum efficiency and profitability of a food production system.

Notable reviews of the impact of such systems include Ruth Harrison's foundational 'Animal Machines' (1964), the equally influential 'Livestock's Long Shadow' (Steinfeld et al. 2006), a major Australian report on the 'Life of the Dairy Cow' (Voiceless 2015),[3] and comparative analyses of the breadth of welfare harms by Hampton et al. (2021), and of the intensity of environmental harms by Poole and Nemecek (2018). An excellent extended autoethnographic account by Gillespie (2018) discusses relational harms within the dairy industry. The critical work of Greta Gaard (2013, 2015) is very illuminating. Capilé and colleagues (2021) provide a succinct review of research on why people might care about animals yet not change food attitudes and practices in their favour.

Environmental damage

Dairy production entails greenhouse gas emissions (in particular methane), land clearing, water use and water pollution, all of which reduce biodiversity, directly increase the risk of species extinction, and contribute to climate change. The existence of significant environmental harms from dairy is generally accepted as a concern by the industry (see e.g. Dairy Australia 2022). A major meta-analysis[4] by Oxford scholars Poore and Nemecek (2018) estimated that, taken together, dairy, meat, aquaculture and eggs use 83 per cent of the world's farmland and contribute 56–58 per cent of food-based emissions, but provide only 18 per cent of our calories and 38 per cent of our protein. Poore and Nemecek concluded that excluding animal products from our diet would reduce food's land use by 76 per cent and its GHG emissions by 49 per cent, delivering 'benefits on a scale not achievable by producers' through changing farming practices (2018: 5).

Human health impacts

It is important to note, although there is no space here for a nuanced account, that dairy consumption has been directly associated in major epidemiological studies with breast, ovarian and prostate cancer and – via its contribution to saturated fat intake – with heart disease, Alzheimer's and adult onset diabetes (PCRM nd). Projecting mortality reductions under various food consumption scenarios suggests that health benefits increase as the fraction of animal-sourced foods in our diets reduces, with 75 per cent of all benefits occurring in developing countries (Springmann 2016: 4146). In this study, the (dairy-free) vegan scenario reduced deaths more than the vegetarian scenario. Given the increasing uptake of dairy in China and the Global South (Clay & Yurco 2019), these are very major concerns.

Alongside effects on consumers, health effects on farm workers are worth considering. For example, Alston and colleagues (2017) report that increased labour demands and entrenched traditional gender roles are associated with increasing farm size and technologization in Australia, with likely impacts on physical and mental health.

Animal welfare

Animal welfare is probably the most controversial aspect of dairy's impact on the bio-ecology because to consider welfare requires a wide range of disciplines and sectors, including activist and advocacy sectors, and engages with political questions such as whether other species are 'ours' to use to produce food (and fibre). Perhaps as a result of this, studies that focus on dairy's effects on cows (rather than human or planetary well-being) are more likely to call for the abolition of dairy farming, though not all do. As an aside, abolition is my personal position as a female and feminist scholar and participant in creaturely life and multi-species interaction.[5] But, since plurality and pragmatism are also important, is it crucial to consider what can best help current and future generations of cows to fare well or at least better (cf. Singer 2008).

Major welfare concerns stem from the extensive genetic manipulation of the dairy cow, starting with the long period of selective breeding from the aurochs which produced the modern dairy cow, and accelerating with more technologized genetic manipulation in recent decades. Cows in Australia now produce 35–70 litres of milk a day, twice the volume of thirty years ago (Wicks 2018: 57), with a work rate that has been compared with a man jogging six hours a day, seven days a week, carrying risk of ketosis.[6] Such genetic alteration, along with standard practices such as near continuous pregnancy/birth cycles to induce lactation, and being milked until the last two months of their pregnancy, places enormous pressure on cows and is linked to high risks of lameness and mastitis (Rémond 1992; Wicks 2018). Dairy cows are generally slaughtered for beef at about four years old, despite a natural life expectancy of about twenty years (Voiceless 2015). Other welfare issues raised by advocacy and industry groups include dehorning/disbudding, tail docking, calving induction, live export and separation of calf from cow (Voiceless, Dairy Australia nd).

A key concern here is the routine slaughter of male calves as waste products, with millions of calves a year killed in their first few weeks of life (e.g. 1.8 million in New Zealand in 2019; see Safe for Animals 2020). This process is in some places being modified by retailer and regulative pressure, and by the availability of sexed semen, a 'promising mitigation strategy' but one that is likely to elicit new ethical concerns (Levitt 2020; Balzani & Hanlon 2021).

A harm not often raised within industry and industry-based science discourses is the repeated social disruption cows are subject to, as individuals are sold in and out of new social groups (Voiceless 2015; Gillespie 2018). Mothers separated from calves, whether slaughtered, sold or just raised separately, can grieve audibly for days, signalling to humans their disagreement and distress (Adams 2017; Boyde 2018). These noises are sometimes heard as worrying by nearby human residents but within the industry cows mooing is more routinely dismissed either as not grief or as insignificant (Gaard 2013; Boyde 2018; Gillespie 2018). Of course most dairy-consuming public live well out of earshot of dairy farms, disrupting any direct lines of communication between cows and the general public that might exist, and yet for those who have the heart to find out more, and can bear to listen, videos of cows and calves in distress are readily available online (Adams 2017, 2018). See also veterinarian Holly Cheever's report (Cheever 2011; Gaard 2013) of a cow she treated who, after four pregnancies where her calf was taken, set up a subterfuge to keep one of her twins a secret, leading one calf to the farmer to be separated, but keeping and feeding the other in hiding.

Raising the topic of cow welfare, and in particular cow perspectives, in food sustainability discourse has often been dismissed as anthropomorphizing, but more recently has become something dairy industry members and agricultural scientists are explicitly addressing (see, for example, Weary and von Keyserlingk's 2017 article titled 'Public concerns about dairy-cow welfare, how should the industry respond?').

Eminent animal behaviourist Marian Stamp Dawkins argues that instead of prioritizing 'natural' behaviours, which she calls a 'shaky concept' that may not have any real benefit to welfare (2023: 988), industry should, and can, find out 'what animals want' (2023: 991).

Studies investigating what cows want in this context manipulate farm environments to, essentially, ask questions of cows, whether they prefer barn or pasture (it depends on the weather), and whether calves prefer solitude or company (generally they prefer company, and 'paired housing' has made calves less fearful and learn faster [Jacobs 2020]).

For the project of ecolinguistics, it seems fruitful to examine this 'conversation' between farm workers/researchers and cows as 'participatory sense-making' (De Jaegher & Di Paolo 2007; cf. Despret 2016). Participatory sense-making could also help explain why calves learn more efficiently when they spend their early lives wandering about paddocks with their mothers and herd (Whalin et al 2021).

While signs of dialogue between industry, science and cows seem promising, these sit among broader changes. A recent systematic review (Bojovic & McGregor 2022) identifies four dairy 'megatrends', shifts in geographical location from North to South; accelerating mechanization, standardization and corporatization; increasing awareness of ecological impacts of dairy; and disruption from plant milks.

For ecolinguistics, it is interesting to consider the ways that such changes resonate with changes in how the industry represents itself and negotiates relationships through languaging. Research on this is outlined in the next section.

Shifting dairy praxis

Many recent shifts in food industry discourses can be understood as responses to developments in food politics and activism. Two important trends regarding dairy marketing are summarized by Linné (2016). The first is that large-scale industry messaging now often addresses the disconnect between people and their food that stems from our increasingly industrialized food systems. The second appears to be one specific strategy to bridge this disconnect, where the 'absent referent' from Carol Adams' critique (2010/1990) is now often reintegrated into industry stories, deflecting critiques about welfare by presenting farmers as caring for animals' quality of life right up until their 'humane slaughter' (see e.g. Cole 2011). Linné gives the example of the 'speaking cows' who 'post' on dairy company social media accounts, presenting them as 'distinctly emotional beings [who] have long distance relationships, … worry about getting back to work, … and care for their children' (2016: 275).

Such trends, however, sidestep more foundational debates about animal exploitation, giving the take-home message that 'if only industrialization can be rolled back, the ethical issues of using animals for food will be resolved' (Linné

2016: 722). On the more productive side perhaps, these shifts are presented as opening up acknowledgement of animals as 'workers' in food industries, another way in which animals traditionally have been absent or shadowy (Haraway 2003; Porcher & Schmitt 2012). But while cows certainly do contribute their physical and emotional labour, this construal of cows as 'co-workers with humans' has been called 'reprehensible' by Gaard (2015: 6) 'for the ways that it obscures the institutionalized oppression of reproductive labor and human responsibility'. Recent critical researchers agree that dairy marketing still typically depicts cows' lives as idyllic and characterized such depiction as romantic, mythical, sentimental, nostalgic and nationalistic (e.g. Linné 2016; Clay & Yurco 2019; Phillipov & Loyer 2019; Andersson 2020; Andersson & Smith 2021; Capilé et al. 2021). Such depictions have been shown to foster beliefs that poor animal welfare is a problem for 'foreign' cultures, not one's own, and appear to reduce willingness to pay extra for higher welfare products, even among those who rate animal welfare as important to them (e.g. Buddle et al 2023), a phenomenon dubbed the 'citizen/consumer paradox' (Aerts 2013).

Although it is well documented that nationalist appeals feature heavily in food advertising and that construing 'place' plays an important role, there is little research on how such places are invoked semiotically, how specific these places are or how their construal and significance vary between nations or regions (Andersson & Smith 2021). One example however is given in Andersson and Smith's comparative study of Swedish and British butter packaging. Swedish packets displayed an arguably more egalitarian conception of 'nature' with dark green forests and unremarkable countryside, whereas British packaging, studied in the lead-up to Brexit, largely featured recognizable architectural icons and the UK flag.

Interpreting their findings, Andersson and Smith suggest that advertising relies on 'tapping into meanings, arguments, emotions and opinions already existing in a culture and among, in this case, consumers' (2020: 12, citing Kjeldsen 2007). This is a regrettably static understanding of how advertising works. Pointing to something that the consumer already thinks/knows/feels raises the question of how the consumer, particularly one who lives in the city, gets 'pre-filled' with meanings.

Some authors distribute the agency of industry and consumers, and the role of advertising, a little differently. Tulloch and Judge, writing from New Zealand, argue that 'dominant discourses of dairying are powerful shapers of public consciousness' (2018: 1). Other writers suggest that dairy's very emergence as a highly organized and industrialized production system acted and still acts to foster and distil nationalist meanings (Cohen 2017). As Cohen makes clear, modern dairying needs to be understood not just as a national project but above all as an ongoing colonial project, beginning in the sixteenth century, in which 'animals have been used to colonize lands, native animals, and people [and to impose] foreign legal norms and practices of human-animal relations upon communities and their environments' (2017: 268).

To give a sense of what this means, the emergence of milk authorities and marketing boards at state and national levels in many countries relied on a political endorsement of the idea that milk was a common good that required an assured supply to the public. This rested on the positive appraisal of milk/dairy as a special food.

For Australia, this idea of milk as a special food brought with it the contradiction of milk being seen as a distinctively Australian natural resource, setting 'us' up in the nineteenth century as a major exporter 'back home' of a product/practice that dated back to the Neolithic in Britain, through shipments of butter and powdered milk. Yet, at the same time, the current (but contested) view of cows' milk as 'normal milk' in Western households and soy, oat, almond, etc. as 'alternatives' rests on a shallower history than many might think, with the frequent consumption of milk as a drink by adults in the United States, for example, traced to the second half of the nineteenth century (Dupuis 2002; Cohen 2017). In Australian context, this can be seen in the fact that the first attempt to 'supply distant country milk to Sydney' (a distance of approximately 100 kilometres) was made in 1856 by farmers from Wollongong, but was not successfully managed until 1900 (Wilkinson 1999).

The ascendency of milk may be attributed to the Industrial Revolution bringing pasteurization, rail and sea transportation to ship a highly perishable substance vast distances (Dupuis 2002; Deckha 2012) but, equally, the causal direction can be seen the other way – with milk's perishability seen as '*inspiring* urban dairy industrialization, railway transport and, ultimately, doorstep delivery' (Gaard 2015; 56, italics inserted). It can probably be simultaneously attributed to economic and symbolic aspects of colonialism including the associations of milk with whiteness, purity, and innocence 'promoting the consumption of cow's milk domestically ... as an everyday nutritious but also nation-building product that inspired nationalist imperialist aspirations to take root' (Deckha 2012).

More recent phenomena worth mentioning that have influenced how stories about dairy have evolved are (i) the consolidation of power into fewer and fewer hands in the dairy industry, including vertical integration with supermarkets; (ii) the related 'milk price war/s' experienced in many countries; and (iii) a small but persistent movement around alternative farming practices. These and their public coverage are discussed by Dupuis (2002), Taylor and Fraser (2019), Phillipov and Loyer (2019), Thompson (2022) and Wicks (2018). Phillipov and Loyer's study is particularly interesting for its observations about how the public can be rallied to help address ecologically unhelpful practices, but things can go wrong when the same prevailing tropes, such as pastoral sentimentality, are used to justify opposing positions.

Although we see some focus in current research on dairy discourses on whether farmed animals experience relational connection or affection, this remains underexplored. One focus group participant in Buddle and colleagues' research, Susie, when asked what constituted a good life for farmed cows and sheep suggested it would be when 'every animal's got a name', which was followed by focus group laughter. Susie continued, 'but some of them *do* do that, like not every animal maybe, but some of their favourite ones. I'm just being silly' (Buddle et al. 2023: 6). Buddle and colleagues do not pick up on this 'being silly' comment but from a linguistic point of view it is salient discourse work that shows how social bonds around values are proposed and sometimes rejected by being 'laughed off' (Knight 2013).

An important question which we will pick up again towards the end of the chapter is the extent to which meanings and interactions around dairy are available for substantial transformation – transformation that could help move towards an ecocivilization that includes cows in the participatory sense-making. The kind of wiggle room demonstrated in Susie's focus group exchange may help identify points of possible transformation.

Text analysis of recent Australian advertising campaign material

The 'Legendairy' video

In this section I present a close analysis of a video from the international award-winning 'Legendairy' campaign, produced by Dairy Australia, current from 2013 to 2020, and still public at time of writing (Dairy Australia 2013a). This video was part of a 'fully integrated communications strategy' and was screened in print, TV, cinema and football sponsorship contexts.

I argue that despite its familiar nostalgia and nationalist tone, the Legendairy campaign represents a significant change from themes appearing in previous Australian dairy promotional texts, as briefly exemplified at the beginning of this chapter. Yet, like previous texts, Legendairy can be read as an industry response to contemporaneous food politics in Australia. Indeed, in launching the campaign, Dairy Australia stressed the goals of 'connecting the farming community with its consumers' and helping to 'restore confidence in the industry' (2013b).

The video analysis relates the 'first order', dynamic nature of 'languaging', where coordination of embodied human (inter)actants is seen as primary, to the 'code' aspect of language treated as 'second-order' – that is, a phenomenon of a longer time scale than instances of interaction, the sedimentation of habits of languaging over time. In the Legendairy text, with its asynchronous interaction between the text producer(s) and audiences, this coordination of embodied selves takes a different form from co-present coordination, but the bodily bases of interpreting the Legendairy advert, and of affiliating or disaffiliating with its people and values, remain crucial as we shall see.

A second resource for analysis is the idea of ecolinguistics as the 'ecological analysis of discourse' (Alexander & Stibbe 2014), which critiques analysis that limits itself to problematic lexical items and grammatical patterns. Echoing Halliday's emphasis on 'syndromes of all kinds of features ... complementarities and contradictions' (2003/1990: 149), Alexander and Stibbe argue for greater focus on 'clustering of grammatical and semantic features within specific discourses' (2014: 8) and for 'whole alternative models/discourses which have greater practical adequacy' (2014: 8).

The three main descriptive tools on the workbench for my analysis were Hasan's model of (linguistic) cohesive harmony as a way of identifying the 'clustering of meanings' that Alexander and Stibbe talk about, especially in terms of how these give a specific text its 'texture' or identity (Hasan 1984); van Leeuwen's work on the (linguistic) representation of actors (1996); and Kress and van Leeuwen's work (2006) on reading images and image-text relations. Linguistic data (all written) were transcribed and parsed into clauses, moving and still images parsed into shots. ELAN multimodal software (Brugman & Russell 2004) was used to coordinate language analysis with image analysis. Soundtrack and action sequences are relevant but beyond the scope of the chapter.

I examine first a transcript of the linguistic elements in the 'Legendairy' video (Table 9.1), then the alignment between linguistic messages and video images.

Table 9.1 Transcription of Legendairy campaign principal video, 2013–20. Source, Dairy Australia (2013a)

Time	Element	Clause/Message No.	Text of Clause/Message
0.01	CAP	1	There's a new story about Australian Dairy
	FPL	2	Dairy Australia
	CAP	3	Dairy has been through some tough times
	CAP	4	Once a hero of our health and wealth
	CAP	5	It has become less valued
0.16	CAP	6	It's time to reclaim our ground
	CAP	7	It starts on the farm
	CAP	8	It's our people
	CAP	9	It's our hard work
	CAP	10	It's our industry
0.35	CAP	11	Creating jobs for generations, careers for life and billions of dollars for Australians
	CAP	12	It's a superfood with ten essential nutrients found in the things we love
0.46	DG	13	MILK ([written on a milk carton])
	CAP	14	It's time to value this amazing product and to place it in the hearts and minds of all Australians
0.59	CAP	15	Only one word captures it
1.00	CAP	16	Australian dairy is ([new frame, 1.04]) LEGENDAIRY
1.11	CAP	17	Here's how we'll do it…
	CAP	18	Legendairy
	CAP	19	Legendairy
	CAP	20	It's the single biggest source of calcium – Legendairy
	CAP	21	Legendairy – Legendairy
1.25	CTD	22	Legendairy – Legendairy ([becomes bus shelter poster])
	CTD	23	It's an industry that directly employs 45,000 Australians – Legendairy ([becomes page print ad in magazine])
1.30	DG	24	Legendairy ([on baseball cap])

Time	Element	Clause/ Message No.	Text of Clause/Message
	DG	25	Legendairy ([on a milk truck])
	DG	26	Each serve has 10 essential nutrients "on mat near the dairy cabinet in a supermarket"
	DG	27	Legendairy ([on same mat near dairy cabinet])
	DG	28	Legendairy ([on back of farmer's shirt])
	DG	29	Legendairy ([on a farm gate])
	DG	30	Legendairy ([a sign above a school tuck shop])
1.49	CAP	31	Legendairy
1.49	FP	32	Dairy Australia

Legend CAP *Bold caption over film*
  FP *Fineprint caption over film / credits etc.*
  FPL *Fineprint logo*
  DG *Diagetic – e.g. writing on milk carton*
  CTD *Caption to Diagetic e.g. text starts as caption on moving image, then becomes incorporated into a moving image e.g. as part of a bus shelter advertisement.*
  ([]) *Comment on location or status of wording in with regard to represented action*

Language choices in the 'Legendairy' text

The first point of interest is that this text relies heavily on equative constructions, called Relational Identifying clauses in systemic functional grammar (Halliday & Matthiessen 2014).[7] This kind of clause generally works to depict one thing as a token of some value, e.g. 'Milk (token) is life (value)'. In the Legendairy text, examples of this equative construction include '*It's our people*', '*It's our hard work*', and '*It's our industry*' where '*our people*', '*our hard work*' and '*our industry*' are on the 'value' side of this verbal equation.

But what is this '*it*' and what's its significance? Readers will no doubt have noticed that the Legendairy text introduces '*dairy*' as an explicit element in the first few clauses, e.g. 'There's a new story about Australian Dairy'. This is followed by a string of clauses in which the pronoun '*it*' is the subject, referring back to '*dairy*' in some cases but in other cases perhaps referring forward. In any case the referent is somewhat unclear. This ambiguity seems to be a key rhetorical strategy in the text, beginning explicitly in clause 5 ('*It has become less valued*') but casting a shadow much earlier.

Using the linguistic technique of cohesive harmony (Hasan 1984; Moore 2014), we can help clarify the sources and flows of such ambiguity in the text and explore how the text is working to offer values for readers to align with. Chains of lexical meaning that run through a text can be displayed, showing the way that different chains persist, or get interrupted, or re-enter the discourse. We can also map how different chains or vertical strands of meaning in the text are woven together horizontally, including their ambiguities, to produce the 'fabric' of a text. Such an analysis brings out the way dairy is construed predominantly as an industry or a human collective in the 'Legendairy' text, unlike the 1911 'Milk in sealed bottles' poster or the 1960s 'Only butter with fish' poster, each of which presents a particular dairy product as its promotional target.[8]

A cohesive harmony analysis of the 'Legendairy' text is given below in Figure 9.1.

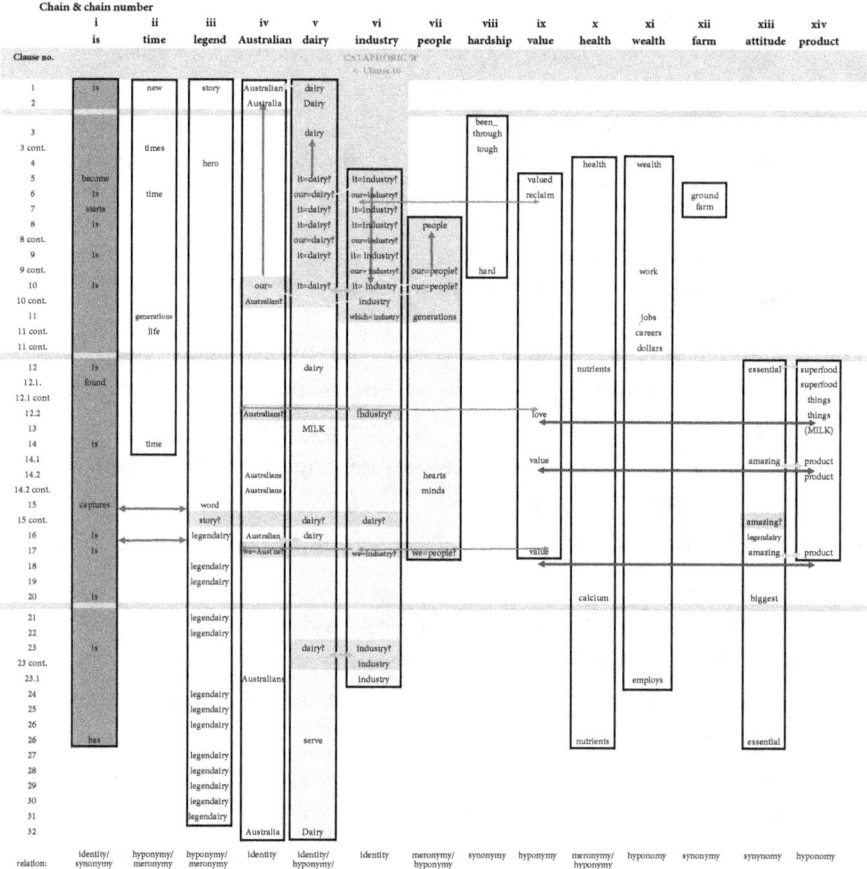

Figure 9.1 Cohesive Harmony of Legendairy Text.

The first step in mapping the cohesive harmony of a text is to allocate words in the text to lexical/semantic chains on the basis of

a. identity relations, where
   - lexical items refer to the same entity, event or circumstance in a text e.g. the cow … the cow; or
   - lexical items are pronominally substituted or likewise need interpreting and 'rendering' from the actual text wording, e.g. The cow stood quietly and chewed her cud; and

b. similarity relations
   - where words are related via sense relations such as synonymy, hyponymy metonymy etc – e.g. She loved her calf and valued her freedom, where 'to value' is treated as a hypernym of 'to love'.

Figure 9.1 represents the Legendairy text as consisting of fourteen lexical chains concerning the semantic items is, time, legend, Australian, dairy, industry, people, hardship, value, health, wealth, farm, positive appraisal/attitude, and finally product. For example, the chain for 'is', in the pink column, consists of 'is' in clause 1, its synonym 'become' in clause 5, then many more instances of is and a handful of other synonyms or repetitions. Other ways of organizing all the words in this text into chains could be valid and would indicate a different reading path as it were.

Key initial points from the diagram in Figure 9.1 include:

- The chain for *Australia(n)* is introduced in the first clause and persists to the end (clause 32).
- the chain for *dairy* is also introduced in the first clause and persists to the end.
- The chains for *industry* and *people* are introduced soon after and persist to near the end (until clause 23 and clause 17 respectively).
- The *industry*, *people*, *dairy* and *Australia* chains are also quite permeable in terms of some items being ambiguous with regard to which chain they help form (for example, the pronoun *our* might refer back [or forward] to *dairy*, *industry*, or *Australians*).
- The chain for dairy as a *product* comes in late and dies away quickly.
- In the chain for dairy as a product, the word *milk* is not actually spoken or written into the primary text of the advertisement, nor are the words 'cheese', 'yoghurt'; only generic words such as *things, product* and *superfood* are in the advertisement itself.
- The word *milk* does appear in the ad, but only printed on a carton handled by an actor (this is included as an available meaning in the cohesion analysis).

In Figure 9.1 the shading represents those pronouns (*it, our*, etc.) that cannot be conclusively resolved. One effect of such ambiguity is that '[o]ur interest is immediately engaged, since we inevitably start searching for some interpretation of the "*it*". This type of false or unresolved cohesion creates an effect of solidarity with the hearer or reader. It puts him [sic] on the inside, as one who is assumed to have shared a common experience with the speaker or writer' (Halliday & Hasan 1976: 298).

A similar effect is achieved by all but omitting any reference to milk, butter and so on: the reader is again assumed to share an understanding of what '*products*' and '*things*' might mean in this context of positive appreciation. Such rhetorical strategies are bound to be deliberate on the part of the text's creators, given the goal of bringing consumers and farmers together and restoring confidence in the industry, because (i) vagueness can create room for a wide range of 'someones' to read the text in terms of shared values, and (ii) avoiding explicitness creates an 'emic' sense that producers and audience already know what their shared values are and do not need to declare them (cf. Knight 2013; White 2020; Zappavigna 2011 on bonding, alignment and affiliation).

The second step in cohesive harmony analysis is to look at the horizontal interaction between the vertical chains, as indicated by horizontal arrows in Figure 9.1. This involves identifying how the tokens of a chain relate to tokens of some other chain(s) grammatically, rather than in terms of lexical semantics. Within this approach, two chains are said to interact when at least two members of one chain stand in the same experiential relation to two members of another chain (Hasan 1984) – for example two members of the *attitude* chain act as epithets where members of the *product* chain are head nouns, as in '*amazing product*' and '*essential superfood*'.

The linguistic strategy of ambiguity outlined in previous paragraphs works in synergy with the chain interaction patterns. Probably the most important patterns are:

- There are multiple interactions between the '*industry*' chain and the '*value*' chain where '*industry*' is grammatically the undergoer of the processes of '*valuing/loving/reclaiming*'.
- There are multiple interactions between the other possible referents of '*it*' and the possible referents of '*we/our*' in the text.

The whole overall effect is an apparently fluid text fabric that construes a very ambiguous concept of 'us'. If you're one of the 'us' that is offered up to the compliant reader of the Legendairy text you are offered an identity that is fused across being Australian, being part of the dairy industry, loving dairy and embodying or at least aligning with all the awesome things ascribed to this industry and its products in the text.

It is perhaps surprising that there is no chain in the Legendairy text for 'cows'. On reflection this is arguably a manifestation of what we see in the language at large: the word 'cow' is not a very common modifier (or top collocate) of 'milk' (Moore 2015) because cow's milk is still the default kind of milk consumed by humans. A deeper reason underlying these linguistic patterns may be that to maintain its social licence the dairy industry requires the textual absence of those whose physical presence and manipulation is necessary for producing milk and milk products. The absences of the lexemes 'milk' and 'cow' in the advert instantiate Adams's concept of absent referent (2010[1990]). The absent referent is a powerful force for the 'natural mystification' of dairy because it helps keep milk from being seen as a 'relational substance' (Cohen and Otomo, 246) made by a someone, for another someone – who is not a human.

Language-image relations and appraisal in 'Legendairy'

There are, however, degrees and types of absence. The power of the absent referent in naturalizing dairy can be more fully appreciated when we turn to the relation between linguistic elements and images. Figures 9.2–9.5 show stills from the Legendairy video and how they align with multiple 'tiers' of textual analysis.

In the video, human figures are prevalent throughout. In most shots humans are represented as differentiated persons, either as individuals or in collectives (after van Leeuwen 1996). That is to say, even if a human appears in a group in the advert, they have been constructed visually in such a way that their individual identity or role can be recognized in different shots. This helps to position readers to first empathize with the people shown and then later to admire them, especially those shown in farm settings.

As the video opens, a man in a lush pastoral setting is shown from behind; he is standing on a hill looking out over a ridge (see Figure 9.2). With the man's gaze entirely denied, the viewer is positioned to observe this figure rather than engage directly with him, and the high shot implies the viewer is in some way in a position of greater power than the figure (Kress & van Leeuwen 2006). Over this image the caption appears, 'Dairy has been through some tough times.' This configuration begins a sequence of verbal appraisals in which dairy is represented as human collective/industry, as detailed above, but evaluated as if

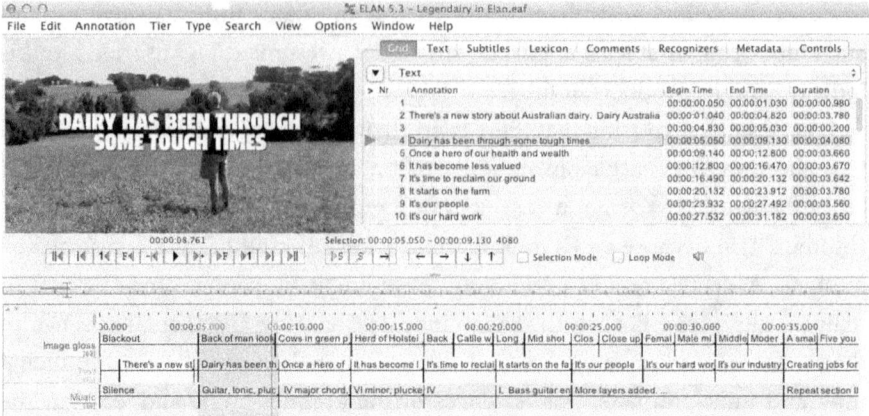

Figure 9.2 'Dairy has been through some tough times', still from 'Legendairy' video with partial analysis in ELAN software.

it were a person, via the resources of judgement, which are typically reserved for construing attitudes towards humans (Martin & White 2005).

One particular appraisal motif in 'Legendairy' is tenacity, inscribed here through tokens *been through, tough times, hard work* and *hero*. Tenacity is also evoked through lexical items such as *reclaim,* and the semantics of persistence in 'creating jobs *for generations,* careers *for life*'. A cumulative effect of these and other linguistic choices is to depict dairy both as agentive and as an affected party, and no doubt this is designed to promote solidarity between consumers, farmers and possibly other sections of the dairy industry. It is worth noting that several human groups seem to be linguistically and visually excluded here, including large-scale dairy processors, international dairy companies, possibly farm hands, vegans, people who are not lactase persistent (a non-Euro-centric way of denoting 'lactose intolerant'), and indeed people from non-Caucasian backgrounds and other diversity groups – all of this echoing Hall and colleagues' description of how the media maintain 'strategic areas of silence' (1978).

Cows, despite their absence in the text's wording, do appear in Legendairy's images, beginning with the second shot in the video (Figure 9.3). Here several cows are shown as individuals with close-mid shot length and level shot height on flat and very green pasture, under the caption '*Once a hero of our health and wealth*'. Taken together with further linguistic choices nearby, this patterning frames cows as part of the industry and possibly sharing the lost heroic status depicted in Clause 4/Figure 9.2.

The shot in Figure 9.4 is captioned '*It's our people*'. It frames and individuates a single young, white, male, human farmer/worker, operating part of the rotary

Figure 9.3 'Once a hero of our health and wealth', still from 'Legendairy' video with partial analysis in ELAN software.

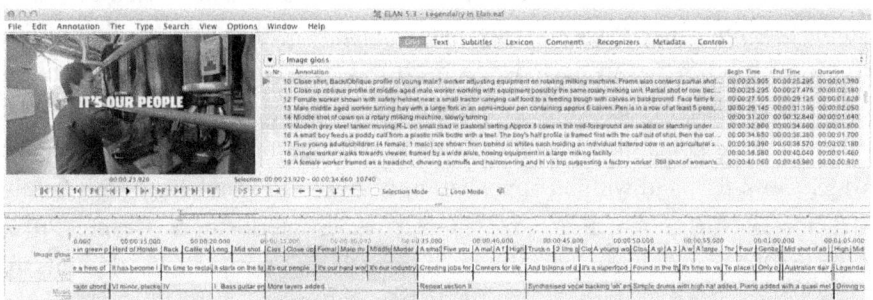

Figure 9.4 'It's our people', still from 'Legendairy' video with partial analysis in ELAN software.

milking 'parlour'. Viewers are presented with the young man's oblique gaze, allowing us to observe the apparent slight frown of concentration on his face and his clean and tidy presentation. He is clipping the milking clusters to one cow's teats while his gaze moves on to another cluster, which he will soon place on the next cow's teats.

This shot also depicts three cows who are having the clusters attached, but the cows are on a raised platform (the circulating part) on the other side of some safety fencing, facing away from the camera and slightly out of focus. The shot presents only an observational engagement from the worker to the cows' relevant body parts and there is no reciprocal interpersonal engagement construed between the cows and worker, audience and worker, or cows and audience.

The complex coherence between the very white and predominantly though not entirely male visual representation of human Australians in 'Legendairy' with the deceptively open but in fact very prescribed linguistic construction of 'us' outlined earlier suggests a highly worrying interpretation of who counts as 'us' and 'our people' according to this very recent messaging.

Figure 9.5 shows one cow, a calf in fact (bottom right), offering a fairly direct gaze allowing some interpersonal engagement with the viewer, but this is brief and unusual for the video overall. More commonly, cows in 'Legendairy' are genericized, represented as undifferentiated and/or aggregated through the use of long shots, oblique angles, being out of focus and other aspects of framing as in Figure 9.4 (after Kress and van Leeuwen; van Leeuwen). It is also interesting to note that the shot capture in Figure 9.5 is not static but opens with the caption *'Creating jobs for generations'* on the human boy alone, with a dynamic vector from the boy's gaze moving downward towards the calf's face and mouth as he or she suckles the bottle.

By themselves some images in this video appear to depict individual engagement between cows and humans, as seen in Figure 9.5 between the calf and young boy. But when image and language are taken together, we see an important way in which the cows are occluded from ethical view. Figure 9.5, with its caption of *'creating jobs for generations'* is one of many jarring shots whose visual-verbal relations lack empathic coherence with knowledge of the conditions under which cows live, and with an appreciation of cows as social beings with family structures, which research on cows as interspecies interlocutors (Despret 2016; Cornips 2022) and alternative calf-rearing practices (Thompson 2022) points to.

In other words, where Adams's absent referent is reinstated in the Legendairy video into the context of dairy in the way that Linné has observed, slogans such as *'careers for life'* and *'jobs for generations'* could suggest cows as workers who contribute physical and emotional labour, intelligence and collaboration, a view of species relations on farms which has been promoted as true to life and

Figure 9.5 'Jobs for generations', still from 'Legendairy' video with partial analysis in ELAN software.

ethically sound by some scholars (e.g. Haraway 2003; Porcher & Schmitt 2012) but criticized by others (Gaard 2013; Adams 2017; Boyde 2018). However, when the actual conditions cows live in are brought to mind, wordings such '*jobs for life*' carry connotations of endless endurance and repeated suffering, stretching from mother to child, on and on. There is no holiday, retirement or generational aspiration in sight, no choice over where one 'works' and no opportunity to 'resign' – echoing Derrida's critique of animal agriculture as an 'infernal, virtually interminable survival' (2002: 394). Adams (2017) also reminds us that like human females in the domestic sphere, cows cannot 'go home' from work.

Through such coordination of meanings across modes, the Legendairy video presents cows as not persons, their actual labour as insignificant and their situation as unremarkable, while visually appreciating them and entailing them within the industry (cf. Linné). These patterns also serve, like other advertisements for dairy products, to 'reconceptualise the relationship of milk production as being between the cow and us, not the cow and her calf' (Adams 2017: 23).

Thus instead of engaging with issues that increasingly concern consumers and are caused by current standard dairy praxis – such as early death of individual 'spent' cows at around four years old, and the disruption of bovine social bonds – the dairy industry itself, as a human collective, is positioned through this multimodal languaging to invoke empathy and admiration from audiences, as a set of attitudinal couplings around which consumers are invited to bond with dairy producers and with each other (there is no productive distinction in this multimodal text between consumers and citizens).

These recurring interpersonal-to-ideational couplings in the Legendairy text are one type of Alexander and Stibbe's clusters (2014) and Halliday's syndromes (1990). This analysis is related to but, in important ways, distinct from Berger's (1980) and Baker's (2001a, 2001b) arguments: where they exhort us to look to the visual, especially in high art and the mythical, the present analysis highlights the cultural meanings that can only be understood by considering (at least) wording and images together, particularly in quotidian contexts, and using a fine-grained analysis of such multimodal languaging.

Implications for dairy and for ecolinguistics

Cuffari writes:

[A]s humans we must tell ourselves, and we must believe, that habits can change, and that what is exceptional about our kind of being can be good and not only deadly for the rest of the universe ... We find the power to transcend our inherited perspectives in our defining ability, as linguistic bodies, to *decentre* from our ego-point, to dually embody (incorporate and incarnate) the voices of others. To the extent that we can receive utterances from nonhuman others, we hold open the possibility of shifting our own habitual ways of being. (2020: 245)

In weighing which new habits around dairy should be considered, it will be necessary to look at tensions between proposed alternatives to the status quo, but it seems to me important to do so while keeping in mind Cuffari's possibility of listening to the utterances of cows (cf. Adams 2017 and others). Although a discussion of the alternatives in any depth is beyond the scope of this chapter and my scholarship, following Clay and Yurco (2019), we can identify three broad options: we can consume *more* milk, *better* milk or *less* milk (perhaps none).

With regard to the 'consume more milk' option, mitigation strategies such as feeding seaweed to cows to reduce methane emissions are gaining attention; but it seems unlikely that expanding traditional dairy would suit the ecocivilization project because so many other causes of environmental harm are involved, in particular land clearing; and, as noted in this chapter, there is an increasing recognition of harms to cow and calf welfare with large-scale dairy.

Going organic and mitigating the harms with methods such as cow-calf contact rearing seems appealing and reassuring. Yet the relative climate impacts of going organic may be small or even negative, even before cow welfare is considered. For example, a recent assessment of a 100 per cent switch to organic production including dairy in the UK found that direct greenhouse gas emissions are reduced but, after accounting for increased land use, net emissions are greater (Smith et al. 2019).

Consuming less cow's milk and dairy is a good option in my view except in a very small number of regions of the developing world as a strategy to combat malnutrition, although scholars caution that it is hard to establish or expand dairy in such scenarios without commercialization, which disrupts smaller farming operations (Clay & Yurco 2019).

The 'less milk' option can sometimes be rejected on the grounds that dairy alternatives, especially soy and nut milks, have 'entrenched reliance on agri-business' and consumers 'need to drink more of [them] to get the same nutrition as dairy milk' (Clay and Yurco 2019: 5). An important factor that does not seem to be addressed very often is the assumption apparent here that the nutrition provided by cow's milk is best replaced by foods that resemble cows' milk; but many cultures thrive without dairy or similar items in their diet and foodways, and epidemiological and modelling research indicates that replacing animal protein with plant protein in human diets may lead to health improvements (Willett & Stampfer 2013; Capilé et al. 2021). It may be profitable for many of us to give up our adult devotion to the 'white river of life' in animal *or* plant form. (At a consumer choice level I try to do this myself sometimes by channelling the scorn an Australian gets in Italy asking for a cappuccino after breakfast.)

There are many scales on which decisions need to be made beyond the consumer or citizen level, and questions that those working in and around dairy need to consider, which reciprocally influence decisions at all the other scales, whether to exit the industry, get bigger, go niche, or change to food crops or even cotton (Ruddick 2020; Moeller Gorman 2023).

What can ecolinguistics contribute to such decisions and conversations? Can the kind of close text analysis presented in this chapter throw new light on how to promote meaningful private and public conversations about the challenges of dairy? The text analysis presented is only one account of one text from one campaign in one traditional dairy-producing-and-consuming country. But it is place-based and relation-oriented and arguably it suggests some new points or hypotheses about how dairy industry languaging works towards its goal of keeping milk in its 'proper' position. Perhaps its key contribution is to demonstrate the need to get beyond the trope of 'truth in advertising'. The ad is meticulously crafted, but the text analysis helps identify worrying disjunctions that appear underneath the smooth surface. Finding these disjunctions helps get a closer picture of the discursive work this languaging performs in this context, not all of which is deliberate, but it is designed.

There is a particular resonance here with the work of Vigors et al. (2023), who find that farm animal welfare research lacks attention to the sociocultural and relational aspects of the livestock workplace. They advocate tapping into ideals and symbols unconsciously embedded in farmers' practices – values that farmers show but may not be able to express – using on-site 'skilled performances' rather than attitude surveys. They argue that farmers and whole supply chains are more likely to change within this skilled performance framing.

Conclusion

Against the background of dairy's long but now quite problematic role in human civilization, this chapter discusses the languaging observed in a recent, carefully coordinated media campaign by the Australian dairy industry. Analyses show some unusual ways in which this industry messaging works to deflect the kind of public concern for cows' well-being, and the well-being of the planet, that might help bring about and constitute a willingness to change habits of purchasing and consumption.

Changing our current dairy habits is a necessary element of promoting positive bio-ecological change, which should work to maintain biodiversity AND promote the flourishing of individuals of different species, thus moving on from a neoliberal freedom for humans only.

The focus on languaging explored here, although it is by no means all that is needed, can help us rethink connections between formal and practical ways of knowing, and foreground action.

Notes

1. This is not to say that no good linguist could drink milk, but that reflection on what it means (and who it affects) to consume dairy is essential, particularly for moving towards an ecocivilization.
2. A challenge for ecolinguists here is using language that increases engagement outside ecolinguistics but also takes seriously the fact that our language, thought and action is not really 'about' dairy: despite grammatical clunkiness it may be more helpful to say that we need to change how we speak, think and do dairy – which explicitly construes 'languaging' as agentive and helps combat the 'aboutness' bias.
3. Voiceless is an animal justice institute. Patrons include Jane Goodall and Mark Bekoff.
4. Based on 40,000 farms in 119 countries and covering 40 food products that represent 90 per cent of all that is eaten (Carrington 2018).
5. A reviewer asks for clarification. I consider myself currently cohabiting and co-becoming with human, canine and cavy family members, some of whom have been 'rescued' from research laboratories, and I have also lived in this way with alpacas and budgerigars, and at other times in regular interaction with and/or responsibility for chickens, sheep, cows and horses, as well as welcoming many 'wild' others as regular interactants including lorikeets, kangaroos, lizards, snakes, insects and beautiful but troubling baby rats. Beyond this direct interaction, my multi-species entanglement includes animals that might be displaced or otherwise affected by my actions, including travelling, eating and clothing myself. The categories I have used to organize this mini-account of my multi-species relations are woefully problematic: writing an unproblematic statement would take another paper at least.
6. John Webster, Emeritus Professor of Animal Husbandry, Bristol University (cited in HSUS 2009).

7   I use 'systemic functional grammar' to refer to the framework for describing features and (largely paradigmatic) patterns at clause level, and 'systemic functional linguistics' for the overarching theory of language developed by Halliday and others, including tools for describing features at other levels such as the level of 'semantics' (e.g. Hasan 1984; Halliday 1990) or 'discourse semantics' (e.g. Martin & White 2005).

8   See Moore and Evans (forthcoming) for discussion of diachronic changes in Australian dairy promotion texts. The limits of comparing videos with posters are of course acknowledged.

References

Abbott, M. (2015). 'Margarine and the origins and timing of microeconomic reform in Australia'. *Australian Journal of Agriculture and Resource Economics*, 60: 22–38. https,//doi.org/10.1111/1467-8489.12100.

Adams, C. (2010/1990). *The sexual politics of meat: A feminist-vegetarian critical theory*. 20th Anniversary Edition. New York and London: Bloomsbury.

Adams, C. (2017). 'Feminized protein, meaning, representations, and implications'. In Mathilde Cohen & Yoriko Otomo (Eds.), *Making milk, the past, present and future of our primary food*, 19–40. London and New York: Bloomsbury.

Adams, C. (2018). 'Provocations from the field, female reproductive exploitation comes home'. *Animal Studies Journal*, 7(2): 1–8. ro.uow.edu.au/asj/vol7/iss2/2.

Adams, C., & Donovan, J. (2007). *The feminist care tradition in animal ethics, A reader*. New York: Columbia University Press.

Aerts, S. (2013). 'The consumer does not exist, overcoming the citizen/ consumer paradox by shifting focus'. In H. Rocklinsberg & P. Sandin (Eds.), *The ethics of consumption, the citizen, the market and the law*, 172–5. Wageningen: Wageningen Academic Publishers.

Alexander, R., & Stibbe, A. (2014). 'From the analysis of ecological discourse to the ecological analysis of discourse'. *Language Sciences*, 41: 104–10.

Alston, M. (2017). 'Gender and climate change in Australia'. *Journal of Sociology*, 47(1): 53–70. https//doi.org/10.1177/1440783310376848.

Andersson, H. (2020). 'Nature, nationalism and neoliberalism on food packaging, the case of Sweden'. *Discourse, Context and Media*, 34: 100329.

Andersson, H., & Smith, A. (2021). 'Flags and fields, a comparative analysis of national identity in butter packaging in Sweden and the UK'. *Social Semiotics*.

Baker, S. (2001a). *Picturing the beast, animals, identity, and representation*. Champaign: University of Illinois Press.

Baker, S. (2001b). 'Animals, representation, and reality'. *Society & Animals*, 9(3): 189–201.

Balzani, A., Aparacida Vaz do Amaral, C., & Hanlon, A. (2021). 'A perspective on the use of sexed semen to reduce the number of surplus male dairy calves in Ireland, a pilot study'. *Frontiers in Veterinary Science*, 7: 623128.

Berger, J. (1980). Why look at animals? *About looking*. New York: Pantheon, 1–26.

Bojovic, M., & McGregor, A. (2022). 'A review of megatrends in the global dairy sector, what are the socioecological implications?' *Agriculture and Human Values*, 40: 373–94.

Boyde, M. (2018). 'Practicing the art of war'. *Animal Studies Journal*, 7(2): 9–24.

Brugman, H., & Russel, A. (2004). 'Annotating Multimedia/ Multi-modal resources with ELAN'. In, *Proceedings of LREC 2004*, Fourth International Conference on Language Resources and Evaluation.

Buddle, E., Bray, H., & Ankeny, R. (2023). 'Values of Australian meat consumers related to sheep and beef cattle welfare, what makes a good life and a good death?' *Food Ethics*, 8: 5.

Carrington, D. (2018). 'Avoiding meat and dairy is "single biggest way" to reduce your impact on Earth'. *The Guardian*, 1 June 2018. https://www.theguardian.com/environment/2018/may/31/avoiding-meat-and-dairy-is-single-biggest-way-to-reduce-your-impact-on-earth. Last accessed 15 June 2023.

Cheever, H. (2011). Animal sentience: Intelligence, social nature, and emotionality. Panel address, National Conference to End Factory Farming, Arlington Virginia, 27–9 October 2011. https://www.youtube.com/watch?v=q-031z5U5hw.

Clay, N., & Yurco, K. (2019). 'Political ecology of milk: Contested futures of a lively food'. *Geography Compass*, 2020: 14: e12497.

Cohen, M. (2017). *Animal colonialism*: The case of milk. Symposium on Global Animal Law (Part 1). *AJIL Unbound* 111: 267–71.

Cohen, M., & Otomo, Y. (Eds.) (2017). *Making milk: The past, present and future of our primary food*. London and New York: Bloomsbury.

Colclough, G. (2008). The measure of the woman: Eugenics and domestic science in the 1924 sociological survey of white women in North Queensland. Unpublished PhD thesis, James Cook University.

Cole, M. (2011). 'From 'animal machines' to 'happy meat'? Foucault's ideas of disciplinary and pastoral power applied to 'animal-centred' welfare discourse'. *Animals*, 1: 83–101.

Coleman, G. (2019). 'Monitoring public attitudes to livestock industries and livestock welfare'. Final Report. APL Project 2018/0014. https://www.awstrategy.net/uploads/1/2/3/2/123202832/nawrde_no._2018-0014_final_report.pdf.

Cornips, L. (2022). 'The animal turn in postcolonial linguistics: The interspecies greeting of the dairy cow'. *Journal of Postcolonial Linguistics*, 6: 209–31.

Cowley, S. J. (2022). 'Ecolinguistics reunited: Rewilding territory'. *Journal of World Languages*, 7(3): 405–27.

Cuffari, E. (2020). *Habits: Pragmatist approaches from cognitive science, neuroscience, and social theory*. Cambridge: Cambridge University Press.

Dairy Australia (2013a). Australian Dairy – it's Legendairy! Video advertisement. DA YouTube Channel https://www.youtube.com/watch?v=UDjl5RRa7Qo. Last accessed 15 June 2023.

Dairy Australia (2013b). Dairy Australia celebrates a Legendairy industry in a new campaign via CumminsRoss Melbourne. Media Release. https://campaignbrief.com/dairy-australia-celebrates-a-l/. Last accessed 15 June 2023.

Dairy Australia (2022). Annual Report for 2022.

Dairy Australia (2023). Aussies still love dairy and farmers see high farmgate milk prices. https://www.dairyaustralia.com.au/news-repository/2023/03/07/aussies-still-love-dairy-and-farmers-see-high-farmgate-milk-prices. 7 March 2023. See 'For Industry' section of website. Last accessed 10 May 2023.

Dairy Australia (no date). Website section for consumers 'separating cows and calves' https://www.dairyaustralia.com.au/animal-management-and-milk-quality/approach-to-animal-welfare/separating-cow-and-calves. Last accessed 15 June 2023.

Deckha, M. (2012). 'Toward a postcolonial, posthumanist feminist theory: Centralizing race and culture in feminist work on nonhuman animals'. *Hypatia*, 27(3): 527–45.

De Jaegher, H., & Di Paolo, E. (2007). 'Participatory sense-making'. *Phenomenology and the Cognitive Sciences*, 6: 485–507.

Derrida, J. (2002). 'The animal that therefore I am (more to follow) (Trans. David Wills)'. *Critical Inquiry*, 28(2): 369–418.

Despret, V. (2016). *What would animals say if we asked the right questions?* Minneapolis: University of Minnesota Press. Last accessed 15 May 2023.

Dupuis, E. M. (2002). 'The perfect food story'. In *Nature's perfect food: How milk became America's drink*, 17–45. New York: New York University Press.

Gillespie, K. (2018). *The cow with ear tag #1389*. Chicago: University of Chicago.

Gaard, G. (2013). 'Toward a feminist postcolonial milk studies'. *American Quarterly*, 65(3): 595–618. Special Issue on Race, Gender, Species.

Gaard, G. (2015). 'Ecofeminism and climate change'. *Women's Studies International Forum*, 49 (March–April 2015): 20–33. doi.org/10.1016/j.wsif.2015.02.004.

Hall, S., Critcher, S., Jefferson, T., Clarke, J., & Roberts, B. (1978). *Policing the crisis: Mugging, the state, and law and order*. London: Macmillan.

Halliday, M.A.K. (2003/1990). New ways of meaning: The challenge to Applied Linguistics. Reprinted in *On language and linguistics*, 139–74. Volume 3 in the Collected Works of M.A.K. Halliday. London and New York: Continuum.

Halliday, M. A. K., & Hasan, R. (1976). *Cohesion in English*. London: Longman.

Halliday, M. A. K., & Matthiessen, C. M. M. (2014). *An introduction to functional grammar*, Fourth Edition. London and NY: Routledge.

Hampton, J., Hyndman, T., Allen, B., & Fischer, B. (2021). 'Animal Harms and Food Production: Informing Ethical Choices'. *Animals*, 11: 1225.

Haraway, D. (2003). *The companion species manifesto: Dogs, people, and significant otherness*. Chicago: Prickly Paradigm Press.

Harrison, R. (1964). *Animal machines. The new factory farming industry*. Boston: Vincent Stuart.

Hasan, R. (1984). 'Coherence and cohesive harmony'. In James Flood (Ed.), *Understanding Reading Comprehension*, 181–221. Delaware: International Reading Association.

HSUS (Humane Society of the United States) (2009). *The Welfare of Cows in the Dairy Industry*. HSUS Report no. 20. Retrieved from animalstudiesrepository.org/hsus_reps_impacts_on_animals/20.

Capilé, K., Parkinson, C., Twine, R., Kovalski, E. L., & Paixão, R. L. (2021). 'Exploring the representation of cows on dairy product packaging in Brazil and the United Kingdom'. *Sustainability*, 13: 8418.

Jacobs, A. (2020). 'Is dairy farming cruel to cows?' *New York Times*, 29 December 2020. https://www.nytimes.com/2020/12/29/science/dairy-farming-cows-milk.html. Last accessed 9 January 2024.

Kjeldsen, J. (2007). 'Visual argumentation in Scandinavian political advertising: A cognitive, contextual, and reception-oriented approach'. *Argumentation and Advocacy*, 43(3–4): 124–32. Special Issue on Visual Argumentation.

Knight, N. (2013). 'Evaluating experience in funny ways: How friends bond through conversational humour'. *Text & Talk*, 33(4–5): 553–74.

Kress, G., & van Leeuwen, T. (2006). *Reading images: The grammar of design*. 2nd edition. London and New York: Routledge.

Levitt, T. (2020). The end of dairy's dirty secret: Farms have a year to stop killing male calves. *The Guardian*, 10 December 2020.

Li, J., Steffensen, S., & Huang, G. (2020). 'Rethinking ecolinguistics from a distributed language perspective'. *Language Sciences*, 80: 101277.

Linné, T. (2016). 'Cows on Facebook and Instagram: Interspecies intimacy in the social media spaces of the Swedish dairy industry'. *Television & New Media*, 17(8): 719–33.

Martin, J. R., & White, P. R. R. (2005). *The language of evaluation: Appraisal in English*. Hampshire and New York: Palgrave.

Moeller Gorman, R. (2023). 'How dairy farmers are turning manure into money'. *Smithsonian Magazine*. https://www.smithsonianmag.com/innovation/dairy-farmers-turning-manure-into-money-180981809/. Last accessed 10 June 2023.

Moore, A. R. (2014). 'That could be me: Identity and identification in discourses about food, meat, and animal welfare'. *Linguistics and the Human Sciences*, 9(1): 59–93.

Moore, A. R. (2015). Talking up milk. Paper presented in a panel session at the Australian Animal Studies Association conference, University of Melbourne, July 2015.

Moore, A. R. (2019). The linguistics of individuation in the ecological and ethical framing of animals. Invited presentation, ICE-4, Odense, Denmark, 15 August 2019.

Moore, A. R., & Evans, N. (forthcoming). Talking up milk: Australian dairy advertising in the 20th and early 21st century. Under review.

PCRM (Physicians' Committee for Responsible Medicine) (no date) Health concerns about dairy. https://www.pcrm.org/good-nutrition/nutrition-information/health-concerns-about-dairy. Last accessed 14 May 2023.

Phillipov, M., & Loyer, J. (2019). 'In the wake of the supermarket 'milk wars': Media, farmers and the power of pastoral sentimentality'. *Discourse, Context & Media*, 32: 100346.

Poore, J., & Nemecek, T. (2018). 'Reducing food's environmental impacts through producers and consumers'. *Science*, 360(6392): 987–92.

Porcher, J., & Schmitt, T. (2012). 'Dairy cows: Workers in the shadows?' *Society & Animals*, 20(1): 39–60.

Rémond, B., Ollier, A., & Miranda, G. (1992). 'Milking of cows in late pregnancy'. *Journal of Dairy Research*, 59(3): 233–41.

Royal Commission on Milk (1913). '*Science of man and journal of the Royal Anthropological Society of Australasia*' 14(41): 19. Last accessed 28 September 2018 via Trove online Archive https://trove.nla.gov.au/version/250878033.

Ruddick, B. (2020). Dairy profits are still so weak that Mark Cowley has gone from milking cows to picking cotton. *ABC News*, 13 June 2020. https://www.abc.net.au/news/2020-06-13/dairy-farmers-experiment-diversify-cotton-goats/12344558. Last accessed 10 June 2023.

Safe for Animals (no date). Every glass of cow's milk comes at the expense of the calf. https://safe.org.nz/blog-articles/every-glass-of-cows-milk-comes-at-the-expense-of-the-calf/. Last accessed 17 August 2021.

Singer, P. (2008). 'Forward'. In M. Stamp Dawkins & R. Bonney (Eds.), *The future of animal farming: Renewing the ancient contract*. Oxford: Wiley-Blackwell.

Smith, L., Kirk, G., Jones, P., & Williams, A. (2019). 'The greenhouse gas impacts of converting food production in England and Wales to organic methods'. *Nature Communications*, 10: 4641.

Springmann, M., Godfray, H., Rayner, M., & Scarborough, P (2016). 'Analysis and valuation of the health and climate change cobenefits of dietary change'. *PNAS*, 113(15): 4146–51.

Stamp Dawkins, M. (2023). 'Natural behaviour is not enough: Farm animal welfare needs modern answers to Tinbergen's Four Questions'. *Animals*, 13(6): 988.

Steinfeld, S., Gerber, P., Wassenaar, T., Castel, V., Rosales, M., & de Haan, C (2006). Livestock's long shadow: Environmental issues and options (Report). FAO. ISBN 978-92-5-105571-7. https://www.fao.org/3/a0701e/a0701e00.htm. Retrieved 27 September 2019.

Taylor, N., & Fraser, H. (2019). 'The cow project: Analytical and representational dilemmas of dairy farmers' conceptions of cruelty and kindness'. *Animal Studies Journal*, 8(2): 133–53. https://ro.uow.edu.au/asj/vol8/iss2/10.

Thibault, P. (2011). 'First-order languaging dynamics and second-order language: The distributed language view'. *Ecological Psychology*, 23(3): 210–45.

Thompson, M. (2022). Alternative visions of 'ethical' dairying: Changing entanglements with calves, cows and care. *Agriculture and Human Values*.

Thorley, V. (2014). 'There is absolutely NO SUBSTITUTE for fresh milk: Dairy marketing in Australia, Twentieth Century'. *International Journal of Liberal Arts and Social Science*, 3(2): 1–14.

Tulloch, L., & Judge, P. (2018). 'Bringing the calf back from the dead: Video activism, the politics of sight, and the New Zealand dairy industry'. *Video Journal of Education and Pedagogy*, 3: 9.

van Leeuwen, T. (1996). 'The representation of social actors'. In Carmen Caldas-Coulthard (Ed.), *Texts and Practices: Readings in Critical Discourse Analysis*, 32–70. London: Routledge.

Voiceless (2015). *The life of the dairy cow: A report on the Australian dairy industry*. Sydney: Voiceless Animal Protection Institute.

Vigors, B., Wemelsfelder, F., & Lawrence, A. (2023). 'What symbolises a "good farmer" when it comes to farm animal welfare?' *Journal of Rural Studies*, 98: 159–70.

Weary, D. M., & von Keyserlingk, M. (2017). 'Public concerns about dairy-cow welfare: How should the industry respond?' *Animal Production Science*, 57(7): 1201–9.

Whalin, L., Weary, D., & von Keyserlingk, M. (2021). 'Understanding behavioural development of calves in natural settings to inform calf management'. *Animals*, 11(8): 2446.

White, P. R. R. (2020). 'Attitudinal alignments in journalistic commentary and social-media argumentation: The construction of values-based group identities in the online comments of newspaper readers'. In M. Zappavigna & S. Dreyfus (Eds.), *Discourses of hope and reconciliation: On J.R. Martin's contribution to Systemic Functional Linguistics*, 22–38. London: Bloomsbury.

Whorf, B. L. (1956). *Language, thought, and reality: Selected writings of Benjamin Lee Whorf* (B. Carroll John Ed.). Cambridge, MA: MIT Press.

Wicks, D. (2018). 'Demistifying dairy'. *Animal Studies Journal*, 7(2): 45–75. Retrieved from ro.uow.edu.au/asj/vol7/iss2/5.

Wilkinson, J. (1999). Dairy industry in NSW: Past and present. Briefing Paper No 23/99, NSW Parliamentary Library Research Service.

Willett, W., & Stampfer, M. (2013). 'Current evidence on healthy eating'. *Annual Review of Public Health*, 34(1): 77–95.

Zappavigna, M. (2011). 'Ambient affiliation: A linguistic perspective on Twitter'. *New Media & Society*, 13(5): 788–806.

10

Learning About, Learning From, Learning With: Towards a Critical Practice and Theory of Situated Language Sciences

Chris Sinha and Vera da Silva Sinha

Introduction

Our aim in this chapter is to critically examine the sciences of language as practices/theories in a complex of interrelated social, cultural, political and ideological ecologies. The specific topic around which we try to disentangle and illuminate this web of practice/theory is the study of endangered (especially, Indigenous minority) languages and cultures. The motivation for this exploration is our conviction that understanding languages as ecological phenomena necessitates a reflexive, deconstructive examination of the presuppositions underlying conventional answers to two key questions: 'what is [a] language?' and 'how do languages articulate their ecological grounding?' The plural notion of 'situated language sciences' implicates, simultaneously, the ecology of scientific practices/theories, and the ecology of social and cultural practices embedding *languaging*.[1] In respect of both these perspectives, our interrogation is *ontological*: we want to understand what language sciences are *about* – that is, what do language sciences set up and analyse as their *objects*, and in what kinds of *worlds* are *practices of languaging* ecologically enmeshed?

Already in 1952, Frantz Fanon, one of the pioneers of what would become post- and decolonial theory, delineated the field of forces that forms the backdrop to this ontological interrogation:

> The colonized has no ontological resistance in the eyes of the colonizer. From one day to the next, the colonized have had to deal with two systems of reference. Their metaphysics, or less pretentiously their customs and the agencies to which they refer, were abolished because they were in contradiction with a new civilization that imposed its own. (Fanon 2021: 90)[2]

Our exploration starts from the conventional framing in language sciences of 'endangered language research', ending with a sketch of how the cultures and languages of Indigenous minority peoples can be re-framed as sources for the revitalization of ecologically grounded, socioculturally situated language sciences. We first attempt to understand the situatedness of language sciences in terms of the production, reproduction, and contestation of a nexus of intersecting presuppositions, practices and power relationships; within which scientists, the linguistic 'objects' of their research, and communities of speakers of Indigenous languages are jointly implicated and intermeshed. We shall be concerned in the first instance to understand how views of 'what is language' are related to the interests of actors in the ecology of language sciences – that is, for whose benefit is the recording, analysis and description of endangered languages conducted? Our contention is that a great deal of such research is practised and conceptualized for the benefit of actors and institutions other than the communities that employ the languages that are the 'objects' of endangered language research. We identify two influential rationales, both of which conceptualize endangered languages as heritage objects disconnected from speech communities that frame and support the practice of what we characterize as *extractive linguistics*. These rationales mesh with the theoretical construction of the 'object' of linguistic science – Language – as constituted by abstraction from a totality of language objects derived from description and analysis of socioculturally situated performances of languaging.

We contrast these two rationales, or perspectives, with a third approach, that acknowledges the heritage dimension of endangered languages, but conceptualizes this in relation to the valorization of cultural and linguistic diversity. This motivates the practice of documentation for the preservation and revitalization of languages in the context of cultural dynamics and the empowerment of communities. Such a practice further demands *rethinking* language sciences in ways consistent with the overall approach encapsulated in the title of this volume – language as an ecological phenomenon. We argue for a transdisciplinary approach in which 'linguistics' is not pre-eminent, but rather one strand of an ensemble of socio-ecologically informed practices/theories.

A transdisciplinary language science is necessarily pluralistic, requiring a willingness by researchers to learn the perspectives of disciplines other than the one(s) in which they were trained. This is one meaning of the title of this chapter. If *multi*disciplinarity implies learning *about* other disciplines, and *inter*disciplinarity implies learning *from* other disciplines, critically learning *with* practitioners of other disciplines is the foundation for the creation of a *trans*disciplinary community of knowledge exploration and construction. Our contribution to realizing this situates our and others' research on Indigenous cultures/languages of Amazonia in the exploration of differing cultural ontologies and their associated 'ecologics'.

Equally fundamental, however, is the reference in our title to the changing relationship implied by a situated, socio-politico-ecological language science between the researcher(s) and the language community. The role of the language scientist is not just to learn *about* the language/culture, but also to learn *from* the community about how to forge effective strategies for cultural and linguistic empowerment (Dobrin 2008), and to learn *with* the community about how shared knowledge has relevance for multiple academic disciplines and for practices of social, political and environmental justice.

Linguistics, languages as objects and the claims of heritage

Mainstream theoretical approaches in linguistics view languages from an external or third person perspective (Sinha 2017a: 496). This perspective, in which languages are *objects* whose systematic and comparative analysis will lead to the progressive refinement, through reflective abstraction, of the ultimate theoretical object of linguistics (*la langue*, the language faculty, or one of their variants) is explicitly adopted by enterprises such as linguistic typology, and it also implicitly informs most linguistics-based endangered languages research (Grinevald & Sinha 2016). Such research commonly involves description of a language by the writing of grammars, compiling of word lists and dictionaries, and recording of interactions and narratives. This general approach to language documentation has a venerable history, going back to the pioneering work of Franz Boas (1911) and his students on Native North American languages. For Boas, however, the description and analysis of endangered languages was not a sub-discipline of linguistics. He regarded linguistics as one of the constitutive fields of anthropology, and the study of endangered languages as inseparable from ethnographic studies. So it was, too, for Bronislaw Malinowski, often cited as the founder of the British school of social anthropology and one of the founders of linguistic pragmatics.[3] Malinowski coined the term 'ethnolinguistics', and argued:

> [T]he conception of context must burst the bonds of mere linguistics and be carried over into the analysis of the general conditions under which a language

is spoken [...] the study of any language, spoken by a people who live under conditions different from our own and possess a different culture, must be carried out in conjunction with the study of their culture and their environment. (Malinowski 1923, cited by Senft 2007: 79)

For both Boas and Malinowski descriptive and documentary linguistic research was always in the interdisciplinary context of ethnographic description and theorization, viewing language as a window for understanding cultural practices, social structure and cultural concepts. Both men lived and worked in the era of still-ascendant Western colonialism, although it should be noted that Boas was an outspoken anti-racist, and both were proclaimed anti-Nazis.[4] The embeddedness of both anthropology and linguistics in nineteenth- and twentieth-century colonial projects has been addressed by many authors.[5] This embeddedness should not be simplistically understood as consisting solely of a veil of ideological justification for imperial rule (although this was indeed manifested in concepts of 'primitivity', 'backwardness' and 'vernacular dialects'). Equally important was the way in which the practice of colonial ethnographic and linguistic investigation defined the disciplinary theories and methods simultaneously with the subjects/objects of their deployment. In terms of the science of linguistics, 'representations of linguistic structure and colonial interests shaped and enabled each other ... such that language difference could become a resource – like gender, race, and class – for figuring and naturalizing inequality in the colonial milieux' (Errington 2001: 20). For the colonial power to map the territory, both geographical and demographic, over which it commanded, and to enable the differential negotiation of the distribution – including for the purpose of 'divide and rule' – of authorities and privileges:

> Language, ethnicity, and territory were supposed to coincide, and to define population units on an administratively manageable scale ... Whatever shapes [colonized] societies had taken previously, and however variable or multifarious their populations' ways of speaking, the moment of colonization is when they were given that particular inflection that turns cultural tradition and genealogies into 'ethnicity', turns linguistic practices into named 'languages' corresponding (supposedly) to ethnic groups, and interprets multilingualism as a secondary effect. (Irvine 2008: 338)

Our claim here is not that this interweaving of the moulding of ethnographic and linguistic theory with the imperatives of imperial power invalidated the fruits of the labours of (often 'amateur') researchers.[6] Take, for example, the post-First World War work of the indomitable Emily and David Lorimer (the latter was a political agent of the British Raj) in the Gilgit region of the Himalayan Karakoram highlands (Lorimer 1929; Lorimer 1939):

> They are said to have learned and recorded a different local language every year, much the most difficult being the scriptless Burushaski [a linguistic isolate[7]] [...] With its seven words for 'mother', its four genders, twenty-eight plural endings [...] the Lorimers gained some facility in this demanding tongue and put it to use quizzing the Hunzakuts on their practices and traditions. Emily Lorimer concentrated on domestic lore, David collected folk tales and beliefs. (Keay 2022: 165)

What is striking in this account is that the documentation of the language was combined, in true Boasian fashion, with ethnographic study of the speech community.[8] Over time, however, the connection that was empirically established in early ethnolinguistic research between language and community morphed and crystallized in linguistic theory into an *assumption* that languages are idealized, complete and consistent unities that are paired with idealized homogeneous communities of speakers. Languages can then be thought of as 'symbolic packages', handed down from generation to generation, whose transmission is ideally both complete and accurate. Any deviation from these normative ideals (such as those arising from language contact, from multilingualism, or from intergenerational differences in contexts of acquisition and use) is liable to be viewed as being both inconvenient noise in the data and evidence for the endangerment of the language.[9]

This assumption set the scene for a further step, towards a purist, exclusively monodisciplinary approach to research in endangered, minority and 'lesser known' languages, in which the language is thought of as 'floating free' from the community. In other words, although it might be acknowledged that the language is integral to the community, the community and its diverse range of languaging practices is *not* considered to be integral to the *language* that is being documented and described. Given this research model, engagement with communities to develop practices of language and culture preservation, revitalization and renewal came to be seen by some linguists as optional add-ons (Austin & Sallabank 2018: 210), at times disparagingly designated as 'linguistic social work' as opposed to 'real' (scientific) linguistics (Newman 2003).

Fortunately, current approaches to best practice in language documentation emphasize the importance both of drawing on interdisciplinary knowledge and practices, and of designing language documentation projects and archives for and with language revitalization (Austin 2016; 2021). The issue remains, however, of the relationship between language ideologies and the fundamental purpose of language description and language documentation. For many linguists, its raison d'être is primarily the enhancement of the empirical base for linguistic theory development and testing, and language documentation research is primarily a data collection and archiving enterprise. This is buttressed by the 'language as object' view, in which languages may be conceptualized as *heritage objects* – which inevitably raises the question: *whose heritage, in what context?* In the remainder of this section, we identify and critically examine three different rationales framing endangered language research in terms of different answers to this question.

'Save it for science': Commodification and extractive linguistics

The first rationale views the data resulting from language documentation research as a *heritage resource for science*. Existing, and documented but sleeping, languages are vital resources for scientists to study the nature of, and the constraints on, crosslinguistic and language-internal variation – and thus the human language faculty and the human mind more generally. The languages and language varieties of interest to endangered language documentation researchers may not be there to study in vivo in the future, and if they are not documented now, they will not be available for future generations of scholars. This is what we can call the 'save it for science' rationale.

It is self-evident that both current and future scholarship will be hugely enhanced by the availability of diverse language archives. However, when languages (and language diversity) are viewed exclusively through the lens of scientific heritage, there exists the danger that the communities from whose languaging practices the data are acquired are 'de-privileged' and rendered invisible.[10] Such de-privileging is reinforced by the framing of language documentation as a technical procedure to be conducted by an external, supposedly scientific observer, who is equipped, by virtue of training and material resources, to document, describe and analyse the language and then to disseminate the results of their analysis to other members of the scientific community. It is further buttressed by the conceptualization of languages as not merely objects of analysis, but objects with commodity value in the academic marketplace. 'Subtle and pervasive kinds of commodification – that is, reduction of languages to common exchange values – abound, particularly in competitive and programmatic contexts such as grant-seeking and standard-setting' (Dobrin et al. 2009: 40-41). Consequently, 'community members report sometimes feeling that the linguist comes in, reifies the language, turns it into a commodity, and then takes it away' (Bowern 2011: 468).

This is the material and ideological matrix within which the theoretical perspective of 'language as an object', coupled with the 'save it for science' rationale, operates as a motor for the reproduction of what we call *extractive linguistics*: the production, through abstraction from ecologically and socially situated practices, of a resource that is extracted from its context of use in order to circulate as a commodity within a *different* material and symbolic ecology – that of academic value.[11] Extractive linguistic practices/theories

> alienate the language from the community as a form of symbolic and cultural capital (Bourdieu 2010). For the communities and their members, the loss of this symbolic cultural capital usually has mainly negative material consequences … For the scientist, however, language-as-databank is a form of capital that, once 'put to work', can yield symbolic and material benefits in terms of continuing success in grant applications, citations and promotions … while the combination of language documentation with language maintenance and revitalization can result in a 'win-win' situation, in which there is mutual benefit to both researcher and community, language documentation in [its] absence is an *unequal exchange* (Emmanuel 1972) in which the benefit to the researcher is not accompanied by an equivalent benefit to the community, and may in fact result in disbenefits. (Grinevald & Sinha 2016: 34–5)

The unequal exchange that is intrinsic to extractive linguistics extends beyond the relations between researcher and community. It can also distort the relations between 'local' researchers and 'non-local' researchers, who are supposedly within the same scientific community. In reality, the 'scientific community', like the 'international community', is to a significant degree a fiction, masking systemically unequal power and resources between researchers from the Global North and the Global South, where many of the 'sites of interest' for endangered language documentation are to be found.[12]

> 'Northern' linguists receive disproportionately greater funding than 'southern' linguists; they generally enjoy better research infrastructures; have networks that help them update their theoretical, methodological and technical knowledge and skills; and are more likely to have publications in international (Anglophone) journals. These facts generate an ideological construction of unequal competence, to the further disbenefit of researchers from the global south. The beneficiaries, linguists from the global north, too frequently seek to

maximize their material advantage by laying claim to the intellectual territory of ELDR and its technical wherewithal; by acting as gatekeepers to funding; and by asserting the principle that 'data are for everyone', which sometimes boils down to 'let me have your data'. (Grinevald & Sinha 2016: 35)

This can result in unequal exchange between scientists of the Global North and scientists of the Global South, even when they are engaged in supposedly collaborative projects (for further analysis and case studies, see Grinevald & Sinha 2016). Furthermore, the framing of endangered language documentation research only in terms of data collection for the purposes of archive construction introduces a further dimension of inequity, because of the way certain kinds of skilled practices ('theory', 'pure research') are more valued, and better rewarded, than others ('applied' research, 'data collection'). The latter is often viewed as 'a purely mechanical, cognitively "light" activity; and local and contextual knowledge gained through personal experience of field work is devalued in comparison with theoretical knowledge. All of this amounts to the devaluation, familiar to many experienced field workers, of *knowledge as practice* and *practice as knowledge*' (Grinevald & Sinha 2016: 28).

Knowledge as practice/practice as knowledge is based upon the (often tacit) 'know-how' that is necessary for field research. It is emphatically not restricted to knowledge of how to use technical equipment and software tools, necessary as such knowledge is. Knowledge as practice/practice as knowledge also implicates the reflexive stance that is intrinsic to research in all disciplines that employ qualitative research methods, including the theory and practice of ethnographic research, intercultural communication, field research ethics, Indigenous rights and intellectual property.

Historicizing languages and cultures – heritage as a 'museum of mankind'

The second widely expressed rationale for documenting endangered minority languages is also grounded in the notion of heritage. Heritage arguments are frequently conceptualized in terms of an immaterial or intangible heritage whose value (analogously, in this context, with material heritage artworks and artefacts) is understood in terms of larger demographics (nation states and their citizens, humanity as a whole), rather than for the still-existing cultural and/or language communities.[13] Grounded in a view of minority (especially Indigenous) communities as 'living relics' of a passing age, and as the source of a vanishing stock of knowledge of cultural and linguistic diversity, this rationale is what we call the *museum of mankind* perspective.

Indigenous minority peoples (those communities known in different parts of world as Aboriginal, Adivasi, First Nations, Indigenous peoples, Tribal people) survive, more often than not, in conditions of material, social, cultural, educational and linguistic disadvantage. These can range from state and majoritarian violence, oppression and exclusion to neglect, lack of recognition, under-resourcing, and failure to address, and redress, past injustices. The consequences of this deprivation and disadvantage can be seen, in Indigenous communities on every continent, in elevated rates of poverty and poor physical and mental health, exclusion from education and employment and training opportunities, violence perpetrated by non-community members (including police and the judicial system) against community members, violence (including domestic violence) within the community, alcohol and drug use, self-harming, and suicide.

It is noteworthy that language vitality *vs* language morbidity is a powerful predictor of the severity of such consequences. A striking example is the prevalence of adolescent suicide. Michael Chandler and his colleagues (Chandler et al. 2003; Hallett, Chandler & Lalonde, 2007) investigated adolescent suicide rates in Canadian First Nations communities. They found that the variable with the single strongest predictive value of low rates of suicide, when comparing different bands, was language vitality. These authors' use of the trope of individual, cultural and community 'death by language' is a salutary corrective to the reifying metaphor of 'language death', the latter being cast as an event that is frequently conceptualized as being of concern principally to the scientific community.[14]

Disadvantaged conditions for the living members of Indigenous communities often go hand-in-hand with idealized representations of their traditional ways of life, in texts and images intended primarily for consumption by non-Indigenous people, communicated via national and international media. In many cases, such representations serve a real educational purpose. In others, they may involve the exoticization and 'othering' of Indigenous peoples, their lifeways and languages. A common message that can be taken from such representations, intended and explicit or not, is that there is a contrast between an authentic and original culture, located in the recent or distant past, and a less 'pure' contemporary culture that has been contaminated by the surrounding majority culture and by modernity in general.

Social, cultural and linguistic change are real, and the adaptation of tradition as a consequence of such change is equally real. We can also note the astonishing time depth of some material cultural traditions – there is evidence, for example, of continuity of artefacts made and used by San communities of South Africa going back 44,000 years (D'Errico et al. 2012); with respect to language/culture mediated knowledge, there is evidence that oral histories in Australia relate to events which took place over 10,000 years ago (Peter Austin, p.c.). There can be no culture without tradition, and no language variation without the transmission of language down through generations. However, the framing of 'traditional ways' (including language and languaging) as more 'authentic' than 'modern ways' is problematic, implying as it does that there once was a 'time before change', and that the original state of things at this time was what constituted (and, where possible, continues to guarantee) the essence of the identity of the group. In reality, while it is true that the closer we come to the present day, the more social, cultural and linguistic change accelerates, there never was a 'time before change' – all myths of origin are just that: myths.

In the perspective framed by the 'museum of mankind' rationale, cultural practices frequently become transmuted into performance for the enlightenment and entertainment of outsiders, sometimes for the material benefit of the community, but sometimes for the material benefit of external actors, state or private. This may be coupled with the establishment of national and regional museums for the display of artefacts, sometimes in the context of recreated settings of village and domestic life. In this context, language documentation practices and objectives can be conditioned by a view of diversity and indigeneity as historical, with their current manifestations fated to wither and die along the road to a future of national resurgence and 'progress' towards less linguistic diversity. This can lead to a focus on the identification and recording of the language of the past, which is seen as more 'authentic' and less inflected by contact with majority languages.

Just as we acknowledge the importance of culture and language documentation for scientific knowledge, we also acknowledge the importance of actual and virtual museums: for science, for public understanding, and as resources for practices by communities of culture and language preservation and revitalization. We also accept that documenting pre-contact varieties of endangered languages is of value both for language sciences and for communities. The key critical issue here is similar to that we have noted for the 'save it for science' rationale – are the products of documentation practices fully available to the communities, and, more generally, do the communities have effective control over the way in which artefacts (including linguistic artefacts) and practices are presented and displayed for the wider public? This leads us to the consideration of the third rationale for culture and language documentation, that is based upon a clearly affirmative answer to the question just posed, and places preservation and revitalization at the heart of its practice/theory.

Dynamics of change: Beyond archive and museum

We have acknowledged that the two long-standing rationales for endangered language documentation that we have discussed above, 'save it for science' and 'museum of mankind', can each claim legitimate justifications. However, each of them is also ideological, and as such may motivate discourses that suppress, to a greater or lesser extent, the historical, political, sociocultural and institutional relations within which language documentation practices are situated. These discursive formations include the conceptions of science, and of the desired scope and format of data, that inform endangered language documentation projects. The point of critiquing these two ideological positions is not to deny the validity of the dimensions of 'heritage' to which they speak *in themselves*. Rather, it is to unmask the power relations in which they are embedded, and to clarify the complex relations between practices and theories in the ecology of the language sciences.

The third rationale is also ideological, inasmuch as it takes a position in relation both to language diversity and to Indigenous peoples' struggles for justice and survival. It sees endangered languages as heritage resources for *continuing* human diversity and for the communities that use them in languaging. In this perspective, language diversity has intrinsic value, analogously with biodiversity, because languages are the most important bearers of the cultural heritage of the communities that speak/sign/write them (or even have largely ceased to use them). As such, they are vital (as demonstrated by the research cited above by Chandler and his colleagues) for community and individual health and well-being, as well as for cultural transmission. Our aim in the rest of this chapter is to explore some preconditions for the realization of this rationale in practice/theory.

Both the 'save it for science' and the 'museum of mankind' ideologies have as their goals constructing an archive of a past (and 'purer') era, rather than a record of contemporary appropriation and adaptation strategies towards a fragile language, employed by speakers who *language* with varying degrees and mixes of linguistic resources, occupying diverse positions in the contemporary political and sociocultural ecology. The third alternative, constructing a heritage *for the community*, does not reject the importance of either recording/ reconstructing vanishing language varieties, or understanding the lifeways that have shaped them in the past. However, it situates its practice firmly in a present in which both languages and communities are fractured, interwoven and inflected with other languages and varieties spoken by diverse social groups. While recognizing that languages (like other knowledge systems and artefacts) 'belong' fundamentally to the people who speak them, in all their diversity, it goes beyond the notion of 'intellectual property' to insist that what needs to be supported are neither the restoration of an imagined Edenic scenario of perfect inter-generational transmission nor a perfect replication of the genres of languaging practised in the past, but communities' own strategies for coping with a changing world.

As we have said, in this perspective, the role of the language scientist is not just to learn *about* the language/culture resources of the community, but also to learn *from* the community about how to forge effective strategies for cultural and linguistic empowerment, and to learn *with* the community how their knowledge has relevance for multiple academic disciplines and for wider movements for social and environmental justice. Our argument is not an appeal to 'make linguistics relevant', or to 'revalue applied linguistics'. Taken seriously, it challenges the boundaries between disciplines, and between 'objective' academic knowledge and the 'traditional' knowledge of minority Indigenous communities. In sum, we argue for a transdisciplinary approach in which 'linguistics' is re-imagined as one contributory strand of an ensemble of socio-politico-ecologically informed and engaged practice/theories.

Language sciences and cultural ontologies

Rethinking language sciences as a transdisciplinary, multi-stranded enterprise means rejecting the monodisciplinary ideal of theory-building as the construction of models that are explanatory within the confines of abstract objects that are conceptualized as discipline-defining. This is especially important – and controversial – with respect to linguistics, in which the language-as-object view is explicitly cast in the Generative Linguistic paradigm as an axiom of the *autonomy* of the 'language object/faculty' both from domain-general cognition and from cultural setting and social organization.

As we have alluded to above, this has not always been the case in language sciences. Boas, for example, not only designated linguistic analysis as one of the 'four fields' of anthropology, but also made explicit its place within the sciences of mind, stating that '[t]he purely linguistic inquiry is part and parcel of a thorough investigation of the psychology of the peoples of the world' (Boas 1911: 63). Boas's near-contemporary Karl Bühler ([1934] 1990) rejected *langue* as the basis for language science, though not as a basis for linguistic description, which he considered to be a necessary precondition for a transdisciplinary science of language.[15] Building on this tradition, we advocate an approach to language sciences that takes as axiomatic the *interdependence* of language, culture and mind (Sinha 2017a, 2021). In accordance with this perspective, we provide a brief overview of recent research on Amazonian languages that exemplifies the way in which understanding languaging is dependent on an understanding of the way in which they are embedded in the *ontologies* of the language communities. Since this reference to 'cultural ontologies' may be unfamiliar to language scientists more accustomed to discussion of 'cultural models' and 'worldviews', we need to clarify its disciplinary provenance and theoretical status.

The 'ontological turn' is a name that denotes an influential theoretical orientation shared by various anthropological writings in the last two decades (for an overview, see Holbraad & Pedersen 2017).[16] One way to clarify this turn is to say that it signifies an exploration of the plurality of worlds (including the *diversity of natures*) that are *lived in* by people in different cultural settings. These worlds, and their multiplicity – that is, the multiplicity of ways of organizing the fundamental categories of being (*ontological pluralism*) – can be considered as principal sources of variation in the experiential envelope that holds the 'being-in-the-world' of members of the cultural community. It is relevant to our discussion below to note that one of the foundational theorists of the ontological turn, Philippe Descola (e.g. Descola 2013a,b; Descola 2017) was prompted to accord a central role to cultural ontologies by his ethnographic research on Amazonian societies, for whom there is no categorical distinction between human and non-human being.

The ontological turn can be seen as a reaction to the potential for concepts such as 'worldview' to be uncritically anchored in philosophical presuppositions about the nature of reality derived from Western philosophies, and especially the assumption of a universally applicable *nature vs. culture* opposition (Viveiros de Castro 2015). In a related vein, ontological pluralism has been counterposed to what many theorists view as a 'sterile and paralyzing' opposition between universalist (including cognitivist) realism and cultural relativism (Descola 2013b: 76).[17] In our interpretation, the ontological turn implies an acceptance of ontological pluralism as a proposition about societies, rather than about 'reality in itself'. Ontological pluralism differs from relativism in that the latter attributes 'living in different worlds' to different 'ways of seeing', or representations (worldviews, cultural models). Ontological pluralism, in contrast, attributes 'living in different worlds' to the different constraints imposed on practices by different embodiments of agency (human and non-human), and different modes of action and co-action.[18]

The ontological turn has significant theoretical and methodological implications for socio-ecologically situated language sciences. First, it turns the primary attention of the analyst from the 'structure of the language', including both its grammar and its language-internal semantics, to *the world that languaging is about*. In this respect, the ontological turn is consistent with a world-oriented interpretation of embodied cognition and language (Sinha 1999). Second, this orientation to the *world as presupposed in languaging* (the culturally recognized ontological manifold, to put it philosophically) permits the language scientist to explore more deeply the *cultural grounding* of language-specific linguistic construals (in the sense of Langacker 1987).[19] It must be conceded that, up to now, research exploring the relationship between ontological pluralism and language variation is rare. However, and not by accident, recent research on Amazonian languages and cultures has provided examples of the insights that such research can offer for the language sciences.

Amazonian perspectivism: Appearance, being and transformation

The languages of Greater Amazonia present what at first sight appears to be a paradoxical profile. On the one hand, '[t]he region comprises over 350 extant languages grouped into over fifteen language families, in addition to a number of isolates' (Aikhenvald 2022: 426; see also Aikhenvald 2015). On the other hand, this enormous linguistic diversity is accompanied by striking similarities of features shared by genetically unrelated, sometimes geographically widely separated languages, so that 'the whole of Amazonia may be considered a linguistic area' (Aikhenvald 2015: 428). The research that we summarize in this and the following section makes the case that such commonalities in linguistic areal features are due to a shared system of cultural ontology: thus, Amazonia can be considered to be a cultural as well as a linguistic area (Darnell 1998: 283).

The cultural ontology shared by many Indigenous Amazonian communities, as expressed in myth, ritual and customary practices, has been designated 'perspectivism' (Viveiros de Castro 1998). The 'western ontology', argues Viveiros de Castro [VdC], is predicated upon there being a singular non-human natural world, and a plurality of cultures, each with different ways of representing this singular nature. Amazonian ontology, in contrast, is predicated upon *multinaturalism*: there are many non-human worlds, corresponding to different (differently embodied) beings, all of which share the same kind of psyche/soul. Instead of the Western opposition between 'the unity of nature and the plurality of cultures', Amerindian perspectivism is based on 'a spiritual unity and a corporeal diversity' (VdC 1998: 470).

This implies that different beings (animals, for example, but also spirits, and other kinds of what Western philosophy calls 'natural kinds', such as plants and bodies of water, and even some artefacts) are different embodiments of the *same kind of soul with the same cultural worldview*. 'Whatever possesses a soul ... is capable of having a point of view ... Whilst [in a western constructionist epistemology] *the point of view creates the object* – the subject being the original, fixed condition whence the point of view emanates – Amerindian ontological perspectivism proceeds along the lines that *the point of view creates the subject* ... all beings see ("represent") the world in the same way – what changes is the world that they see ... Animals see in the *same* way as we do *different* things because their bodies are different from ours' (VdC 1998: 476–8). It is because the *same* kind of perceiving soul inhabits *different* kinds of bodies that 'animals and spirits see themselves [in the same way that humans see themselves] ... they see their food as human food (jaguars see blood as manioc beer, vultures see the maggots in rotting meat as grilled fish, etc.), they see their bodily attributes (fur, feathers, claws, beaks etc.) as body decorations or cultural instruments' (VdC 1998: 470).

Crucial to Amazonian perspectivism is the principle that in certain circumstances (e.g. in shamanic rituals, and in mythological time) the individual human body may metamorphose or transform into another embodiment, either living or dead: the soul retains its powers, even while the being (nature) of the person may or may not change. Transformability, or if you will, fluidity of embodiment, is a potential that remains latent under normal circumstances, but is made actual in ritual ceremonies and enactments. The *plurality of beings*, with different embodiments and inhabiting different worlds, but with the same kinds of spiritual, cognitive and representational capacities, and circumstantially (potentially) capable of transforming into each other, also implies a *plurality of similar societies*: '[Animals] see their social system as organized in the same way as human institutions are (with chiefs, shamans, ceremonies, exogamous moieties, etc.)' (VdC 1998: 470). A consequence (or, in fact, an intrinsic part) of this cultural ontology is an understanding of interacting and corresponding human and non-human ecologies that is quite different from that in Western thought:

> [Indigenous Amazonian peoples] think that there are many more societies (and, therefore, humans) between heaven and earth than are dreamed of by our anthropologies and philosophies. What we call 'environment' is for them a society of societies, an international arena, a *cosmopoliteia*. There is, therefore, no absolute distinction of status between society and environment, as if the first were the 'subject', the second the 'object'. Every object is always another subject and is always more than one. (Danowski & Viveiros de Castro 2015: 94, trans. the authors)

We address below what this cultural ontology means in the context of the construction of a practice/theory that is simultaneously *ecological* and *decolonial* (Radvanskei & Silva 2020). For now, we want to draw attention to the fact that not only is it expressed in discursive genres such as mythic narratives, but it also motivates many areal features of the grammars of diverse Amazonian languages. Aikhenvald (2022: 430) mentions 'patterns of nominal classification (classifiers and gender) and kinship systems', which may apply to human and non-human beings alike. Aikhenvald (2022: 432–4) discusses in detail the centrality of visual perception and of the distinction between 'appearance' (or 'clothing') and what she calls 'essence', but we suggest is better called 'truly named being': 'a transformation from one visual form into another involves entering a "skin" or "clothing". Numerous Amazonian languages with extensive systems of classifiers have a special form for '[an] extended piece of cloth which can refer to an "outward appearance" in transformative contexts.'

Aikhenvald also cites Carlin (2018: 316), who describes how Cariban languages have 'a grammatical truth-tracking system [of nominal markers] that allows us to know whether a protagonist is in essence that expressed in the noun – for example, jaguar – or … something else entirely, and simply appearing in jaguar clothes having undergone a transformation'. Testimony of witnessing of events and beings is grammaticalized in many Amazonian languages by evidential markers. For example, it may be obligatory for the speaker to mark whether they witnessed a particular happening, or they are reporting it as hearsay, but evidential systems may be more complicated: '[The Arawakan language] Tariana has five evidentials – visual, nonvisual, inferred, assumed, and reported' (Aikhenvald 2022: 434). The distinction between what is referentially *true* (truly named being) and what is *apparent* (referring on the basis of appearance) is complementary to the distinctions between the *reliability* of the truth-claim performed by the referential act, and this complementarity attests to the centrality of visual perception in the language-specific construals privileged in many Amazonian languages. Perception is, of course, intrinsically perspectival, and in the perspectivist ontology *what is seen* depends upon the being who sees it. Shamans are different beings (at least when they are 'being shamans') than ordinary humans, so it is logical that a 'shaman is licensed to use the visual evidential when talking about their own prophetic dreams, their own actions, and events in the spirit world. A common mortal is not – and if they do so, they make themselves vulnerable to potential accusations of hidden access to unseen powers' (Aikhenvald 2022: 436).

Naming, personification, metaphor and time

Aikhenvald (2022) discusses another areal feature of Amazonian languages – the prevalence of small number systems, ranging from three or less to twenty numerals (for a survey of twenty-three Amazonian languages, see Silva Sinha et al. 2017). One consequence of this is that the ages of individuals are not (in fact cannot be) counted in terms of years. Rather, Indigenous Amazonians consider life as being a process of learning, punctuated by events that normatively define stages of life. In our research in several Amazonian communities (e.g. Sinha et al. 2011; Silva Sinha et al. 2012; Silva Sinha 2019, 2022), we have documented lexicalized systems of life stages.

The life stages should be thought of as social status categories, not as points on a lifeline. A certain body of knowledge or skill, and certain defined social responsibilities, are appropriate and necessary for each stage of living. The transitions between these stages may involve rites of passage and organized learning. The knowledge associated with one life stage category is not strictly restricted. The knowledge of each stage can be acquired during previous stages. For example, a young person, if they have acquired 'adult' knowledge and responsibility (such as being a skilled fisherman or taking on household responsibilities, with a level of knowledge recognized by the entire community) will be regarded and respected as a fully grown person. Physical and biological changes also index the stages, and in many cases motivate their names (see Table 10.1). For example, a girl will be considered a fully responsible adult after her first period, when she passes through the rite of passage in which she will acquire the knowledge and skills of a grown woman. After the first signs of puberty (breaking of the voice), boys will pass through the rite of passage in these communities. In the stages of life, a girl who is very 'young' (in 'our' terms), but is married, is an adult, but an older woman who has never married or had children will still be considered and treated as a youth unless the biological signs of ageing are very evident.

Table 10.1 Life stage names in three Amazonian languages. Reproduced from Silva Sinha (2019: 6). © Vera da Silva Sinha.

Huni Kuĩ (Panoan, Acre State, Brazil)

Feminine	Masculine
a. *Baku ixta* c. *Umã* Newborn girl child (female, human)	b. *Shuku* d. *bake ixta ewa* Newborn boy child (male, human or animal)
e. *Txipax* Lit. 'hot fire': (female who works in the household, has had her first period, ready to get married)	f. *Beruna* Lit. 'keen eye' (boy who works, ready to get married)
g. *Aibu ewa* grown up woman	h. *Huni ewa* grown up man
i. *Yushabu* woman with grandchildren	j. *Mestbu* man with grandchildren
l. *Ikayushã* Lit. 'very wrinkled' (f.) (old woman who does not work anymore)	m. *Ikameste* Lit. 'very wrinkled' (m.) (old man who does not work anymore)

Awetý (Tupian, Xingu National Park)

a. *Kuňa kyt* newborn (f)	b. *Kaminoat* newborn (m)
c. *Tonti* girl child	d. *Pi'a* boy child
e. *Kapia'jyt* grown up girl, not a child	f. *Kamino at raiwyt* Lit. 'broken voice' (grown-up boy)
g. *Kujãperyt* grown up unmarried girl	h. *komino at peryt* grown-up unmarried boy, still dependent on their parents
i. *Aripi* adult woman, with (grand)children or not	l. *Myrã* adult man, with (grand)children or not
m. *Aripi'jyt* old woman, shrunken, very wrinkled	n. *Myrã jyt* old man, shrunken, very wrinkled

Huni Kuĩ (Panoan, Acre State, Brazil)	
Feminine	**Masculine**
Kamaiurá (Tupian, Xingu National Park)	
a. *Kujã-taimet* newborn (f)	b. *Kunu'um* newborn (m)
c. *Ta'yi* girl child	d. *Ta'yi* e. *Pitang* boy child children (non-gendered)
f. *Kujã-muku* young [grown] woman	g. *Awowajá* Lit. 'broken voice' (grown-up boy)
h. *Kujãyman* unmarried grown-up woman	i. *Yman awawuja* grown-up unmarried boy, still dependent on their parents
j. *Matyt* Adult woman, with children of their own and / or grandchildren	l. *Myrã* Adult man with children of their own and / or grandchildren
m. *Matyri* Old woman, shrunken, very wrinkled	n. *Myra'i* Old man, shrunken, very wrinkled

In the Tupian language Amondawa, the transitions from one life stage to another are marked by changes in the name of the individual. Traditionally, each Amondawa person changes their name during the course of their life, and the rules governing these name changes form a strict onomastic system, based upon sequentially ordered cross-cutting category systems of life stage, gender and moiety. It is obligatory for each individual to change his or her name when 'moving' from one life stage to another, and each name is selected from a finite inventory of names, from which one can infer the individual's status in terms of moiety, gender and life stage. The name inventory that we documented in 2004–5 numbered exactly twenty-eight names (Sinha et al. 2011).[20] The principal event which triggers a change of name is the birth of a new member of the family. The new baby will be given a 'newborn' name, that may be a name previously held by the youngest existing family member. All the existing children will acquire a new name. The other situation that can provoke the changing of names is a change in the role of the individual in the family or in the group. No individual can be a child forever, in other words no-one can have a child name beyond a certain life stage. They have to grow up and assume responsibilities in the family. For example, when an older son changes his name, the father will change his name too. An adult woman will change her name when she is married, and her previous name will go to the youngest sister (Peggion 2005: 132).

Changing names in response to life events is not unique to Amazonian cultures/languages. What is unusual is for the name to be both categorial in terms of intersecting dualities (gender, life stage, moiety), and obligatory for all members of the society. In assuming a new name, the individual does not become identified with the personality of previous living or dead bearers of the name. The change of name signifies a transformation from being one kind of person, with a particular social status, to another kind of person, and is thus analogous to a rite of passage. Both mark a change of state of being. We may conjecture, then, that personal identity for Amondawa people (and perhaps other Indigenous Amazonian people) is in some way discontinuous, a sequence of transitions within a determinate categorical framework. If so, it is consistent with Amazonian concepts of time, which we address below. It also, however, needs to be viewed in the context of the 'perspectivist' cultural ontology that distributes human-like personhood among a much larger variety of beings than is the case in Western thought, in which only humans can be persons.

Our colleague Wany Sampaio led our team's research on ontological metaphors of *personification* in Amondawa, noting that 'if personification metaphors are seen as a subtype of embodiment metaphor, it should be acknowledged that it is a subtype that focuses, or at least implies, the psychic and vital aspects of human ontology, rather than its physical structure' (Sampaio et al. 2020: 186–7). The following example is from a narration of the 'origin of the moon' story (the moon is a salient being in the mythic inventory of Amondawa and other Amazonian communities), and illustrates personification in relation to perspectivized vision (Sampaio et al. 2020: 189):

1. *Jatata'ia hea awape ipieka. .... ngã repieka ....*

Jatata'ia	hea	awa	pe	epieka	ngã	r-epieka
star	she	persons	in	look	they	REL-look

    'The star is looking at the persons … they (the persons) are looking (at the star)'

If we analyse this narrative fragment in terms of conceptual metaphor theory we could say that it exemplifies the conceptual metaphor CELESTIAL BODIES ARE PEOPLE (Lakoff and Johnson 1980: 192). Compare example 1 with example 2 produced in the context of speakers' participation in a game using a model of the village, constructed to represent the buildings in the village, such as family houses, the clinic, the school, the manioc storage house; together with animals, trees, cars, etc.

2. *Inambutinguhua apyryrym awowo tapyia tombeakaty apytawo*

inambutinguhua	a-pyryrym	awowo	t-apyia	-tombea-katy	a-pytawo
hen	3s-surround	going	REL-house	rib-next to	3s-stop

'the hen went around and stopped at the side of the house [lit. next to the rib of the house]'

Examining example 2, noting the use of the body part, 'rib', we naturally view it against the background of diverse languages that employ body part metaphors for spatial relations. In some languages, such as Zapotec (an Otomanguean language of Southern Mexico) (MacLaury 1989; Jensen de López 2002), body part metaphors have been grammaticalized to form closed classes of adpositions on the basis of the projection of a human body schema to all landmark objects. However, there are constructional features of example 2, particularly relating to the marking of inalienable human possession, that suggest that the house is personified, that is, it is conceptualized *as a being like a human being*.

For the Amondawa, the house is not only a place to live, it is (like celestial bodies) also a living being, entrusted with 'guarding and preserving the living and the dead' (Sampaio et al. 2020: 193). In this cultural ontological context, we must question whether the characterization of examples 1 and 2 as 'metaphorical' is correct. The methodological construct of a conceptual metaphor such as CELESTIAL BODIES ARE PEOPLE is only intelligible in relation to the assumption that the source domain of HUMAN BEING is projected to an INANIMATE WORLD target domain. This duality itself maps to, or is perhaps one expression of, the foundational Western ontological opposition CULTURE VS. NATURE, which is, we argue, inapplicable to Amazonian cultures/languages.[21] More generally, we must recognize that the 'domains' presupposed not only in conceptual metaphor theory, but in many other areas of cognitive science, are not immutable units of scientific analysis, but projections of Euro-American-centric assumptions about the world, and its construal, that simply do not hold in other cultural settings. In passing, we should once again clarify that this is not to revisit the 'realism vs. relativism' debate. The question is not whether a house is 'really' a person. Rather, it is whether our analytical concepts are adequate to the world presupposed in the languaging and other cultural practices of the Amondawa people.

We turn now to another foundational ontological domain in Western thought, namely, *time*. Amazonian communities and individuals, like all of us, live in a world of change. However, these changes are not calibrated against the metric time intervals represented in calendars and clocks. In the Amondawa,

Kamaiurá, Awetý and Hãtxa Kuĩ languages, there are no lexical translation equivalents for 'time', no names for days of the week or months of the year (Silva Sinha 2019, 2022; Silva Sinha et al. 2012; Sinha et al. 2011).[22] Temporal change is conceptualized in terms of *events and happenings*, in nature and the social world. The resulting *event-based time intervals* are indexed by environmental happenings (water level and animal songs), celestial bodies (sun, moon and stars) and activities. Parts of the day, for example, are indexed either by activities, for example, 'return from the field time' means before lunchtime; or by the sun's position: 'the sun is on top of the head' means midday (see Table 10.2).

In these cultures/languages, the completion of events and activities, not the counting of metric time intervals such as minutes or hours, is the way the passage of time is kept track of. However, this does not mean that counting is absent – there is even a Kamaiurá word for it, *paparawaw*.[23] In Awetý and Kamaiurá, event-based time intervals can be counted, using and naming

Table 10.2 Event-based time intervals of day and night in Kamaiurá. Reproduced from Silva Sinha (2019: 8). © Vera da Silva Sinha.

a. *Ara pota koyt* day almost assertive almost day/dawn	b. *Ara ohom* day go dawn	c. *Arimé koyt* day assertive day[break]	d. *Kuema mué* morning/sub when morning
e. *Jaiweté* early morning			
f. *Ko-pe-wara* field-loc-source [Back] from the field	g. *Apyter-uwaj ipota koyt* Head-half almost assertive Almost midday		h. *Apyter uwaj* Head half midday
i. *W-ero-aparap* 3-AG-lean [The sun] is leaning; just after midday			
j. *Kaa-ruk amue* forest-is the when the forest [is in shade]	l. *Kaa ruk kóyt* forest is assertive marker It is later, [there is shade] in the forest		m. *Kwara itse* Sun enter The sun entered (disappeared)
n. *Ypy-tunim* Beginning-dark The beginning of the dark [night]	o. *Ypy -pipaw -amue* Beginning- silence -when when the silence begins [later in the night]		
p. *Ypy ajei ipota kóyt* Beginning half almost Assertive Marker Almost half way through [the night]	q. *Ypy ajei* Beginning half Half way through [the night]		

hands, fingers and toes. Although the 'basic' constituent words for number expressions (one and two, hand and foot, fingers/toes) are employed across contexts, they may be combined with other words (e.g. verbs of motion) and meaningful gestures (e.g. showing fingers) in ways which are specific to particular contexts.

Time 'reckoning' (time-keeping or time-tracking) is embodied, not only in body parts and actions, but also in a specific cognitive artefact. The duration of a fishing or hunting expedition is traditionally estimated by untying knots on a string (Figure 10.1). The activities for each day are planned and organized beforehand by the expedition leader, and then the information is communicated to his family and to the community. The leader estimates the length of string that will be necessary to complete the expedition in terms of the expected catch of game or fish, tying a knot in the string for each day. Each knot on the string represents the completion of one day's activities and a night spent on the hunting or fishing expedition. During the expedition, one knot will be untied every day. The knots are never counted before the expedition sets out – the knotted string is not a count or tally of the number of days. In fact, the number of knots tied at the beginning is just an estimate, which should be enough for the string to be used during the expedition.

The knotted string is used only in certain contexts. An individual knot is not a 'unit' in a calendar system, and the string is not an instrument that can count days in any and all situations. It is an artefact that indexes the completion of an event in a sequence of events. Unlike a calendar, the knotted string does not visually-perceptually *spatialize* temporal sequence as straight line or a circle. Rather, the knotted string supports an *embodied* practice of event-based time-tracking. Some cognitive scientists have claimed that time is innately spatialized in human cognition, and that the conceptualization of time as a linear dimension or 'timeline' is a human cognitive universal (Hoerl and McCormack 2019). We have found no evidence that this is the case in the communities in which we have investigated it. It has also been claimed that spatial metaphors for time are universal in language and thought (Fauconnier and Turner 2008). We have found no evidence for this claim, either.

In fact, in Awetý and Kamaiurá, metaphors for time are not derived by mapping from the spatial domain, but by mapping from the domain of embodied perception and cognition. Languaging in these communities situates past and future events in embodied cognitive and perceptual processes, rather than locating them along an oriented timeline. For Awetý and Kamaiurá speakers, the

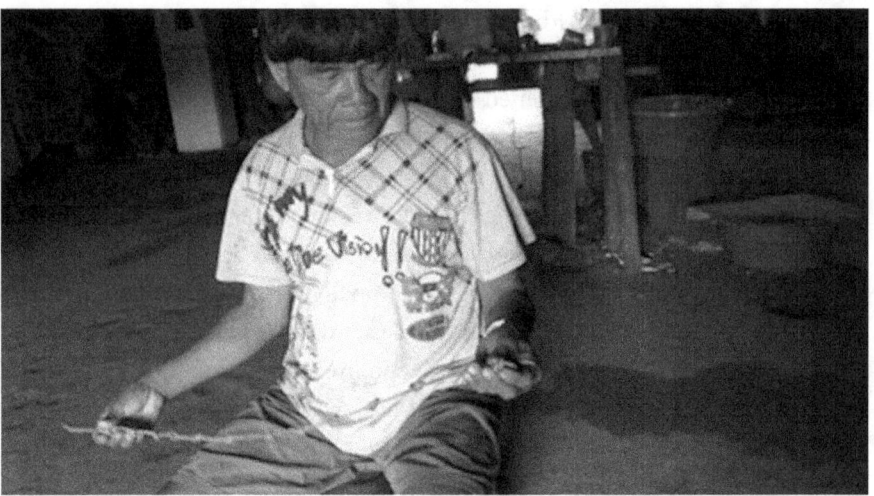

Figure 10.1 Tamahet Kamaiura demonstrates the use of the knotted string for counting days (2016). Image © Vera da Silva Sinha.

past is not behind the speaker, but *in their eyes*. The past consists of memories, and memories can be 'seen' in 'the mind's eye'. If we want to express this in terms of a conceptual metaphor, it would be one that reflects the cultural salience of visual perception: 'REMEMBERING IS SEEING'. Consistently with this, the future for Awetý and Kamaiurá speakers is in front of the eyes, but not far away – it is located in the immediate visual field. In Huni Kuĩ, past events are located in the *heart* (the seat of feeling), and future events and plans are located in the *head* (which is thought of as the location of the mind and thinking). In all of these cultures/languages, past and future are conceptualized in terms not of spatial direction, but of embodied mental capacities: *memory, anticipation, intention* and *imagination*.

We conclude this section by attempting a generalization from the research on Amazonian languages that we have briefly surveyed here (for more details, consult the referenced works). The generalization can be simply (perhaps simplistically) stated. In the Western cultural ontology, NATURE is organized in terms of the fundamental categories of OBJECT, SPACE, TIME, CAUSALITY. This is in opposition to the human domain of CULTURE, characterized by AGENCY and EXPERIENCE. In contrast to this, the cultural ontology of Indigenous Amazonia is organized around the fundamental categories of STATE OF BEING and EVENT (CHANGE OF STATE OF BEING); all BEINGS potentially possessing AGENCY and EXPERIENCE.

Ontologies, ecologics and the rights of the earth

Is it implausible to suggest that this perspectivist ontology (or something like it) is not restricted to Amazonian peoples, being found amongst Indigenous peoples around the globe? Perhaps not. Physicist, philosopher, ecofeminist and activist Vandana Shiva (2020: 254) writes:

> Indigenous knowledge by its very nature defies all attempts at its compartmentalization ... 'Original participation' is a concept expressed by the worldview of Indigenous cultures which means that their members are born into an integral world community where they speak on behalf of the four-legged ones, the winged-ones, the finned-ones, the forest, the mountain, the bees, the river, and the seas. This is a reflection of a consciousness that is supremely evolved, not 'primitive' or 'backward', and it is more crucial than ever to safeguard the increasingly precarious future of our planet.

Figure 10.2 Untitled painting by Rahul Shyam, part of the Gondwana Art Project, an initiative of Craft and Community Development Foundation, New Delhi www.ccdfindia.org. Image © Chris Sinha, art © the artist and Craft and Community Development Foundation.

In the painting by Indigenous Indian artist Rahul Shyam (Figure 10.2), the mother tiger is *fused in embodiment* with the tiger cub. They are one, but not one, because the mother has a protective hand (like a human hand) where the paw 'should' be. We could see the painting as a visual metonym, the hand standing for caring. Or we could, in a 'perspectivist' way, see it as a representation of *how a tiger itself* sees the embodiment of the mother–cub pair, and the maternal caring relationship. Or we could take one step further, and see the painting not as a representation, but as a signpost, indicating how the differing cultural ontologies of the Western world and Indigenous worlds imply different *ecologics*, with divergent implications for the *rights* of beings.

> **Western ecologic:** *different* bodies => *different* cognition/sensibility => *different* experiential world => different rights and obligations (*only humans have rights*)
>
> **Participatory ecologic:** *different* bodies BUT *same* cognition/sensibility => *same* experiential world => similar rights and obligations (*all beings have rights according to their embodiment*)

To further articulate the participatory 'ecologic of rights' that is 'worlded' (Descola 2013b: 78) in Indigenous societies, we can do no better than once again to quote Shiva (2020: 303–4):

> Natural rights are Indigenous, common rights shared by every being, including human beings. They have come before man. They will remain after man ... it is interesting how many languages and cultures don't have a word or language for rights ... There is no language for rights because rights simply are ... [they exist] by the very fact of being born into the earth family.

Conclusion: Situated language sciences as transformative practice/theory

Both theoretically and in relation to language documentation practices, the language-as-object view is constricting and incomplete. While it may represent the historically dominant paradigms of linguistics, it does not represent those research enterprises that are primarily interested in languaging as a social practice, that regard language sciences as *social* sciences, and that encompass interventionist practices as central, and not peripheral to 'theory'.

People belonging to endangered language/culture communities are not just sources of data, but agents with constantly emerging, future-oriented agendas. To use the terminology developed and promoted by the Indigenous peoples' movement of Brazil, they are *protagonists* in a struggle for recognition and empowerment. This struggle includes the recognition of the empowering possibilities of the *re-contextualization* of endangered languages in diverse modes of languaging. As an example, we can cite the inclusion in the inauguration celebrations of Brazil's re-elected President Luiz Inácio Lula da Silva (Lula) on 1 January 2023 of Indigenous language raps by Indigenous artists.

The role of the language scientist is not just to document and analyse languages, but to support, without controlling, the exploration by communities of avenues and modes of emancipation and empowerment. It is to engage, jointly with communities, in the exploration of how language sciences can be not only rethought, but (re-)worlded as practices/theories of transformation. This includes the reflexive transformation of theory, to positively accommodate Indigenous knowledge systems (including Indigenous accounts of language and languaging). It also includes situating transformative practice/theory as a strand of resistance to the grievous damage to our world inflicted by the systematic destruction, extraction and exploitation that is the continuing inheritance of colonial capitalism.

Acknowledgements and responsibilities

We thank Peter K. Austin, Luna Filipović, Joaquim Kaxinawá, Wary Kamaiurá Sabino and Wany Bernardete de Arujo Sampaio for their indispensable contributions to this chapter. We thank an anonymous reviewer for their helpful and insightful suggestions. All deficiencies are the responsibility of the authors. The authors are equally responsible for the content, which we have discussed, organized and presented, individually and jointly, in various fora; and both have contributed to the text.

Notes

1 We employ the term 'languaging' to signify not just 'use of language' but also the general approach in language sciences that emphasizes the priority of embodied, situated multimodal communication practices.
2 We have substituted the words 'colonized' and 'colonizer' for the phrases 'black man' and 'white man' in the published translation of Fanon's text.

3   See the brief biography of Malinowski by Katherine Fletcher (2017) https://blogs.lse.ac.uk/lsehistory/2017/06/13/bronislaw-malinowski-lse-pioneer-of-social-anthropology/
4   Malinowski used terms such as 'primitive', and some comments in his notebooks were racialized, but he recognized that these were unscientific.
5   We thank Peter K. Austin for directing us to the two following quotations.
6   The qualification 'amateur' is not wholly accurate, since much of this linguistic and ethnographic work was in the hands of either colonial officials for whom it was a recognized part of their work, or Christian missionaries who regarded saving souls as intrinsic to the 'civilizing mission' proclaimed by the imperialists (Errington 2001).
7   For a recent descriptive account of Burushaski, see Munshi (2018).
8   In anthropology, too, historic ethnographies continue to be a crucial resource for contemporary scholarship (see, for example, Flannery & Marcus 2012; Graeber & Wengrow 2021); but see also Austin (2021) for a discussion of the potential challenges in using legacy materials in language documentation and revitalization.
9   The idealized one-to-one mapping between language (*langue*) and speech (*parole*) community, viewed geographically and in terms of national entities, with deviations viewed as an exception, is fundamental to Saussure's structuralist linguistics and to the distinction between synchronic and diachronic analysis. Even he conceded, however, that it could be supposed that 'during ancient times unilingual countries in the Mediterranean basin were the exception' (Saussure [1916] 1966: 195). The normative assumption of monolingual linguistic acquisition, despite noise in 'degenerate' input, is fundamental to Chomsky's argument from the poverty of the stimulus (Chomsky 1980).
10 Austin (2018) argues that some current hi-tech annotation and archiving systems are in some respects continuations of colonial appropriation, replicating colonial hierarchies of language and power, for example through the use of metadata language conventions that exclude the members of the 'documented' communities.
11 Austin (2013) proposes a typology of language documentation that includes 'plantation linguistics', corresponding in many ways to our notion of 'extractive linguistics'.
12 It should be recalled that the 'Global North' vs. 'Global South' distinction is not geographical in the strict sense. Some countries geographically situated in the southern hemisphere belong socio-economically to the Global North and vice versa. Furthermore, territories with a local majority of a national minority Indigenous community in the Global North (or South) (sometimes referred to as 'fourth world contexts') may be considered part of the Global South.
13 The abstraction of the notion of intangible cultural heritage from actual practices, and the anchoring of policies in nation states, is laid down in the UNESCO Convention for the safeguarding of the intangible cultural heritage: 'The

importance of intangible cultural heritage is not the cultural manifestation itself but rather the wealth of knowledge and skills that is transmitted through it from one generation to the next. The social and economic value of this transmission of knowledge is relevant for minority groups and for mainstream social groups within a State, and is as important for developing States as for developed ones.' UNESCO expert meetings are usually conducted only in English and/or French. What is Intangible Cultural Heritage? – intangible heritage – Culture Sector – UNESCO.

14 See also the project 'language as a cure: linguistic vitality as a tool for psychological well-being, health and economic sustainability'. Center for Research and Practice (uw.edu.pl).

15 Bühler was familiar with Boas's (1911) *Handbook*, citing Edward Sapir's description in his chapter in it on the Takelma language of body-part locatives (Bühler [1934] 1990: 166, n.4). We are not aware of any evidence that Boas knew Bühler's work, but this is not impossible, and both undoubtedly were well acquainted with Wilhelm Wundt's *Völkerpsychologie* (Sinha 2007).

16 The 'ontological turn' in anthropology shares features and orientations with similar recent developments in philosophy and in other social sciences.

17 Descola (2013b: 77ff) goes on to clarify the relationship between the rejection of the universality of the ontological nature–culture distinction and the rejection of the opposition between universalism and relativism by comparing gene therapies and shamanic cures. While acknowledging that the former 'has more chance of success', he rejects an interpretation in which 'the former [is] anchored in positive reality and the latter in the imaginary and the symbolic'.

18 This interpretation is not meant as a definition, and nor is it intended to convey a consensual view. Our interpretation of the notion of ontological pluralism is coloured by our broad acceptance of the basic principles of *practice theory* and its key concept of *habitus* (Bourdieu [1972] 1977). Others, including Descola and Viveiros de Castro, see their work as being more in the Lévi-Straussian tradition; our own position is to see these traditions, taking into account the foundations of the ontological turn in studies of Amazonian societies, as complementary.

19 Although one of the foremost proponents of the ontological turn in anthropology, Eduardo Viveiros de Castro, stresses the distinction between ontological pluralism and a pluralism of 'ways of seeing', we would argue that ontological pluralism cannot but entail culturally distinctive construals, that in turn motivate language-specific lexico-grammatical patterns.

20 The changing of names in Amondawa society is now falling into disuse, being incompatible with state requirements for each individual to document their identity.

21 We draw attention here, although we do not have space to further explore the issue, to the ecological anthropology of Tim Ingold (see especially Ingold 2020), which

resonates with many of the points we make here, while originating from a different theoretical tradition from that animating the work of Descola and Viveiros de Castro.
22 Hãtxa Kuĩ is the language spoken by the Huni Kuĩ community.
23 Our evidence here contradicts Aikhenvald's (2022: 436) claim of a consistent 'lack of a counting routine' in Amazonian languages.

References

Aikhenvald, A. Y. (2015). *The Languages of the Amazon*. Oxford: Oxford University Press.

Aikhenvald, A. Y. (2022). 'Perspectivism through language: A view from Amazonia'. In S. Völkel & N. Nassenstein (Eds.), *Approaches to Language and Culture*, 425–42. Berlin: Walter de Gruyter.

Austin, P. K. (2013). 'Language documentation and meta-documentation'. In Mari Jones & Sarah Ogilvie (Eds.), *Keeping Languages Alive: Documentation, Pedagogy and Revitalization*, 3–15. Cambridge: Cambridge University Press.

Austin, P. K. (2016). 'Language documentation 20 years on'. In L. Filipovic & M. Pütz (Eds.), *Endangered Languages and Languages in Danger: Issues of Documentation, Policy and Language Rights*. IMPACT Series 42: Studies in Language and Society, 147–70. Amsterdam: John Benjamins.

Austin, P. K. (2018). 'Colonialism in language documentation and revitalization – the times they are a changing'? University of Malaya'. invited talk 6 December 2018. http://www.peterkaustin.com/docs/teaching/2018-12-06_UM.pdf

Austin, P. K. (2021). 'Language documentation and language revitalization'. In J. Olko & J. Sallabank (Eds.), *Revitalizing Endangered Languages: A Practical Guide*, 199–212. Cambridge: Cambridge University Press.

Boas, F. (1911). *Handbook of American Indian languages*. Vol. 1. Smithsonian Institution Bureau of American Ethnology, Bulletin 40. Washington: Government Print Office.

Bourdieu, P. ([1972] 1977). *Outline of a Theory of Practice*. Cambridge: Cambridge University Press.

Bourdieu, P. (2010). 'The forms of capital'. In I. Szeman & T. Kaposy (Eds.), *Cultural Theory: An Anthology*, 81–93. New York: John Wiley & Sons.

Bowern, C. (2011). 'Planning a language-documentation project'. In Peter K. Austin & Julia Sallabank (Eds.), *The Cambridge Handbook of Endangered Languages*, 459–82. Cambridge: Cambridge University Press.

Bühler, K. ([1934] 1990). *Theory of Language: The Representational Function of Language*. Amsterdam: John Benjamins.

Carlin, E. B. (2018). 'Evidentiality and the Cariban languages'. In Alexandra Y. Aikhenvald (Ed.), *The Oxford Handbook of Evidentiality*, Oxford Handbooks

(2018; online edn, Oxford Academic, 7 March 2018), https://doi.org/10.1093/oxfordhb/9780198759515.013.16, accessed 4 January 2024.

Chandler, M. J., Lalonde, C., Sokol, B., Hallett, D., & Marcia, J. (2003). 'Personal persistence, identity development, and suicide: A study of native and non-native North American adolescents'. *Monographs of the Society for Research in Child Development*, 68(2): i–138.

Chomsky, N. (1980). 'Rules and representations'. *Behavioral and Brain Sciences*, 3(1): 1–15.

Danowski, D., & Viveiros De Castro, E. (2015). *Há mundo por vir: Ensaio sobre os medos e os fins*. Florianópolis: Cultura e Barbárie/ISA.

Darnell, R. (1998). *And Along Came Boas: Continuity and Revolution in Americanist Anthropology*. Amsterdam: John Benjamins.

Descola, P. (2013a). *Beyond Nature and Culture*. Chicago: University of Chicago Press.

Descola, P. (2013b). *The Ecology of Others* (G. Godboud & B. Luley Trans.). Chicago: Prickly Paradigm Press.

Descola, P. ([2014] 2017). 'La diversité des natures'. In *La Composition des Mondes III*, 195–278. Paris: Flammarion.

D'Errico, F., Backwell, L., Villa, P., Degano, I., Lucejko, J. J., Bamford, M. K., et al. (2012). 'Early evidence of San material culture represented by organic artifacts from Border Cave, South Africa'. *Proceedings of the National Academy of Sciences of the USA*, 109: 13214–19.

Dobrin, L. M. (2008). 'From linguistic elicitation to eliciting the linguist: Lessons in community empowerment from Melanesia'. *Language*, 84(2): 300–24.

Dobrin, L. M., Austin, P. K., & Nathan, D. (2009). 'Dying to be counted: The commodification of endangered languages in documentary linguistics'. In *Language Documentation and Description*. 6: 37–52. London: SOAS https://lddjournal.org/articles/10.25894/ldd238

Emmanuel, A., Bettelheim, C., & Pearce, P. (1972). *Unequal Exchange: A Study of the Imperialism of Trade*. New York: Monthly Review Press.

Errington, J. (2001). 'Colonial linguistics'. *Annual Review of Anthropology*, 30(1): 19–39.

Fanon, F. ([1952] 2021). *Black Skin, White Masks* (R. Philcox Trans.). London: Penguin.

Fauconnier, G., & Turner, M. B. (2008). 'Rethinking metaphor'. In Raymond Gibbs (Ed.), *The Cambridge Handbook of Metaphor and Thought*, 53–66. Cambridge: Cambridge University Press.

Flannery, K., & Marcus, J. (2012). *The Creation of Inequality: How Our Prehistoric Ancestors Set the Stage for Monarchy, Slavery, and Empire*. Cambridge, MA: Harvard University Press.

Graeber, D., & Wengrow, D. (2021). *The Dawn of Everything: A New History of Humanity*. London: Allen Lane.

Grinevald, C., & Sinha, C. (2016). 'North-South relations in linguistic science: Collaboration or colonialism?' In Filipovic, L. and Pütz, M. (Eds.), *Endangered Languages and Languages in Danger: Issues of Documentation, Policy and Language*

Rights. IMPACT Series 42: Studies in Language and Society, 27–43. Amsterdam: John Benjamins.

Hallett, D., Chandler, M. J., & Lalonde, C. E. (2007). 'Aboriginal language knowledge and youth suicide'. *Cognitive Development*, 22 (3): 392–9.

Hoerl, C., & McCormack, T. (2019). 'Thinking in and about time: A dual systems perspective on temporal cognition'. *Behavioral and Brain Sciences*, 42: e244.

Holbraad, M., & Pedersen, M. A. (2017). *The Ontological Turn: An Anthropological Exposition*. Cambridge: Cambridge University Press.

Ingold, T. (2020). *Correspondences*. Cambridge: Polity.

Irvine, J. T. (2008). 'Subjected words: African linguistics and the colonial encounter'. *Language & Communication*, 28(4): 323–43.

Jensen de López, K. (2002). 'Baskets and body parts: A cross-cultural and cross-linguistic investigation of children's development of spatial cognition and language'. PhD dissertation, Aarhus University.

Keay, J. (2022). *Himālaya: Exploring the Roof of the World*. London: Bloomsbury.

Lakoff, G., & Johnson, M. (1980). *Metaphors We Live By*. Chicago: University of Chicago Press.

Langacker, R. W. (1987). *Foundations of Cognitive Grammar, Vol. I*. Stanford, CA: Stanford University Press.

Lorimer, D. (1929). 'The supernatural in the popular belief of Gilgit region'. *Journal of the Royal Asiatic Society of Great Britain and Ireland*, 110(3): 512–13.

Lorimer, E. O. (1939). *Language Hunting in the Karakoram*. London: Allen and Unwin.

MacLaury, R. E. (1989). 'Zapotec body-part locatives: Prototypes and metaphoric extensions'. *International Journal of American Linguistics*, 55: 119–54.

Munshi, S. (2018). *Srinagar Burushaski: A Descriptive and Comparative Account with Analyzed Texts*. Leiden: Brill.

Newman, P. (2003). 'The endangered languages issue as a hopeless cause'. In M. Janse & S. Tol (Eds.), *Language Death and Language Maintenance*. Current Issues in Linguistic Theory 240: 1–13. Amsterdam: John Benjamins.

Peggion, E.A. (2005). Relações em perpetuo desequilibrio: a organização dualista dos povos Kagwahiva da Amazonia. São Paulo: Universidade de São Paulo PhD thesis.

Radvanskei, I. A., & Silva, M. dos R. L. (2020). 'Ecologia de saberes e perspectivismo: epistemologias decoloniais/Ecology of knowledge and perspectivism: decolonial epistemologies'. *Brazilian Journal of Development* 6(10): 80801–17.

Sampaio, W., Silva Sinha, V. da, & Sinha, C. (2020). 'Embodiment, personification, identity: Metaphor and world view in a Brazilian Tupian culture and language'. In Silva Sinha, V. da, Moreno Núñez, A. & Zhen, T. (Eds.), *Language, Culture and Identity – Signs of life*. Amsterdam: John Benjamins.

Saussure, F. de ([1916] 1966). *Course in General Linguistics* (W. Baskin Trans.). New York: McGraw-Hill.

Senft, G. (2007). 'Bronislaw Malinowski and linguistic pragmatics'. *Lodz Papers in Pragmatics*, 3(1): 79–96.

Shiva, V. (2020). *Reclaiming the Commons: Biodiversity, Indigenous Knowledge and the Rights of Mother Earth*. London: Synergetic Press.

Silva Sinha, V. da (2019). 'Event-based time in three Indigenous Amazonian and Xinguan cultures and languages'. *Frontiers in Psychology*, 10: 454. DOI: 10.3389/fpsyg.2019.00454.

Silva Sinha, V. da. (2022). 'Time: Sociocultural structuring beyond the spatialization paradigm'. In Svenja Völkel & Nico Nassenstein (Eds.), *Approaches to Language and Culture* (Series Anthropological Linguistics Vol. 1), 75–306. Berlin, Boston: De Gruyter Mouton. https://doi.org/10.1515/9783110726626

Silva Sinha, V. da, Sinha, C., Sampaio, W., & Zinken, J. (2012). 'Event-based time intervals in an Amazonian culture'. In Luna Filipović & Kasia Jaszczolt (Eds.), *Space and Time in Languages and Cultures II: Language, Culture, and Cognition*, 15–36. Amsterdam: John Benjamins.

Silva Sinha, V. da, Sampaio, W., & Sinha, C. (2017). 'The many ways to count the world: Counting terms in indigenous languages and cultures of Rondônia, Brazil'. *Brief Encounters* 1(1) DOI: h9p://dx.doi.org/10.24134/be.v1i1

Sinha, C. (1999). 'Grounding, mapping and acts of meaning'. In T. Janssen & G. Redeker (Eds.), *Cognitive Linguistics: Foundations, Scope and Methodology*, 223–55. Berlin: Mouton de Gruyter.

Sinha, C. (2007). 'Cognitive linguistics, psychology and cognitive science'. In D. Geeraerts & H. Cuyckens (Eds.), *The Oxford Handbook of Cognitive Linguistics*, 1266–94. Oxford: Oxford University Press.

Sinha, C. (2017a). 'Getting the measure of meaning'. In Barbara Dancygier (Ed.), *The Cambridge Handbook of Cognitive Linguistics*, 493–7. Cambridge: Cambridge University Press, 493–7.

Sinha, C. (2017b). *Ten Lectures on Language, Culture and Mind: Cultural, Developmental and Evolutionary Perspectives in Cognitive Linguistics*. Leiden: Brill.

Sinha, C. (2021). 'Culture in language and cognition'. In X. Wen & J. R. Taylor (Eds.), *The Routledge Handbook of Cognitive Linguistics*, 387–407. New York: Routledge.

Sinha, C., Silva Sinha, V. da, Zinken, J., & Sampaio, W. (2011). 'When time is not space: The social and linguistic construction of time intervals and temporal event relations in an Amazonian culture'. *Language and Cognition*, 3(1): 137–69. DOI 10.1515/langcog.2011.006

Viveiros de Castro, E. (1998). 'Cosmological deixis and Amerindian perspectivism'. *Journal of the Royal Anthropological Institute*, 4(3): 469–88.

Viveiros de Castro, E. (2015). 'Who is afraid of the ontological wolf? Some comments on an ongoing anthropological debate'. *The Cambridge Journal of Anthropology*, 33(1): 2–17.

Woodbury, A. C. (2011). 'Language documentation'. In P. K. Austin & J. Sallabank (Eds.), *The Cambridge Handbook of Endangered Languages*, 159–86. Cambridge: Cambridge University Press.

Index

abstracta of language 86, 93–4
agency 158
   biological 6, 14, 75
   distributed 89, 92, 94–9
   human 12–16, 69, 73, 75, 77, 138
Aikhenvald, A. Y. 236–7
Alexander, R. 160–1, 201, 211
amateur 224, 248 n.6
Amazonian languages 223, 233–41, 244–5
ambiguity 203–4, 206
Amondawa (Tupian language) 239–42, 249 n.20
Andean community case 67–70
animal(s). *See also* dairy cows
   chena and wild 179, 181–2
   humans and 20–1, 107, 110–12
   non-human 31–3, 111
   populations of 115–16
   production 33–4
   welfare 195–7
Anumethirala 180, 187 n.2
applied linguistics 2–4, 88, 232
Austin, P. K. 248 n.10–248 n.11
Awetý language 242–4

Bang, J. C. 130–41, 142 n.3
Becker, A. 88
Becker, H. 154
bioecology 8–9, 11–22, 73, 85, 93–6, 100, 170
bio-logics 138–41, 142 n.3
Boas, F. 223–5, 232–3, 249 n.15
bophelo 170
Brown, M. E. 153–5
butter 191–2, 198–9

capitalism 78
Carlin, E. B. 236
Cascaded Tank-Village system 180
chena cultivation 178–81

chocolate spot (*Botrytis fabae Sardiña*) 68–9
classical theory of perception 59
climate change 58–60
   Andean communities to 70
   anthropogenic 55–7, 67, 76
   Canada high temperature 66
   and global warming 97
   human-caused 55–8, 67, 78
   spiral case 61–6, 74, 77, 79 n.4
CO_2 concentrations 62–3, 98
cognition 71, 74, 76–7
   culture and 56–7
   enlanguaged 134–7, 140–1
   human and animal 112
   language and 134–7, 140–1
cognitive ability 36, 110
cognitive devices 56–60, 64–7, 69–70, 74–5, 77
   ecolinguistics of 70–5
   and linguaculture 71–3
cognitive linguistics 1
cognitive process 130, 169
Cohen, M. 199
cohesive harmony analysis 201, 204–6
commodification 226–7
communicative modes 158–9
'consume more milk' option 212
Cornips, L. 17
'corridor' 174–5, 178
Courtice, P. 155
Couto, H. H. d. 3
Cowley, S. J. 84, 88, 92, 100 n.3, 130, 137–8, 186
cows. *See* dairy cows
creatura 93
Crown Land Ordinance 181
Cuffari, E. 211–12
cultivation 171–2, 175, 177–81, 187
cultural heritage 57, 172, 231, 248–9 n.13
culture 56–8, 107, 117–18, 152–3, 161–2, 230–1

dairy cows 30–1, 33–4, 207–14
   advertisements 192–3
   animal welfare 195–7
   'cattle-cookies' 39–44
   environmental harms from 194
   ethnographic fieldwork 37–8
   human health impacts 194–5
   languaging 35–7
   neck-chain stuck 44–8
   sociolinguistic study of 34–5
   vocalizations 39–49
dairy praxis 197–200
Darwin, C. 111
Dawkins, M. S. 196
de-privileging 226
Descola, P. 21, 233, 249 n.17
dialectical ecolinguistics 130–41
discourse analysis
   critical 13, 148
   ecological 13
   environmental 84, 86
   harmonious 14, 96
discursive practices 69, 127
distributed cognition 77, 186
distributed language 128, 130, 142 n.4, 170
divide and rule 224
Døør, J. 130–41, 142 n.3

Earth Democracy 161
ecocultural identity 162
ecolinguistics 4–8, 21–2, 148–50, 163
   of cognitive devices 70–5
   contemporary 1, 10
   in discontinuity 2–4
   and ethical leadership 159–60
   implications for 73–5
   practices 11–16, 85–7
   radicalized 128–30
   regeneration 98–100
   theory of practices 94–8
ecological niche 19, 114–15, 119
ecology 5, 18–19, 113
ecosophy 9–10, 148–54, 158, 160–4
ecosystem 1–4, 6, 8, 30, 67, 69, 83, 93, 98, 114–15, 147–9, 152, 155, 157, 164, 169, 181
ELAN multimodal software 201
elephants 20, 170–82, 186

endangered language 21, 222–3, 226–8, 230–1, 246–7
environmental damage 194
environment effect 7–8
ethical leadership 148, 150, 153–9, 162–3
   ecolinguistic approach to 159–60
ethnography 37–8
ethnolinguistics 223–5
event-based time intervals 241–2
evolution 109–19
expression 128–33, 136–7, 141
extractive linguistics 222, 227, 248 n.11

Fanon, F. 221
fauna and flora 72–3, 181
Filemyr, A. 184, 186
Fill, A. 83–4, 86–7, 127–8
Finke, P. L. W. 131, 134, 142 n.2
fragrance 184
full-blown theory of practices 95–6

Gahrn-Andersen, R. 19
genetic determinism 113, 115
Ghorbanpour, A. 3
Gibson, J. 58–61, 64, 71, 78, 118
global atmospheric CO_2 concentration 62–3
globalization 73, 183
Globally Important Agricultural Heritage Systems (GIAHS) 180
Global North 227–8, 248 n.12
Global South 194–5, 227–8, 248 n.12
global surface temperature 61–2
global warming 66, 97
Goatly, A. 97
Goodwin, C. 69
greenhouse gas emissions 194, 212
Green Revolution 161–2
growthism 83, 86, 94, 96
Guattari, F. 128–33, 136–7, 141, 150

habitus 86, 249 n.18
Halliday, M. A. K. 2, 14, 85–7, 90–1, 99, 127, 139–40
Harrison, K. D. 72
Hãtxa Kuĩ language 242, 250 n.22
Haugen, E. 3, 5, 7–9, 84–7, 90, 93, 95
Heizmann, H. 155–8

heritage
    as museum of mankind 228–31
    resource for science 226
heteroscalar description 58, 61, 66–7,
    71–2, 74–5, 79 n.2
He, W. 3
Heyes, C. M. 79 n.1
Homo sapiens 76, 107, 109, 112, 116, 120
homoscalar description 58, 60–1, 66–7,
    72, 74–5, 79 n.2
Hosking, R. 183, 185
Hovens, D. 36
Huang, G. 3, 16
human-elephant conflict 170–82, 186
humanity 78, 100, 110, 148, 155
humans
    ability 109
    agents 12–16, 69, 73, 77, 138
    and animal 20–1, 34, 107, 110–12
    behaviour 56–7, 70–1, 73, 76–7,
        149–50
    cows and (*See* dairy cows)
    engagement 85
    health impacts 194–5
    niche 116–17
    and non-humans 20, 30–1, 33
    organism 111–12, 114, 116, 118–20
    populations of 56–7, 116–18
human-wildlife conflict 170, 181
Hutchins, E. 60–1, 77

ideo-logics 133–4, 142 n.3
Indigenous 229
    cultures 161
    knowledge 245, 247
    languages 222
    minority peoples 239
individual perceiver 59–60
Industrial Revolution 107, 199
Ingold, T. 170, 249–50 n.21
integrity 151
intrinsic value 227–8, 231

Kamaiurá language 242–4
Kaptein, M. 154
Kiley-Worthington, M. 33
knowledge as practice/practice as
    knowledge 228
Knudsen, S. 95

Kramsch, C. 3, 57
Kravchenko, A. V. 142 n.2

land/landscape 169–75, 182–3
    communications 184
    languages of 183–5
    listening to 185–6
    Sri Lanka 178–80
    use 174–5, 177, 187, 212
language(s)
    and communities 231–2
    death 229
    and discourse 85–6
    documentation 223, 225–8, 230–1,
        246
    first-order 119, 138–9, 191–2
    in human organisms 112
    and linguistics 131–2
    morbidity 229
    myth 119–20
    ontologies of 233
    sciences 74, 221–3, 230–4, 246–7
    second-order 90, 115–16, 119, 139,
        201
    use 3–4, 18–19, 84–7, 91, 93, 96, 129,
        131–8
    vitality 229
languaging 35–7, 83–5, 87–96, 116–19,
    149–50
Larsen-Freeman, D. 3
Latour, B. 13, 95–6
leadership 148, 157.
See also ethical leadership
    dynamic approach 156
    sustainability 155
    theory 157
    transformative 157
Legendairy
    appraisal in 207–11
    campaign 200–3
    text 203–7
'less milk' option 212–13
Levisen, C. 73
life-significant 133, 137
life stages 237–9
life-sustaining relations 1–2, 4, 6, 8–12,
    15–16, 18, 20, 30–1, 48, 75, 83–7,
    94–100, 149
linguaculture 71–3

linguistic
  diversity 70, 73, 222, 229–30, 234
  meaning 74, 128, 130–1
  reification 9
  semiosis 116
  techniques 74, 149, 163, 204
Linné, T. 197, 210
Liu, H. 155–9
Living! 150–1
living systems 6, 14, 84–5, 95, 100 n.1, 111–20
long-term cultural classification system 68
Lorimer, D. 224–5
Lorimer, E. O. 224–5
Lytton, British Columbia case 66–7

MacWhinney, B. 57
Malinowski, B. 223–4, 248 n.4
maps/mapping 9, 60, 65, 136–7, 141, 173–6, 204–5, 224, 241, 243, 248 n.9
Marxism 78
Maturana, H. 36, 87–9, 137
Mead, G. 160
meaning-making process 19, 30, 32, 34, 37–8, 43, 48, 88, 129, 133–4, 156
Meyerson, D. 158
Michell, P. 67
milk 20, 30, 37–9, 191–5, 197, 199–200, 205–13
monodisciplinary approach 225, 232
Moore, A. R. 20–1
moral entrepreneur 154
Mühlhäusler, P. 4
Mulcaster, R. 88–9, 99
multimodal(ity) 30, 33, 89, 201, 211, 247 n.1
museum of mankind 228–31

Nabhan, G. 184–6
Næss, A. 150
narrative framing 66–7, 74, 77
narrative leadership 160
natural innovation (Shapiro) 6, 14
natureculture 29–31
neurobiological evidence 33
niche construction 19, 93, 98, 113–19
non-humans
  animals 31–3
  humans and 20, 30–1, 33

non-metaphorical analysis 83–4, 86–7
'Northern' linguists 227

ontological pluralism 233–4, 249 n.18–249 n.19
ontological turn 233–4, 249 n.18–249 n.19
organisms 23 n.4, 60, 71, 74
  adaptive interactions 111
  and environment 79 n.2, 113–16, 119–20, 192
  language role 112

Panamura 181
participatory ecologic 246
participatory sense-making 197
Penz, H. 87, 97–8
percaction 90, 92–4, 99
perception 7, 18, 56–60, 64, 69–72, 77, 86, 90, 136, 170, 236–7, 243–4
Petrollino, S. 72
politics 97
Popper, K. 117–18
posthuman ethnography 37–8
Postigo, J. C. 67–70
practice theory 95–6, 221, 231, 236, 246–7, 249 n.18
praxis-logic 140–1
professional vision 69

radical embodied ecolinguistics 186–7
Radical Enactivism 136
radicalized ecolinguistics 129–30
regeneration 98–100
Relational Identifying clauses 203
Rosen, R. 14

Saussure, F. de 9, 84, 133, 248 n.9
scientific knowledge 64–5, 99, 110, 230
Sellars, W. 89–90, 93
semogenesis 84–6, 88, 90–3, 95–7, 99
Shields, C. 157
Shiva, V. 160–3, 245
Shyam, R. 245–6
simplex tricks (Berthoz) 6
snapshot theory of perception 60
social brain hypothesis 111
Social Representation Theory 74

sociolinguistics 29–32
  of dairy cows (*See* dairy cows)
  knowledge 33–4
socio-logics 133, 137–41
South Asia 170, 186
Southwest Ethiopian Hamar people 72
Sri Lanka 178–82
state-of-the-art 5, 127
Steffensen, S. V. 76, 87, 127–8, 186
Stibbe, A. 10, 19, 73–4, 152, 201, 211
stimulus-sequence theory of perception 60
'stories' 152–3, 160–1
sustainability 30, 78, 148, 154–8, 162, 164, 181
systemic functional grammar 9, 21, 85, 192, 203, 215 n.7

temperature anomaly 62–3
tempered radical (Meyerson) 158
temporal(ity) 6–7, 17–18, 41, 57–60, 64–5, 69, 162, 172, 174–8, 187, 242–3
territories 20, 171, 173–4, 178, 248 n.12
Thibault, P. J. 142 n.4
three worlds (Popper) 117–18
time reckoning (time-keeping/time-tracking) 243
Trampe, W. 4

transdisciplinary approach 16–17, 98, 222–3, 232–3
transformative leadership 157
Transport Safety Board of Canada 66
transposition 60–1, 68–9, 77
Trappes, R. 115
Tutu, D. 151

Uda Walawe National Park 182
Umwelt 73, 113, 119
urbanization 73

vayal-nad (Wayanad) 172–8
Visser, W. 155
visual perception 59, 71–2, 236–7, 244
vital process 6–7, 13–15, 91–6, 99–100, 100 n.1
Viveiros de Castro (VdC) 235
Viveiros de Castro, E. 249 n.19
Voiceless 214 n.3

Wayanad. *See vayal-nad* (Wayanad)
western ecologic 246
wild animals 179–81
Wittgenstein, L. 131, 137

Yako, T. 183–5

www.ingramcontent.com/pod-product-compliance
Lightning Source LLC
Chambersburg PA
CBHW071815300426
44116CB00009B/1320